Diversity, Conflict, and State Politics

Diversity, Conflict, and State Politics

Regionalism in Illinois

Edited by

Peter F. Nardulli

University of Illinois Press
Urbana and Chicago

Publication of this book was supported in part by a grant from the Institute of Government and Public Affairs at the University of Illinois.

This book is printed on acid-free paper.

Library of Congress Cataloging-in-Publication Data

Diversity, conflict, and state politics : regionalism in Illinois /
   edited by Peter F. Nardulli
      p.   cm.
   Includes index.
      ISBN 0-252-01576-2 (cloth : alk. paper).   ISBN 0-252-06036-9
(paper : alk. paper)
      1. Regionalism—Illinois.   2. Illinois—Economic conditions
   —Regional disparities.   I. Nardulli, Peter F.
   JK5729.R44D58 1989
   306′.2′09773–dc19   88-18719
                                                              CIP

Dedication

To Samuel K. Gove,
for forty years of dedication and service
to the State and University of Illinois.

Contents

Preface

This book is a collection of original essays examining various aspects of geo-political cleavages in Illinois. In recognizing the importance of regional differences within states and examining their origins, development, and implications for state politics, it builds on the conceptual contributions of such scholars as Frederick Jackson Turner and V. O. Key. Most contemporary students of American state politics implicitly recognize the significance of geographically based, intrastate political rivalries (north-south, tidewater-uplands, urban-rural, etc.) but, since the mid-1960s, most rigorous research on state politics has been explicitly comparative, using the state as the unit of analysis. This body of research has contributed much to our understanding of state politics by sensitizing researchers to important differences among states. At the same time, however, this comparative tradition has largely ignored the interplay of intrastate forces in the political process. In doing so it has ignored many of the insights based on the works of scholars such as Turner and Key, insights that were fertile for systematic examination as early as the 1950s.

The void left by the macro focus of most of the recent research on state politics became evident as changes in the environment of state governments produced local crises of varying proportions. In the largely insulated economies and the highly localized politics of a bygone era, the battle lines in most state matters were drawn along geo-political cleavages that separated different cultural groups or regions with distinct economic or political interests. The enemy was from within. The demise of the rust belt states and the emergence of the sun belt, combined with the differential impact of the oil crisis, led many to realize that a fundamental reordering, both economic and political, was taking place among the American states. The competition for new business ventures, with their attendant consequences for growth and fiscal health, reached unprecedented levels. These developments were compounded by the emergence of a new, truly global economic order, one that threatened the preeminence of the United States in economic matters and drained individual states of jobs and industrial development funds.

This series of events led many to realize that the real threat to the continued viability of many states was from outside their borders, not within. This new environment dictated political and economic strategies that depended on the state acting as a unified political community; the urgency of such strategies was heightened as the "New Federalism" of the Reagan era increased the responsibilities and importance of state governments. Unfortunately, the ability of many states to act forcefully was hamstrung by regional rivalries that have festered for generations. These difficulties, compounded by the realization that we know relatively little about the origins, nature, and current status of these regional strains, prompted the Institute of Government and Public Affairs at the University of Illinois, in cooperation with a group of Illinois-based corporations and foundations, to initiate a set of activities to study and address the problems emanating from geo-political cleavages within Illinois.

These activities included conducting a statewide survey that examined the present status of regional animosities within Illinois, holding a conference attended by people from all sections of the state, and commissioning a set of interdisciplinary background papers that was distributed to conference participants. The background papers, prepared by a group of political scientists, economists, historians, geographers, and sociologists, were developed into scholarly in-depth essays that addressed important aspects of geo-political cleavages in Illinois. The essays included here are substantially revised versions of a selected subset of the full collection of papers. The selected essays stress the developmental character of regionalism in Illinois, without ignoring its contemporary manifestations and foundations.

Acknowledgments

The genesis of this project makes the list of debts and acknowledg-
ments a highly diverse one. This collection could not have come about
without the work of those who made the regionalism project possible
and who did so much to make the statewide conference a success.
The initial idea for the project was the result of discussions among
Samuel K. Gove of the University of Illinois, James D. Nowlan of
Knox College, and Michael Hudson of Illinois Tool Works. J. Fred
Giertz and James Fossett of the Institute of Government and Public
Affairs at the University of Illinois were helpful in finding the authors
and organizing the volume. The efforts of Stanley O. Ikenberry, Pres-
ident of the University of Illinois, were important in getting the project
off the ground.

Without the guidance and sustained efforts of Michael Hudson of
Illinois Tool Works, William Higginson of Chicago United, Robert
Klaus of the Illinois Humanities Council, Michael Lennon of *Illinois
Issues,* John McDermott of Illinois Bell, and David Paulus of the First
National Bank of Chicago, who spearheaded the work of the project's
planning committee and were responsible for much of the fund raising,
the overall project would never have been possible. Patricia Hurley
of the Illinois Ambassadors was responsible for organizing the conference and her contributions were invaluable. The assistance of James
Gallagher and F. Richard Ciccone of the *Chicago Tribune,* and Jeffrey
Miller and Charles Levesque of the Governor's Office of Planning,
in making the statewide survey possible was much appreciated. The
generous support of Robert F. Rich, Director of the Institute of Government and Public Affairs at the University of Illinois, during the
latter phases of this project was also essential in bringing the project
to a timely conclusion.

The invaluable efforts of the administrative staff at the Institute of Government and Public Affairs also need to be acknowledged. Anna Merritt and Jean Baker handled myriad problems in completing this project. Shirley Burnette typed all of the manuscripts. The help of Lorena McClain and Velma Sykes in resolving last-minute difficulties was also appreciated. The heroic efforts of Jane Mohraz in editing and "cleaning up" the original manuscript will be appreciated by all who read this book. Last but not least, the efforts of Larry Malley at the University of Illinois Press in securing a timely review of the manuscript and an expeditious production of it should not go unnoticed.

PART I

Introduction

Geo-Political Cleavages, Conflict, and the American States

1

Peter F. Nardulli

Conflict is an inevitable consequence of communal life that occurs at every level of association. Because of its potentially disruptive impact on many aspects of life (physical well-being, social, economic), people have sought methods to diffuse conflict and to guard themselves against the threats emanating from conflicts or potential conflicts. Governments have been formed for both of these reasons as well as others. They provide a forum for the nonviolent resolution of political conflicts and the force to implement those resolutions. In addition, modern, bureaucratic states were formed to ward off external threats from larger, more powerful neighbors by consolidating smaller, somewhat more homogeneous political entities. Areas that had geographically distinct subentities strong enough to resist pressures to consolidate (e.g., Italy, Poland) were often easy prey for imperious foes.

Although geographic consolidation offers military, economic, and political benefits to a polity, it also makes more difficult the role of the political system in the resolution of conflicts. Simply stated, geographic amalgamation complicates the political matrix with which a political system must deal. There are many sources of intrasystemic (as opposed to international) political conflicts, but most can be fit within one of several broad categories: class-based, ideological, religious, cultural, economic, or geographic (sectional or regional). Obviously, many conflicts are rooted within more than one of these categories, and there is undoubtedly much overlap across these general groupings. The point here is simply that the multiplicity of geographically based areas with strong regional identities within a single governmental unit considerably complicates the political calculus necessary to make the system work effectively.

One could argue that geo-political animosities are not an independent source of political conflict, that regional differences are simply a facade that masks other more fundamental differences. However, the tendency for conflicts (be they economic, religious, or class-based) with geographical overtones to create animosities and coalitions that persist well beyond the duration of isolated confrontations suggests that regional differences are an independent source of political conflict. So does the long history of regionally based conflict—a history that extends almost uninterrupted from a time when the economic, social, and religious fabric of society was much simpler than today.

This volume aims to enhance our understanding of one type of geo-political conflict—intrastate regionalism—the strain that has plagued many American states almost since their inception. Our particular point of reference is regionalism within Illinois. This inquiry comes at a time when states such as Illinois are faced with economic challenges from states in other sections of the United States as well as from developing nations in a new, still emerging, world economic order. States are also struggling to adjust to a new set of responsibilities that emerged as part of the "New Federalism" of the Reagan era. These developments dictate economic and political strategies that depend upon the state acting as a unified political community. Unfortunately, the ability of many states to act forcefully has been hamstrung by regional rivalries that have festered for generations.

Broadly gauged efforts to understand regional cleavages and animosities are painful but necessary first steps in any attempt to confront the challenges facing many states and to develop strategies to deal with the negative effects of regionalism (as well as to capitalize on its beneficial aspects). Each author in this volume addresses a different facet of regionalism in Illinois. This introduction paints with broader strokes to illustrate the ubiquity of geo-political animosities and conflict. It underscores the magnitude of the problems for those seriously concerned with addressing the consequences of regionalism.

This essay begins with a brief historical overview that is no more than a sampling of excerpts from broad surveys of earlier eras (anything more than this would constitute a series of volumes in itself). It then discusses in somewhat more depth the geographic cleavages in the United States, with an emphasis on the origins and evolution of these cleavages. After general comments on the relationship between geographically based animosities and political conflict, it brings the present study into better focus by putting Illinois' regional mosaic into a comparative perspective. Finally, it outlines the approach used in this volume to study this mosaic and its ramifications.

Geo-Political Animosities: A Historical Overview

In his classic work *Ancient Mesopotamia,* A. Leo Oppenheim notes, "This contrast between city-dwellers and those in the open country cuts across the fabric of Mesopotamian society and represents an eternal source of conflict. As such it was of fateful influence on the political development in Mesopotamia. The tension, city against surrounding country, affected the history of the region but should not be regarded as a typically Mesopotamian phenomenon, since the entire ancient Near East had to face this problem in varying intensity and in several periods, and had constantly to strive for any solution, however unstable, that could be found" (1977:82). Oppenheim further explicates the importance of town-country conflicts in early Mesopotamia:

> The anti-urban tendencies in and, for the most part, around Mesopotamia have to be recognized as social and political facts, exactly as does the trend toward living in cities, if one is to achieve a genuine understanding of the history of the time between the first emerging city-states and the conquest of Mesopotamia by the Arabs. In a perennial battle characterized by sudden reverses and a persistent instability of political power, the pattern of the events in this region was shaped by pro- and anti-urbanization tendencies. Urbanization created and tenaciously maintained cities which evolved into centers of political gravity but which evoked in turn anticentralization reactions in certain strata of the population. These strata, because of tradition or previous experience, show definite and often effective resistance not only against living in settlements of greater complexity than the village but also against the power—be it political, military, or fiscal—that an urban center was bound to exercise over them [1977:110].

Regionally based conflict in ancient Greece can be viewed from a couple of different levels. The animosities and conflicts among the Greek city-states (Athens, Sparta, Thrace, Thebes) and their role in the demise of Greek predominance are too well known to require comment here. Less well known, however, are the tensions that existed between the city dwellers and those who lived in the countryside. While there were observable differences between these two groups, they did not always result in conflicts or animosities. As one student of this period notes:

> Except where a native population had been reduced to a subject condition there was generally, in the areas just mentioned, no fundamental difference between those who lived in or near the urban centre of the polis and the peasants who lived in the countryside, even if the latter tended to be noticeably less urbane (less citified) than the former and

in the literature produced by the upper classes are often treated patronisingly as "country bumpkins," an attitude which nevertheless allows them to be credited on occasion with superior moral virtues of a simple kind. Both groups, however, were Greek and participated in a common culture to a greater or less degree [de Ste. Croix, 1981:9].

In the eastern areas of Asia and Egypt into which Greek civilization had penetrated, however, the situation was markedly different. In those areas the *chora*—the term traditionally used for the outlying area around the city proper—was used in a more encompassing sense to include all land not part of a polis (de Ste. Croix, 1981:10). Country dwellers were not members of the body politic and were not entitled to the limited spheres of autonomy enjoyed by members of the polis. The peasants in these *chora* were ruled by autocratic kings. During these times, peasants came to be viewed as unsophisticated, unrefined, and almost subhuman. They were largely uneducated and frequently spoke a language different from that of the upper classes who dwelled in the city (de Ste. Croix, 1981:16). Marriages between peasants and city folks were uncommon and discouraged (de Ste. Croix, 1981:17, 18). De Ste. Croix even cites Aesop's Fables to show that countryside gods were believed to be simpleminded, while city gods were infallible and omnipotent (1981:18).

The relationship between the city and the countryside in the Roman west was very similar to that prevailing in the Greek east. Not only were rural dwellers subjected to derision and ridicule and excluded from political participation (Jones, 1940:270), they were exploited ruthlessly:

> It must further be remembered that industry and commerce mainly served the towns and not the country. Merchants, it is true, bought not only manufactured articles from the towns but also the agricultural produce of the country-side, but they sold both in the main to the well-to-do, who were town-dwellers; the balance of payments to the peasants was completed chiefly in cash, with which they paid their taxes and rents. . . . Throughout the period under review the cities were, it would thus appear, economically parasitic on the country-side. Their incomes consisted in the main of the rents drawn by the urban aristocracy from the peasants, and the trade and industry which flourished in some of them catered largely for this class and were dependent on it for their existence. . . . The wealth of the country-side—and it must be emphasized that the bulk of the wealth of the empire was derived from agriculture—was drained into the towns [Jones, 1940:263–68].

The role played by food in the animosities between the city and the countryside during this early period cannot be overemphasized.

The difficulties of transportation made a fertile *chora* essential for a city to survive and prosper. Given the rudimentary agricultural technology of the day, however, the nutritional support of an urban area was no small task. Droughts and failed crops led to crises in which the peasants attempted to hide their yields while urban dwellers attempted to gather up what they felt they needed for the winter. De Ste. Croix quotes Galen, a noted second-century physician and medical writer, as follows:

> Those who live in the cities, in accordance with their universal practice of collecting a sufficient supply of corn to last a whole year, took from the fields all the wheat, with the barley, beans and lentils, and left to the rustics only those annual products which are called pulses and leguminous fruits; they even took away a good part of these to the city. So the people in the countryside, after consuming during the winter what had been left, were compelled to use unhealthy forms of nourishment. Through the spring they ate twigs and shoots of trees, bulbs and roots of unwholesome plants, and they made unsparing use of what are called wild vegetables [1981:14].

While this episode was clearly exceptional, it is in such situations that the true character of socio-political relationships can be seen most clearly. Experiences under difficult conditions also tend to be the most influential in shaping people's perceptions of one another. Compounding the tensions generated by episodes such as those quoted above was the fact that peasants were often required to perform menial services of various types (de Ste. Croix, 1981:14, 15). In summarizing the relationship between the city dwellers and the peasants, Jones contends that "there was, it would seem, little love lost between them. . . . The gentry regarded the peasants as boors and barbarians, and this was probably the general attitude. . . . Of the attitude of the peasants to the city aristocracy we have little direct evidence, but they had not much ground for liking them. The city magnates came into contact with the villagers in three capacities only, as tax-collectors, as policemen, and as landlords" (1940:295).

In his review of town-country relationships in the Middle Ages, Jacques LeGoff notes, "In ancient Greece and above all in Rome the real dichotomy which lay at the heart of the Greek and Roman cultural world was that between town and country . . . the antithesis urbanus-rusticus was a linguistic legacy to the men of the middle ages; and Christianity, the child of the Jewish and Greek colonies and thus of the towns, reinforced the prejudice against the countryside in making the countryman (paganus) into the pagan, the rebel against the word of the Christian God" (1976:71).

Despite this legacy, LeGoff contends that the town and its immediate surrounding countryside were a fairly well-integrated unit during the early Middle Ages, a period in which towns were in a state of decline (1976:72). The fundamental social and cultural cleavage was between the more civilized areas, including and surrounding the town, and the forest or wilderness. The town was a "den of iniquity," a re-creation of Babylon; the wilderness represented a crude and uncultured existence. At the same time, however, the forest presented hermits and others with a place for reflection and contemplation; the city was the center for commerce and culture.

The resurgence of urban life in the thirteenth century was due to the revival of commercial exchanges. However, urban growth was also nurtured by the emergence of cities as centers of production (LeGoff, 1976:78). This had several important implications for town-country relations. First, the city began to attract peasants, who brought with them their own customs and patterns of thought. They transformed city life and narrowed the gap between the two cultures, which led to a more balanced relationship between town and country. No longer was it wholly a one-sided, parasitic relationship. In normal times the countryside produced enough surplus to meet the demands of the city; now the city itself could produce things of value to trade for these commodities.

On this general point, LeGoff notes, "Certainly the traditional opinion of historians of the towns, above all in Italy, is that the commune did conquer the contado and enslave it. The peasants went from servitude to lords to servitude to townsmen. The thesis is not confined to Italy. But . . . this picture of the town-country relationship should be corrected and to some degree reversed. The countryside, at least in medieval Italy, profited as much as it suffered from the dominance of the towns. . . . The amount of opposition between town and country in the middle ages was often trifling (1976:80).

Despite these encouraging observations, town-country relations ebbed and flowed during the course of European history. As Europe was trying to free itself from the shackles of feudal society and urban dwellers were attempting to assert themselves as a political force to be reckoned with, town-country tensions were rekindled. Townspeople felt tainted in their dealings with the landed gentry and clergy by the servile image projected by rural peasants, with whom they were often grouped socially. In viewing the social conflicts of the time, one observer notes that "one overriding prejudice, stronger probably than the barrier to sympathy between layman and priest, was the townsman's prejudice against the countryman" (Hale, 1978:173).

These prejudices existed even though the townspeople and the country dwellers were highly interdependent in many ways and had a good deal of personal contact at every social level. These ties not withstanding, "there was an emotional gulf between town and country dweller, narrowest among the rich, widest when all other classes contemplated that universal butt, the peasant, most pungently expressed in the most highly urbanized countries, Italy, Germany and the Netherlands, but audible everywhere in literature and almost always visible in art, where the hulking, bent figure of the countryman is rendered commonly in caricature or with amused condescension. 'Country folk are sub-human,' growled Felix Hemmerlin, a humanist canon of Zurich; 'it would do them good if their houses were burned and their farms laid waste every fifty years' " (Hale, 1978:174).

Geo-Political Cleavages in American History

In was what to become the United States, geographic cleavages emerged almost as soon as the individual colonies matured and developed individual identities.[1] By the third quarter of the eighteenth century there were clear sectional groupings among the states. According to Fullmer Mood, "Before the Revolution began, native-born Americans were recognizing the reality of a threefold system of sections, one that was 'American' rather than 'British American.' When the Continental Congress convened, we find the delegates spontaneously using such terms as 'Southern Colonies,' 'Middle Colonies,' 'Eastern Colonies,' and 'New England Colonies' " (1951:25).

In addition to the traditional tripartite distinction (New England, Middle, Southern), there was much discussion of the western territories as a distinct section. Indeed, as eastern trisectionalism evolved into a North-South rivalry over slavery and economic policy, the West became a pawn in the struggle and compounded sectional politics (Turner, 1959:chapter 2). The mere existence of the West drained the East of its labor supply and kept land prices low. The existence of both a developed economy (the East) and a developing economy (the West) under a single government led to other conflicts, such as debates over land policy, interest rates, and internal development. Jacksonian democracy was, in a very real sense, a triumph of the interior over the tidewater (Turner, 1959:25).

The prominence of sectionalism in national political debates cannot be overestimated. According to Frederick Jackson Turner, "sectionalism was the dominant influence in shaping our political history" (1959:323). Its impact can be seen even in the conduct of Congress under the Articles of Confederation. Madison once observed, "The great danger to our general government is the great southern and northern interests of the continent, being opposed to each other. Look to the votes in congress, and most of them stand divided by the geography of the country, not according to the size of the states" (quoted in Farrand, 1911:476).

The early saliency of sectional considerations can be seen in the Constitutional Convention. Reviewing some of the relevant materials, Mood relates that "George Mason, in a discussion of the proposed chief magistracy for the new government, declared: 'If the Executive is vested in three persons, one chosen from the Northern, one from the Middle, and one from the Southern States, will it not contribute to quiet the minds of the people and convince them that there will be proper attention paid to their respective concerns?' " (1951:28). The slavery question was another example of sectionalism in the convention. Also, Gouverneur Morris proposed a representational scheme to the delegates in which the emerging western states would always be underrepresented in Congress to ensure the dominance of the established eastern states (Turner, 1959:26).

These instances were only the beginning of a long history of sectionalism in American national politics. The Civil War and its prelude were the most dramatic of the geo-political conflicts in American history, and, along with the ones involving Indian nations, the only one that its national political institutions were unable to resolve peacefully. But sectionalism did not end with the Civil War or with the conflicts involving Indian tribes. Battles over the regulation of trusts, free silver, banking, tariffs, and political reform all had sectional overtones. As American politics became increasingly nationalized in the twentieth century, sectional strains intensified anew. Nowhere can this be seen more clearly than in the civil rights battles of the fifties and sixties. The energy crisis of the seventies and the economic decline of the "rust belt" states are even more recent examples.

Turner puts this continuing struggle into perspective by noting:

> We must frankly face the fact that in this vast and heterogeneous nation, this sister of all Europe, regional geography is a fundamental fact; that the American peace has been achieved by restraining sectional selfishness and assertiveness and by coming to agreements rather than to reciprocal denunciation or to blows.

> In the past we have held our sections together, partly because while the undeveloped West was open there was a safety valve, a region for hopeful restoration; partly because there were national political parties, calling out national party allegiance and loyalty over all sections and

at the same time yielding somewhat under stress to sectional demands. Party was like an elastic band [1959:46].

In dwelling upon the saliency of geographically based cleavages at the national level, it is all too easy to ignore subnational regionalism which, in some instances, predated national sectionalism. Clinton Rossiter notes in his review of pre-revolutionary society in the United States:

> The basic sectional division during this period was between west and east within each colony rather than between one group of colonies and another. The west was . . . the area of protest; the east was the area of indifference and reaction. Mixed in national origin (with the Scotch-Irish giving the mixture its special flavor), dissenting in religion, democratic in politics, and leveling in social attitudes, the men of the "Old West" felt entitled to a better deal in representation, religious freedom, prices, taxation, debts, protection, and the administration of justice. In many a colony in 1764 civil war seemed more likely than war with Britain [1953:115].

Allan Nevins echoes Rossiter's point about the intensity of intrastate divisions:

> Almost everywhere from Pennsylvania to Georgia a struggle between east and west, Tidewater and uplands, cut in the later Colonial period across the alignment between people and Crown. In each larger Province the self-assertion of the democratic, individualistic settlers of the hill and inland regions marked the decade 1760–1770. . . . In Pennsylvania the "Paxton boys" . . . massacred some Christian Indians, and by an angry march upon Philadelphia, which they thought indifferent to their sufferings, threatened a civil war, which Franklin and others averted. . . . In North Carolina the sufferings of the inland population from corrupt sheriffs, court officials, and tax collectors, from heavy taxes, charges for land-patents, illegal fees, and quit-rents, caused graver and graver disturbances as the sixties wore on. These columinated when the backwoodsmen of a territory comprising all or part of seven counties in what is now the north central part of the State rose in the Regulators' Rebellion; and the vigor with which the lowland militia under Tryon crushed this outbreak at the battle of the Alamance (1771) bred an intense hatred for the coast country among the discontented settlers. Similar disorders in upper South Carolina reached a crisis in 1769, but here bloodshed was averted [1927:11, 12].

Given the importance of these state-level cleavages in American history, and their centrality to this work, we stop here to examine briefly their origin and evolution over time.

Geo-Political Cleavages in the American States

A general understanding of subnational geo-political cleavages in the United States requires, at a minimum, considering separate sets of factors during several periods in American history. We begin by examining the distinctiveness of the initial settlements in the colonies, including how the geographic conditions of the different colonies, or sections thereof, combined with the early pioneer stocks to affect their culture. The second important development concerns the structure of the dominant migration paths of western settlement, especially during the pre–Civil War period. The Civil War intensified the sectional animosities within many states because many migrants from the North and South tended to settle in distinct parts of the newer states, bringing with them their old habits, allegiances, and beliefs. After the war a new set of geo-political cleavages began to emerge, adding another dimension to the cultural and political mosaic that already existed in most states. This cleavage was formed by the spiraling urbanization that occurred in the late nineteenth and early twentieth centuries, a development spurred by industrialization and fed by European immigrants. The latest development in the structure of state regionalism is, of course, the emergence of the suburbs as powerful political forces.

We cannot, and need not, go into a detailed review of the distinctiveness of different sections of the United States in its formative era; many have already dealt with these matters in some detail.[2] Moreover, the general outlines of the differences are quite familiar. Daniel J. Elazar summarizes them quite nicely:

> The first settlers who founded colonies and communities at various points along the Atlantic coast from Maine to Georgia between 1607 and 1732 brought with them a cultural heritage from the countries or areas of their origin in the Old World which was reflected in the institutions—social, political, and religious—which they established on these shores. These colonists of the seaboard and their descendants spent anywhere from two to five generations rooting themselves in the American environment east of the Appalachians and then plunged into the wilderness to start the great westward movement that took them across the continent. As they became Americanized during their period of confinement to the coast, there developed not only the beginnings of a national culture but also three sectional subcultures which flourished within the framework of the emerging American civilization: (1) the Southern subculture of Virginia, the Carolinas, and Georgia, based on slavery, the plantation system, a radically individualist conception of social obligation, and a gentry-dominated political order; (2) the

subculture of the Middle States (New York, New Jersey, Pennsylvania, Maryland, and Delaware) based on commercial enterprise, ethnic and religious pluralism, freehold agriculture, and a political order which, virtually from the first, was maintained by professional politicians; and (3) the Yankee subculture of New England based on Puritanism, with its emphasis on individual enterprise within the context of an organized and powerful community, dedicated to social improvement and individual redemption, and fostering a political order which encompassed a tension between an oligarchy deemed to be the guardians of religious orthodoxy and the fundamentally democratic town meeting [1970:155–56].

Turner would probably add to this a fourth distinct subgrouping important for the appreciation of regional migration patterns and cleavages: the Scots-Irish and German settlers of the Piedmont region.[3]

Prior to 1830 the larger part of the interior of the Union had been colonized from the back country of the South Atlantic section. It was not the tidewater planter who furnished the mass of these settlers, but the nonslaveholding upcountry farmer of the Piedmont region. In an earlier generation, these uplands had been settled by a combined stream of Scotch-Irish and Germans from Pennsylvania and by the yeoman pioneers who had pressed forward the Virginia and Carolina frontiers. Mingled with them were the gentry, but these were far outnumbered by the pioneers with ax and rifle, who crossed the mountains and cut out new homes on the "Western Waters" [Turner, 1950:18].

These western settlers were the first to break with the tidewater society and had the least affinity for European culture. They were contentious Calvinists who placed a high value on self-reliance and who embodied the term "rugged individualist." They were largely small farmers who chafed under the arbitrary constraints of civil government and had little tolerance for the formalities of law (Turner, 1950:19, 20). Elazar points out the import of these subcultures:

The distinctiveness of these various subcultures is important because, when the westward movement began, each section launched its own particular subcultural stream across the mountains. Each was carried westward by the people who were its products and the transmitters of its characteristics, flowing across the continent in the course of the late eighteenth, nineteenth, and early twentieth centuries, separately or together embracing wide bands of territory all the way west and depositing settlers who carried their cultural traits with them. Though these traits were modified in the course of their adaptation to fit into the new geo-historical environments into which they were transplanted, they were also transmitted from generation to generation [1970:156].

The southern stream was the first to penetrate the western wilderness, initially settling Tennessee and Kentucky. Later they went on to southern Ohio, Indiana, Illinois, and Missouri. Even in the new territories the emigres from the Piedmont province settled in areas distinct from the tidewater or slaveholding emigres. The southern stream was followed closely by the stream from the middle states, which came by some of the same migration routes. These settlers left Pennsylvania, New Jersey, New York, Delaware, and Maryland and initially settled in Ohio, Indiana, and Illinois. Finally, the Yankee stream did not begin until after the opening of the Erie Canal in 1825. New Englanders used this route to settle Michigan, Wisconsin, and the northern portions of Illinois (see, Elazar, 1970:156 et seq., and the references cited therein).

John Fenton's analyses of the politics of the border states and the Midwest illustrates the residual effect of these settlements upon regionalism within many states:

> The fundamental structure of Missouri politics is a product of geography and population movements. The initial population movement into the state came largely from the Upper South, and was composed of many slaveholders who settled primarily along the rivers and in the more fertile sections of the state adjacent to or near the rivers. Later population movements stemmed in large part from the north, and tended to settle in the less populated sections of the state, in the northwest corners of the state. Therefore, the areas settled earliest, by Southerners, and which are also the more fertile, tend to be Democratic; and those settled later, by Northerners, and which are largely thin soil sections tend to be Republican.
>
> Exceptions to this generalization are found in some river counties and the western Ozarks section. Many river counties, though settled at an early date by Southerners, have become predominantly Republican because of the Republican-inclined German population which has since settled there. The western Ozarks section, which was also settled at an early date by mountain people from the Upper South, is also Republican; the reason being that Missouri's mountain folk, like their brethren in Kentucky and West Virginia, have been stalwart Republicans since the Civil War. In addition, there was a considerable influx of people from northern states into the Ozarks following the Civil War, and this new population was largely Republican [1957:155–56].

Later, in drawing some contrasts between the political makeup of Ohio, Indiana, and Illinois and that of Michigan, Wisconsin, and Minnesota, he notes:

The differing histories of the six states provide some preliminary insights into the reasons behind their political party patterns. . . .

In 1850 the populations of Ohio, Indiana, and Illinois included a substantial proportion of people who followed the rivers and streams from the South to the Midwest. They came in search of land and settled, first, the bottomland, and then the hills of the southern portions of the three states. The Civil War was particularly painful to the transplanted Southerners and many affiliated themselves with the Democratic party in the 1860s out of opposition to Abraham Lincoln's war.

The northern portions of Ohio, Indiana, and Illinois were originally settled largely by New Englanders. The New Englanders were Whig-inclined before the Civil War and also tended to oppose slavery with some fervor. They supported the Civil War wholeheartedly and found renewed reason in the political conflicts of the period to support the Republican party. . . .

There were few people who traveled directly from the South into Michigan and Wisconsin in search of land (Minnesota was not settled in 1850, but its subsequent settlement conformed to the Michigan and Wisconsin patterns). Most of the early settlers were Yankees or were from bordering states or were immigrants from Europe. Consequently, the reaction of the populations to the Civil War consisted of near-unanimous support for the Union forces against the Southern "rebels." The political result was a virtual one-party system in the three states from the Civil War and until the Great Depression. The one-party character of the states was further buttressed by the tendency of the newly arrived Scandinavians to join forces with Yankees in the Republican party [1966:4–6].

Geo-political concentrations formed by the diffusion of these various subpopulations constituted the basis for many of the within state cleavages in the United States up to, and for a period of time after, the Civil War. But by the time of the Civil War the seeds had already been sown for a new species of intrastate regionalism, one which blossomed fully in the early twentieth century. This was, of course, the urban-rural cleavage. Cities had a long history of political conflict with the western sectors of many of the original colonies as well as with the agricultural sectors of the nation. Anti-urban feelings were based upon religious, political, and even medical foundations (Glaab and Brown, 1976:46–47, 54–57). Moreover, the economic interests of the cities were often opposed to those of the hinterlands.

Several things changed in the middle of the 1800s to elevate cities into a generator of regional animosities of the highest order, one that rivaled the intensity of the "bloody shirt" and would permanently change the geo-political mosaic in the United States. One change was a shift in the function of cities and in population trends. In early U.S. history cities had been a temporary holding area, a point of debarkation from which people set off to stake a claim to cheap western lands. Until about 1820 the urban portion of the nation's population was quite stable, around 7 percent. The drain of the West was such that it was not until 1830 that the urban population in the United States reached the level it had attained 140 years earlier (Glaab and Brown, 1976:21). The percent of the population living in urban areas began to rise markedly in the 1840s. Moreover, the emergence of truly major urban centers began to become apparent, spreading from the East through the Midwest.

By the turn of the century these major cities were beginning to threaten the rural majorities in many state legislatures. The very real threats of urban domination were compounded further by the fact that the composition of city populations had undergone some very marked changes in the last several decades of the nineteenth century. Migration streams from native American settlements were being replaced by European streams (see Elazar, 1970:166 et seq. for a discussion of these various streams). The new immigrants were often Catholic and brought with them their foreign customs and rituals. They frequently did not speak English nor did they always have a sound understanding of, or appreciation for, American democratic traditions. They were too often preoccupied with more basic needs to be overly concerned with the niceties of democratic theory, a tradition that was, in most instances, foreign to them.

Political conflicts over prohibition, political reform, and reapportionment, as well as other issues, kept urban-rural animosities at a high level through the late 1960s. At that point the effects of some pronounced population shifts that had been changing the landscape of urban America gave rise to yet another cleavage in the structure of state politics. The development of a metropolitan wide system of highways facilitated the movement of white urban dwellers to the outer fringes of urban areas, just as blacks from the South began to migrate to the central cities of the industrialized North. Later they were joined by Hispanics. This led to the emergence of the suburban ring as a new regional force in state politics, one that looks as imposing as the burgeoning cities of a century ago. Its ultimate impact on the political alliances within state governments is not altogether clear at this point, but there is every reason to believe that it will have as much impact as the emergence of cities had upon the sectional divisions of an earlier era.

Geo-Politics and Conflict

This brief review suggests that geo-political animosities have, for a long time, been an important source of political conflict. Their independence as a source of conflict is seen most clearly by their prevalence in primitive societies, societies in which geographic distinctions were not compounded by marked differences in religion, ethnicity, race, culture, or economic interests. The rapid development of one distinct region, perhaps as a result of geographic advantages, can breed suspicion and resentment by others, if only because of the fear of potential subsumption or domination.

We have also seen that the suspicions and resentments generated by these fears can be compounded by a number of factors. Economic exploitation and the suppression of legitimate political and human rights are one type of ubiquitous aggravating factor. They are in a very real sense the realization of fears of potential domination. Exploitative strategies tend to transform the misunderstandings that flow from geographically distinctive life-styles into regionally based animosities and hostilities.

Also important is repeated conflict over public policies, even under conditions of political equality across regions. The development of regionally specific comparative advantages often requires a set of public actions (easy money, tight money; the development of a particular type of infrastructure; policies protecting labor unions or regulating industrial or commercial practices). When regional diversity dictates different policies, conflict frequently results. Even when different regions support similar policies, differences can emerge when site specific decisions must be made or when the structure of a government program has distributional consequences for a region.

Another aggravating factor is the regional settlement of distinctive racial or ethnic groups. This occurs when certain geographic features—a harbor, fertile agricultural lands, rich ore deposits—offer special attractions to certain groups or when economic or political discrimination restricts identifiable classes of people to certain areas. Both factors affected the waves of immigrants that flocked to the United States during the nineteenth and twentieth centuries. Some looked for a setting similar to their homeland, others looked simply for immediate economic opportunity. Local enclaves of immigrants from a certain country attracted others, giving rise to immigrant populations that differed from the natives in terms of religion, customs, dress, language, and physical features. Cultural differences triggered regional conflicts that were quite independent of local economic interests. Differences also emerged over how political demands ought to be aggregated and articulated.

The types of regional animosities that these various factors create have important consequences for the operation of the political process, consequences that go beyond conflicts based on concrete differences in regional interests and views. Regional animosities can persist over time—even in the face of social changes that may have narrowed the distinctiveness of regional populations and interests. Social stereotypes and conventional wisdoms die slowly and blind even astute political observers. Regional differences can also spill over into issues that have few regional implications—due in part to the geographic basis of representational systems and the need to form lasting coalitions. Political networks in legislative bodies forged over time create lasting divisions and binding ties that can impede the formation of new coalitions, even when there are short-term gains to be realized.

This brief introduction has clarified somewhat the genre of political conflict we have labeled geo-political or regional, but it has also been useful for the immediate objectives of this work. It underscores the fact that regional animosities and conflicts in the American states are not a manifestation of some transient set of forces reflecting current demographic trends. We know that regionally based hostilities did not originate with the influx of blacks into the urban areas of the North after World War II. Nor did they begin with the great European immigrations that began in the latter part of the nineteenth century, nor even with the rise of the great urban areas in early U.S. history. Rather, the type of geo-political cleavages with which this book is concerned dates to the earliest clusterings of people in western civilization; they have their more immediate roots in sectional differences that predate the American revolution. Any reasoned attempt to understand or deal with these regional animosities must come to grips with these sobering realities or risk vastly underestimating the task at hand.

Regionalism in Illinois: A Comparative Perspective

Partly because of the developments just reviewed, Kenneth Palmer, in his review of state politics in the United States, was able to assert, "All states seem to have on-going conflicts of a sectional nature, either between distinctive geographic regions or between their metropolitan centers and the hinterland" (1972:34). He goes on to review some of these divisions:

Friction has long existed between northern and southern California over such issues as the use of water and legislative apportionment. In recent years, the two sections have manifested distinctive political styles, with northern areas, especially San Francisco, leaning in a liberal direction while southern California has provided a base for right-wing politics. Because of its peculiar shape and topography, Idaho reveals a three-way division in which the northern section of the state is closely linked to Washington, the southwestern to adjacent Oregon, and the southeastern portion, where large numbers of Mormons live, to Utah. Florida has historically revealed north-south tensions that led for many years to northern ("pork chop gang") domination of the state legislature through malapportionment and to occasional discussion of succession by south Florida politicians. Reapportionment and the emergence of a new constitution have eased this particular conflict.

Some long-standing intrastate conflicts seem as lively today as in past years. At the turn of the century, that famous Tammany Hall philosopher-politician, George Washington Plunkitt, allowed that his "fondest dream" was the eventual secession of the City of New York from the State of New York: "The feelin' between this city and the hayseeds that make a livin' by plunderin' it," complained Boss Plunkitt, "is every bit as bitter as the feelin' between the North and South before the war" [1972:34].

Palmer suggests that these regional divisions may be on the wane (1972:35 et seq.), but his observations were made before suburban ring communities began to assert themselves in the legislatures of many states, thereby restructuring and rekindling regional animosities.

If we examine the traditional literature on state politics, we find many other examples of sectionalism within states. Without question the premiere study is V. O. Key's *Southern Politics*. While the sectional cleavages differed somewhat from state to state, the most common division Key finds is between the "black belt" or tidewater or delta regions, where slavery and large plantations flourished, and the upcountry, where small farmers and independent mountain people eked out a living. Lockard (1959) found city, suburban, and small-town cleavages prominent in New England. Fenton (1957, 1966) found sectional differences from distinct migration patterns compounded by urban-rural divisions in the border and midwestern states. In the West a combination of geographic features and barriers, ethnic settlements, and city rivalries form the basis for the regional fissures in many states (Jonas, 1961).

To say that geo-political cleavages exist in most states is not to contend that they are inevitable or that the intensity of the cleavages is similar across states, or even within states over time. It is clear that the types of population migrations that forged the various cleavages discussed here did not affect all states in the same manner. Moreover, the geographic terrain differs from state to state, and its structure can have a marked effect upon the formation and perpetuation of regional cleavages.

Political factors can also affect the intensity and longevity of regional animosities. Broad-based state political parties and cumulative voting for state legislative offices can minimize the intensities of regional conflict because the parties will attempt to broker regional differences before they enter the legislative arena. In Turner's terms (1959:46), the party will act as a rubber band, pulling the sections together. Fenton's notion of "issue-oriented politics" as opposed to "job-oriented politics" (Fenton, 1966:chapter 1) is also relevant here. Issue-oriented politics will cut across regional lines, while issueless politics will be more likely to introduce regional divisions into conflicts as immediate self-interests play a larger role in the formation of public policies. Finally, the availability of highly emotive symbols underscoring a state's political heritage and evoking a sense of statewide political community will have a mitigating effect upon the intensity of sectional cleavages.

Given these various observations we must ask a set of questions relevant to the immediate object of our inquiry here: Where does Illinois stand in relation to the various patterns observed here? Does it evidence distinctive patterns? Are its regional animosities greater or less than those of other states?

With respect to the structure of its geo-political fault lines, it can be said that while no pronounced geographic barriers divide the state, most other factors that have worked to create intrastate cleavages have been operative in Illinois, as will be seen in the essays in Part II of this work. The second question is somewhat harder to answer, as these matters are difficult to quantify and are likely to vary over time. Elazar's analysis (1972:193, 198) of intrastate cleavages based on seven different factors—the diversity of political cultures among various subgroups of the population, the diversity of the state's general culture, and the existence of sectional, urban-rural, metropolitan-nonmetropolitan, local, and interurban cleavages within the states—is suggestive. Despite the limitations of his analysis (lack of quantification and lack of a temporal dimension) and the fact that his data do not conform precisely to the types of strictly geo-political cleavages we have been discussing, Elazar's analysis is generally consistent with what one might expect on the basis of the developments reviewed earlier. They also provide some semblance of a badly needed comparative perspective. Elazar's analysis suggests that Illinois is one of the more deeply divided states. In his scheme it is surpassed only by Missouri and Pennsylvania, which have interurban cleavages. On the other hand, Illinois does not stand out among the other midwestern states, which also have a variety of migration streams and urban-rural splits. These, of course, make them more fragmented than many of the western states, which are divided mainly along geographic lines.

Studying Geo-Political Cleavages

Our efforts to enhance our understanding of regional cleavages, with an eye toward appreciating their virtues and dealing with their diseconomies, were given very little guidance by prior bodies of research. The traditional literature on state politics, beginning with the seminal work of V. O. Key (1949, 1963) and his students (Fenton, 1957, 1966; Lockard, 1959), dealt with regionalism within states but treated it as a given and not as a focus of inquiry. The studies centered on the implications of regional strains for the structure of political parties and on the operation of parties in the democratic process and state policy making.

Key's ideas, and the extension of the "behavioral revolution" into the study of state politics and policy making, spawned a new generation of works (Dawson and Robinson, 1963; Hofferbert, 1968; Dye, 1966; Dye and Hofferbert, 1966; Sharkansky, 1967a, 1967b, 1968; Jacob and Vines, 1965; Sharkansky and Hofferbert, 1969). These works were comparative and highly quantitative. They sought to specify the determinants of state policy outputs as well as to document, rigorously and quantitatively, differences in state political institutions and processes. Some of these studies questioned the conclusions of Key and his followers. In challenging the importance of political factors in the state policy-making process, they generated a good deal of debate and controversy.

This body of comparative studies produced many insights and enhanced our understanding of many facets of state political systems. Its progeny have expanded the scope of inquiry and refined their methods, producing more sophisticated works. Nevertheless, this methodological shift has not been without its costs. In focusing on the state as the primary unit of analysis, most contemporary state politics scholars have ignored many of the most interesting facets of the work done by Key and his students, not to mention the work of historians such as Frederick Jackson Turner. Their insights concerning intrastate cleavages and politics merit further investigation.

To begin to follow up on some of these matters, we chose an interdisciplinary, multifaceted approach—one that stresses the developmental character of geo-political conflict but does not ignore the contemporary manifestations of regional animosities in Illinois. Political scientists, historians (both political and economic), economists, and demographers examined secondary and primary historical materials, as well as census, voting, and expenditures data, to enhance our understanding of the origins, nature, and manifestations of regionalism in Illinois. In addition, we conducted a statewide survey to examine directly the intensity and current underpinnings of regional animosities.

Before previewing these various contributions, a word needs to be said about our definition of regions within Illinois. This entire work is premised upon the belief that Illinois is divided into various regions, which have important implications for the state. We flesh out these implications in the following essays. In doing so, however, we are confronted with a formidable methodological problem with potentially important substantive implications. While there is little disagreement that Illinois is a heterogeneous state, the precise geographic cleavages are less clear. Moreover, the most meaningful divisions of the state may vary depending upon the time frame with which one is concerned or the substance of one's concerns (political, social, economic). One could talk about Chicago and "downstate," but what about the suburbs in the post–World War II era? Is it legitimate to lump the highly segmented and heterogeneous Chicago into one region? What counties are considered part of the suburbs? Does northern Illinois belong in the same category as southern Illinois? What about the central part of the state?

These problems might have been worked out by individual researchers defining their own regions based upon the nature of their concern. The danger here, of course, was that we could have ended up with ten disparate essays, which might not have yielded a cumulative and coherent set of insights and findings. Moreover, many of the research endeavors that we commissioned required an a priori definition of regions, the survey being the primary example here. Therefore, we developed, and asked authors to begin their work with, a common set of regions. These definitions were not relevant for all authors, especially those who focused on the Chicago metropolitan area or purely historical overviews. Also, not everyone could conform completely to our definition because of problems with the organization of existing data. This was especially a problem in trying to isolate Chicago when data were available only for counties. Finally, it should be stated that authors were encouraged, where possible, to experiment with more refined definitions of the state's regional structure after they had used our initial categories to conduct their preliminary examinations.

The regions we began with include the city of Chicago, its suburban collar, northern Illinois, central Illinois, and southern Illinois (see Figure 1–1). The choice of Chicago and its suburban collar was the easiest. Chicago has been at the heart of the regional cleavages in Illinois since the late 1800s; no defensible categorization of the state could exclude Chicago. The most problematic aspect of defining Chicago as a separate region is that it is so diverse that it is really an amalgam of subregions. Indeed, in some essays Chicago is disaggregated. Unfortunately, in a set of essays focusing on the state as a whole, it was simply not feasible or statistically possible to focus consistently on the various subsectors of the city. The suburban collar, while also a set of highly diverse cities and regions, was easy both to justify as a region and to identify. It was defined as suburban Cook county and the five surrounding counties. Even though some of the collar counties contain very rural sections, each contains towns and cities widely regarded as suburbs of Chicago. These towns and cities constitute the bulk of the population in these counties. Moreover, when taken as a whole, the suburban population is a sociologically distinctive part of the state. Politically, the suburbs are quickly becoming the fulcrum of power within Illinois.

The division of the remainder of the state into northern, central, and southern Illinois was more arbitrary and problematic. Because of the history and settlement patterns that characterized different parts of the state, we did not feel comfortable in lumping everything outside the metropolitan area into a "downstate" category. At the same time it was not at all clear how many subsections existed outside the collar counties or where the dividing lines should be drawn. Does a "western Illinois" exist in the minds of some Illinoisans? How far north does southern Illinois extend? We settled these questions in a fairly arbitrary and unsystematic manner, but we asked respondents a question in the statewide survey to check our categorizations.

These results for the most part confirmed our categorizations. Between 75 and 80 percent of the respondents in our southern and central subsamples identified themselves as being from the section of the state in which we had categorized them. About 67 percent of the people in the northern region identified themselves as being from northern Illinois. Nineteen percent of the people in counties we had categorized as "northern," however, said they lived in central Illinois.

Figure 1–1. Regions within Illinois

Only about 1 percent of the respondents labeled themselves as being from western Illinois. Thus, for the most part, the categorizations we used for the nonmetropolitan area were a defensible first attempt at defining the regional structure of the state. Various essays will suggest better categorizations for different purposes; in others the various categorizations do not appear to make much difference.

The first set of essays are historical attempts to define the origins and development of regionalism in Illinois. Frederick Wirt presents an in-depth examination of the various peoples and cultures that have settled in different parts of the state at different points in its history. Jeremy Atack reveals how differences in the development of regional economies within the state have exacerbated the cultural differences and intensified the regional cleavages. Finally, focusing upon the nineteenth century, Robert Sutton recounts the history of regional political conflict in Illinois.

The second set of essays examines developments in the post–World War II era, with a focus on the Chicago metropolitan area. Chiang and Geraci lay the groundwork for these analyses by tracing the population shifts that led to the emergence of Chicago's suburban collar as a potent political force within the state. The following essays make more sense when interpreted in light of the shifts mapped out in their demographic analysis. Alexis and McDonald trace the shifting economic fortunes of the city of Chicago and its immediate neighbors by examining the history of their economic relations. They also discuss the changes in the regional economy of the metropolitan area and Chicago's vital role in that economy. Michael Preston analyzes the changing politics within the metropolitan area by tracing the history of political relations between blacks and white ethnics. He investigates the roots of the growing disaffection between the burgeoning black community and the powerful Democratic machine, the rupture of this once thriving relationship, and its ultimate impact on Chicago's role in metropolitan, state, and national politics. Using the lessons of this history, he suggests what can be done to stem the deterioration of Chicago's political power within the state's new regional configuration.

The final section of the book includes empirical assessments of the political dimensions and manifestations of regional animosities. Frank, Nardulli, and Green examine legislative representation and voting patterns from a regional perspective, pointing out distinct regional patterns and shifts in the balance of political power. Looking at the fiscal dimensions of regionalism (who gets what), Fossett and Giertz examine the equity of state expenditures in different sections of the state and attempt to explain and assess the findings they uncover. Finally, Nardulli and Krassa analyze data from a multi-sample statewide survey concerning regionalism. They first map respondents' views of the state and their perceptions of inhabitants of different parts of the state. Then they examine regional differences in attitudes, perceptions, and political wants.

In a concluding essay Nardulli attempts to summarize the structure and evolution of regionalism within Illinois and suggests four dimensions to geo-political conflict in state politics that are important to understand. He closes with some suggestions for dealing with regional conflicts.

NOTES

1. A good historical introduction into regionalism in American life can be found in Jensen (1951) and Turner (1959).

2. See, for example, Elazar (1970), Rossiter (1953), Turner (1950), and Nevins (1927). Each of these works is well documented and makes references to other basic sources.

3. See Turner (1950:25 et seq.) for the contrast between these "upland folks" and the tidewater aristocracy that seems to be implied in Elazar's characterization of the southern subculture. Much of V. O. Key's work on southern politics in the 1940s (Key, 1949) develops the contrasts between these two groups as well.

REFERENCES

Dawson, Richard E., and James A. Robinson. 1963. "Interparty Competition, Economic Variables, and Welfare Politics in the American States." *Journal of Politics* 25 (May):265–89.

de Ste. Croix, G. E. M. 1981. *The Class Struggle in the Ancient Greek World.* Ithaca, N.Y.: Cornell University Press.

Dye, Thomas R. 1966. *Politics, Economics and the Public: Policy Outcomes in the American States.* Chicago: Rand McNally.

———, and Richard I. Hofferbert. 1966. "Some Structural and Environmental Variables in the American States." *American Political Science Review* 50 (March):73–82.

Elazar, Daniel J. 1970. *Cities of the Prairie.* New York: Basic Books.

———. 1972. *American Federalism: A View from the State,* 2d ed. New York: Thomas Y. Crowell.

Farrand, Max. 1911. *The Records of the Federal Convention of 1787.* New Haven, Conn.: Yale University Press.

Fenton, John H. 1957. *Politics in the Border States.* New Orleans: Hauser Press.

———. 1966. *Midwest Politics.* New York: Holt, Rinehart and Winston.

Glaab, Charles N., and A. Theodore Brown. 1976. *A History of Urban America*, 2d ed. New York: Macmillan.

Hale, J. R. 1978. *Renaissance Europe Individual and Society, 1480–1520*. New York: Harper and Row.

Hofferbert, Richard I. 1968. "Socioeconomic Dimensions of the American States: 1890–1960." *Midwest Journal of Political Science* 12 (August): 401–18.

Jacob, Herbert, and Kenneth Vines. 1965. *Politics in the American States: A Comparative Analysis*. Boston: Little, Brown.

Jensen, Merrill, ed. 1951. *Regionalism in America*. Madison: University of Wisconsin Press.

Jonas, Frank H. 1961. *Western Politics*. Salt Lake City: University of Utah Press.

Jones, A. H. M. 1940. *The Greek City from Alexander to Justinian*. Oxford: Oxford University Press.

Key, V. O., Jr. 1949. *Southern Politics*. New York: Random House.

———. 1963. *American State Politics: An Introduction*. New York: Knopf.

LeGoff, Jacques. 1976. "The Town as an Agent of Civilization 1200–1500." In Carlo M. Cipolla (ed.), *Fontana Economic History of Europe, I: The Middle Ages*. New York: Barnes and Noble.

Lockard, Duane. 1959. *New England State Politics*. Chicago: Henry Regnery.

Mood, Fullmer. 1951. "The Origin, Evolution and Application of the Sectional Concept, 1750–1900." In Merrill Jensen (ed.), *Regionalism in America*. Madison: University of Wisconsin Press.

Nevins, Allan. 1927. *The American States during and after the Revolution 1775–1789*. New York: MacMillan.

Oppenheim, A. Leo. 1977. *Ancient Mesopotamia*. Chicago: University of Chicago Press.

Palmer, Kenneth T. 1972. *State Politics in the United States*. New York: St. Martin's Press.

Rossiter, Clinton. 1953. *The Seedtime of the Republic*. New York: Harcourt, Brace.

Sharkansky, Ira. 1967a. "Economic and Political Correlates of State Government Expenditures: General Tendencies and Deviant Cases." *Midwest Journal of Political Science* 11 (May):173–92.

———. 1967b. "Government Expenditures and Public Services in the American States." *American Political Science Review* 61 (December):1066–77.

———. 1968. *Spending in the American States*. Chicago: Rand McNally.

———, and Richard I. Hofferbert. 1969. "Dimensions of State Politics and Policy." *American Political Science Review* 63 (September):867–79.

Turner, Frederick Jackson. 1950. *The United States, 1830–1850*. New York: Henry Holt.

———. 1959. *The Significance of Sections in American History*. Gloucester, Mass.: Peter Smith.

PART II

The Roots of Regionalism

The Changing Social Bases of Regionalism: Peoples, Cultures, and Politics in Illinois

2

Frederick M. Wirt

"Culture" refers to a group's regular ways of acting and believing about important things in their lives—religion, family, work, government. Different peoples have different cultures, and when these differences come into contact, conflict—political or otherwise—often results. Living with cultural diversity and managing this conflict potential are problems that have challenged people and their institutions throughout recorded history. Conflict arises for reasons stated so eloquently by Rudyard Kipling in "The Stranger within My Gate":

> He may be true or kind
> But he does not talk my talk—
> I cannot feel his mind.
> I see the face and the eyes and the mouth.
> But not the soul behind.

There have been many such strangers in the history of Illinois. Their differences have precipitated political, religious, and economic conflicts that have laid the foundation for regional animosities. In some instances, these regional cleavages have persisted well after the fading of the cultural distinctions that originally created them. These regional animosities have contributed in important ways to the divisions that have characterized Illinois politics for most of its history (Sutton, chapter 4 herein; Frank, Nardulli, and Green, chapter 8 herein). This essay aims to explore the cultural roots of that regionalism and its alteration over time. It starts with the first settlement period and then examines immigration from Europe and the parallel urbanization and industrialization of the state that attracted first these immigrants and later black and Hispanic peoples. Finally, it provides some integrative observations about diversity in culture, regionalism, and politics of the state today.

The Settlement Period

Unlike many other states, Illinois was settled in geographical layers, each with its distinctive ethnic and religious qualities. Historians agree on the basics of what occurred (Jensen, 1978; Pooley, 1968; Power, 1953; Wyman, 1984). At different times and in different places, settlers crowded into the half-saucer-shaped state with its flat prairies of the east-central region surrounded on three sides by low hills.

In the first quarter of the nineteenth century, poor farmers from the southern highlands of Appalachia flooded into southern Illinois. Then for the next quarter-century, Yankees from New England poured into the northern region. While the south and north continued to grow before 1860, other large groups were also arriving to find their niches. Germans moved into counties east of St. Louis and up the Illinois River valley, and Irish were beginning their urban concentration, mainly in Chicago. In the years before the Civil War, the last settled region—the east-central prairies—began slowly filling with farmers from the Old Northwest and Middle Atlantic states. The southern region—called "Egypt" with its commercial center at Cairo—dominated the state's population and politics in this early era. A brief sketch of the cultures in these three regions will enable us to focus sharply upon key cultural differences in this settlement period.

Southern Pioneers: Traditionalists

Prior to 1830, a great corridor from southern Appalachia funneled impoverished, land-hungry Scots-Irish pioneers into the tributary valley systems north of the Ohio River. A starting point for many was up the Wabash River bordering Indiana and then west into the "Shawneetown" region. Widely dispersed, these small farmers settled in family units amid the tall forests; that is what they had known in the forest uplands of Appalachia.

Theirs was a traditionalist culture whose central values were both negative and positive. They distrusted everything outside kith and kin—strangers, laws, education, and progress. Having lost out to large landowners down South and bitterly resentful of it, they doffed their coonskin hats to neither squire nor judge. They lacked education and saw little need for it for their children. The protection of rights, property, and family was often handled individually and violently. Litigation was extensive, but the presence of local enemies on juries often led to dissatisfaction with this process and hence to feuds and vigilantes. Williamson County—"bloody Williamson"—in the heart of Egypt had a fearsome reputation for such violence. Several hundred were killed in just a decade after the Civil War amid industrial violence over creating miner unions (Angle, 1952).

But these pioneers also experienced a closeness to their God; the traditional roles of family and church were the center of their lives. They were sustained by an extended family and by authority figures such as the husband in families, a vengeful God in religion, and (much later) a party boss in politics. For the southerners, freedom in this new land meant cutting all ties to society except those to family and church. An extended family, once in place in the forests, provided a means for bringing other members northward. Once there, family members protected one another against all outsiders as well as natural and personal disasters. Living as isolates, they saw only a physical world bounded by their property lines, and they believed in a "spiritual world [that] encompassed not heaven, hell, and Christ crucified, but spirits, spells, and omens" (Jensen, 1978:23). As late as forty years ago, the folklore of backwoods Egypt was still heavy with stories of ghosts, or "hants," and witchcraft (Smith, 1941; Briggs, 1952). The theology of the dominant Baptists and Methodists centered on a protective and vengeful God. The Bible was interpreted by tiny congregations, which often split over theological points that, while obscure, were passionately felt. Their religion was pietistic; it was not dominated by higher church authorities but rather was decentralized—or fragmented—to an uneducated lay minister who was "called" to preach.

Their religion shaped their views on public policy. Southerners objected to government policies that outsiders claimed were morally imperative. To the pioneer settler, separation of state and church was not merely constitutional law but God's law as well (following from Cole, 1922:207–29). Religion in Egypt could interact with other values to shape policy views. Temperance was opposed for several reasons. There was no clear biblical injunction against drinking, whiskey was a vital commodity in corn-growing areas, and, as a local newspaper put it, "the use of intoxicating drinks seems more natural than the use of water." It was no surprise that a statewide referendum on temperance failed badly in this region. On another policy matter, slavery was condoned in this region more than elsewhere. In this, the pioneers repeated the biblical justification for it that the deep South also expressed. As a result, "race hatred often broke out in southern towns, [and blacks] dwelt in true humility in obscure corners of towns and cities." Also, that era's important feminist issue—discrimination in property rights—was never questioned in Egypt.

This region's culture was reinforced by its ethnic and religious homogeneity and an "attachment to the Democratic party [which] provided, perhaps, the major unifying force within the region" (Raines, 1985:22). Egypt had few blacks, few foreign-born, and few Catholics. Still, some ethnic diversity existed. Many immigrants—mostly Germans—lived close to St. Louis in St. Clair and Monroe counties. In 1860, those two counties had just over 40 percent foreign-born; there were also substantial percentages in the ring of counties surrounding them (Clinton, Perry, Randolph, Washington) and even in river towns in the far southern counties of Alexander and Pulaski. The true Anglo-Saxon traditionalists lay in Egypt's interior (where the Ku Klux Klan originated after the Civil War). The coming of the railroads in the 1850s began to break down this isolation, but the traditionalistic culture was to remain for a century.

Northern Yankees: Moralists

New forms of transportation were crucial for the arrival of the next major cultural group—the "Yankees." Coming into the north after 1830, they arrived first by boats along the Erie and Illinois and Michigan canals and then by trains. These immigrants brought not simply a new population but a new culture. Figure 2–1 shows how, in successive decades of the movement west, the New Englanders reached northern Illinois by the 1840s and the prairie region in the 1850s.

Compared to the southern settlers, these immigrants had drastically different views about most aspects of life. This difference arose from a New England culture that was determinedly "moralist," that is, it was driven by the religious zeal of the New England churches to use secular power to achieve God's will. In this culture, it was imperative for members to make something of this new world economically and to convert the land into a Christian commonwealth. Their churches— mostly Congregationalist and Presbyterian—were organized hierarchically. This meant that religious doctrine was set by higher church authorities and then transmitted to local churches through ministers trained in theology, usually in New England (Sweet, 1939). These ministers, often termed "missionaries," were sent from the East to the northern farmlands and Chicago's belt counties to build this religious structure and to transmit theological doctrine.

As a Yankee, one didn't simply submit to fate but rather used reasonable analysis to find efficient ways of organizing life for the

Figure 2-1. Westward Migration of the People of New England into Lands North of the Ohio, 1820–50

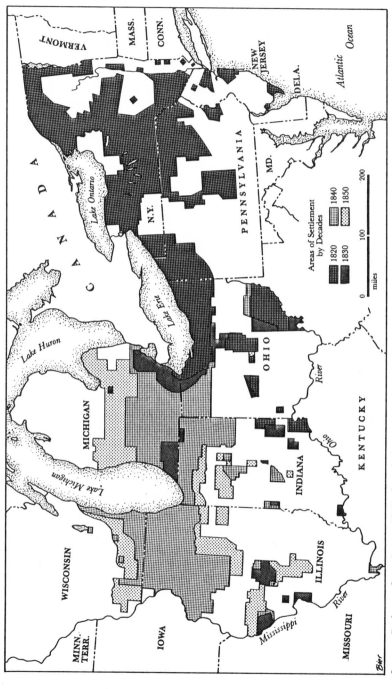

Source: Redrawn from Sweet,,1939, frontispiece.

purpose of fulfilling God's will. One of those ways was to employ the authority of government to provide in law the "right" policies, conceived of as God's work in this land. This culture insisted that women had special responsibilities that were unknown to the southern pioneer women; they were given exclusive authority over household affairs and raising children. That notion, new then, persisted throughout our history until recent decades brought new attitudes about work and parenting (Demos, 1986). Central to the Yankees was schooling, which was clearly viewed as a resource to be developed and employed for good purposes. This belief accounts for the fact that, unlike southerners, they regularly founded numerous schools and colleges, like Grinnell and Beloit. Equally central to this culture was the importance of participating in community life through voluntary groups. As a consequence, Yankees created new forms of organization in many sectors—corporations, banks, and universities. All these forms were ways of combining separate resources into group resources that could be employed for specific tasks within a moralist outlook rooted in religious values.

Possessing more resources than earlier settlers, the Yankee thrived in agriculture, business, and industry in the northern part of Illinois. Their farms flourished, as evidenced by the fact that their income was half again greater than similarly placed farmers. Their industries mushroomed in Chicago and the smaller cities in the northern half of the state. And everywhere, they pushed progress. As a governor of the era noted, "Is a school house, a bridge, or a church to be built, a road to be made, a school or minister to be maintained, or taxes to be paid? The northern man is never found wanting" (Jensen, 1978:48-49).

The Settlement of the Prairies: A Mixture of North and South

A familiar aspect of Illinois geography are those flat, black, rich prairies of the east-central region. Yet this was the last area settled in the early period. In 1830, most settlers lived along a V-shaped sector between the Mississippi and Wabash rivers and bounded by the Ohio River (Atack, chapter 3 herein: Figures 3–2 and 3–3). By 1850, however, settlers had filled in much of the V-shape and were settling in the north and northeast, especially in Chicago. The settlers of the prairie in the 1850s and later moved relatively slowly into the rich of farmlands in east-central Illinois. These settlers were mostly Scots-Irish (with some Germans), often from Mid-Atlantic states or New England.

Their culture was a mixture of the North and South. These new

prairie settlers were often suspicious of new things; new farm implements, like mechanical reapers, were not accepted immediately. But
they were also active businesspeople, always looking for better products and higher profits. Although they were religious as settlers in
other regions, they were not driven, as were Yankees, to imprint every
aspect of living with what was regarded as God's handiwork. There
were fewer prairie folk than either pioneers or Yankees, but later they
often operated pivotally between the regions, particularly in presidential voting.

Yankee-Southern Cultural Differences

These waves of early settlers differed in more than these major cultural
aspects; cultural differences touched even the smallest aspect of life.
For example, pioneers preferred to race horses with a rider on the
animal, while Yankees put the rider in a two-wheeled cart for harness
and trotting races. But more fundamental differences existed between
these two cultures—their origins, work, physical structures, and literacy (following abstracted from Power, 1953). The southern settlers
were poor people seeking free land not controlled by landlords in
the South or England, but the Yankees settlers were prosperous enough
to afford to move. Southerners expected little from God, people, or
nature, while the Yankees had high expectations of all three because
they served God's will. Such conflicting expectations were an underlying factor in regional differences.

Agriculture. The two cultures approached quite differently the dominant way of making a living—farming. Southerners' forest or bottomland had poor soil and was often swampy; it suffered from heavy
rainfall and could produce only thin crops. The Yankees, however,
farmed lands with extremely rich soil, excellent rainfall, and bountiful
crops. Yankees saw the pioneers as "lazy" and themselves as "indus-
trious," although differences in land quality—not personal qualities—
may have been the true cause of Yankee productivity.

Differences in farm organization and methods were striking. Northerners grew hay for cattle fodder, but southerners simply used leaves
of their corn plants. Northerners carried fruit farming and dairying
from New England to Illinois to provide lucrative products (and still
do), but southern settlers did none of this because little had been
done in the Appalachians. Even the type of corn grown—the main
cash crop in both regions—differed (flint versus gourd seed), because
each type had been dominant in their points of origin. As for the
food they ate, Yankees saw buttermilk as fit only for hogs, and wheat

bread and potatoes dominated their diet. Among pioneers, however, buttermilk was a treat for humans, and cornbread and sweet potatoes regularly graced their dinner tables.

Culturally, these differences point directly to the contrasts in agriculture in New England and the American South which were carried to Illinois in the minds and packs of settlers. Settlers turned these differences into a contrasting economic reality on their farms. That experience, combined with differences in energy, land, and climate, produced regional differences in wealth almost from the beginning.

Physical Structures. How we shape our physical environment is affected by how culture tells us to do it; moreover, the presence of those physical shapes comfort the members but antagonize outsiders. A small, significant example of the imprint of culture upon structures is found in the shape of property. In Illinois, Yankees drew their land plats in rectangles, while pioneers avoided square angles. Why? Rectangles had been convenient in measuring boundaries in New England's flatlands, but odd property angles were absolutely necessary in hilly, upland Appalachia. Property lines were marked in northern Illinois by straight, board fences, but in southern Illinois the fences were V-shaped, open, log rails (these were the "worm" rails Abraham Lincoln made famous as "the rail splitter"). This rail was more adaptable to the rough, hilly terrain of Egypt and, earlier, of Appalachia.

A house carries deep emotional feelings for the owner, but it also reflects local culture; the two influences are deeply mixed. Houses, therefore, had different structures in the state. The southern farmhouse was built at the back of the corn field, suggesting a barrier of space against neighbors or visitors passing on the road; however, Yankees placed farmhouses near the road, accessible to community members. The house's interior most visibly marked these cultural differences. A Yankee typically built a two-story, frame, New England-type house, which had internal stairs and was planned for comfort. The pioneer farmer, however, erected a crude, casually assembled, one-story house, which was often unfloored and contained crude furniture. Nearby, the Yankee would build a barn for horses; after all, New England winters had been cruel. Horse barns were rare in southern Illinois because winters had been easier in the South.

The cultural implication of these physical differences is that they gave visible evidence that like-minded persons were living nearby. These structures also enabled people to identify members of their own—and differing—cultures. Physical difference can increase the possibility of conflict between cultures when a structure is a visible reminder to friends and neighbors of "strangers within my gate."

Literacy. The way people converse and the words they use have always marked off different cultures but also have provided another basis for conflict. Literally, the outlander "does not talk my kind of talk"; language becomes another way of classifying "our kind" and every-body else. Even teaching the language will emphasize one's special inflection, accent, and vocabulary. In reading, divisions arise when using one's own books, whose allusions symbolically reinforce com-munity. Even the words for the same object differed. The Yankees went up a "hill," but the pioneers went up a "bluff"; the first crossed a "stream," but the second a "slew"; the Yankees could "guess" where they were, but the other "reckoned" their location. When such lan-guage differences are based in regions, they reinforce other differences based on religion, work, and so on.

Language thus provided yet another regional distinction in early Illinois. Yankee culture had a tradition of letters and printing; as far back as the colonial era, Massachusetts had adopted the first public-schooling law in America. On the other hand, there was very little drive for education in the South, although Thomas Jefferson had (unsuccessfully) urged Virginia to adopt a state university system. Not surprisingly, then, northern immigrants to Illinois left a much larger paper trail of their ideas and times than did southern immigrants. Their letters home to New England regularly reported details of their operations in pursuing God's work, or they requested assistance for that work. Southern expression, on the other hand, was much more oral than written and exhibited a more limited vocabulary; few wrote home to the South so there was little record left of their actions.

Census records document these literacy differences. Although Il-linois regional breakdowns are not available, by comparing the state as a whole in 1850 with the South (the origin of Egypt), Power (1953:chapter 2) found that more resources for achieving literacy were available in Illinois. Illinois had 23 percent of its children in schools in 1850, but southern states had only 6 percent. Similarly, Illinois compared to the South had fewer pupils per school (211 versus 531), fewer borrowers per library book (3 versus 19), and more papers and periodicals printed per person (22 versus 11).

The Impact of These Differences. The Yankees of Illinois injected a re-ligion-driven quality to their work of pioneering; institutions and members were to serve moral purposes through a collective combining of will and resources. Southerners, however, faced the world individually or through the extended family. For them, religion was less a collective experience and was less transformed into public action; rather, it was a private relationship with God which had little community consequence. Overlaying this fundamental difference in regional culture was a relative affluence derived from agriculture and business in the north that was little known to the southerners. Everything else equal between the regions, this economic difference would have generated conflict; that distinction sharpens after the Civil War, as shown later.

Ethnic Arrivals in the Settlement Period: Germans and Irish

Any accounting of settlers in the early period is incomplete if it excludes consideration of the true foreigners, the immigrants from Ireland and Germany. They would be the first of several waves of ethnic-racial migrants in Illinois history who would provide both diversity and social tensions to these regional differences just detailed. After 1880, central and east Europeans would provide another surge, blacks another after each world war, and Hispanics in recent decades. But in the early period of settlement, a special ingredient was provided to the two cultures in the first ethnic wave of "immigrants in the valley" of the Upper Mississippi (Wyman, 1984).

Both Irish and Germans fit the traditionalist culture of southern Illinois, but they expressed it quite differently. Well before 1850, the Germans filled farms and cities in a swath from St. Louis east into Illinois counties and then up the Illinois River to Springfield. For the whole of the nineteenth century, they were the largest immigrant group in St. Louis, Chicago, and the state as a whole. From their earliest days, Germans established a reputation for hard work, prospering in skilled trades, business, and farming. How, then, do Germans fit into the traditionalistic mold of the Appalachian pioneers? While Germans were more prosperous and varied in their economic activity than traditionalist pioneers, like the latter they were just as strongly rooted in the large extended family and their religion. Whether Roman Catholic or Lutheran, religion was of the deepest importance to Germans, and God was a dominant, authoritarian figure in their lives. Unlike the southern pioneers but like the Yankees, however, their religious structure was hierarchical, and it directed many aspects of their lives.

As for the Irish, the familiar history of oppression that drove them to the Atlantic shore also brought them inland as unskilled labor to build canals and railroads. Usually they clustered in cities, especially

Chicago, but some railroad workers left to buy or work farms along the rail lines. Wherever they lived, the Irish were mostly unskilled labor; by the end of the nineteenth century, however, the men would staff the urban services and the women the domestic services. How were they traditionalist? Like southern pioneers, the Irish had deep roots in the extended family, and their Roman Catholicism furnished traditional norms for all aspects of life. The city also provided another hierarchy to structure their lives, namely, the political party machine; as early as the mid-1850s, one in five elected or appointed Chicago officials was an Irishman.

Ethnic-Religious Tensions

If Yankee-southern divisions were severe in this early era, the ethnicity and religion of these new arrivals generated a fierce reaction—"nativism," a hatred of everything foreign, especially Catholic. These immigrants infuriated the Protestants, particularly the Yankees. Without exaggeration, the Yankees hated everything about them—their religion, politics, manners, speech, and morals. In the 1840s, this Protestant reaction led to a national, nativist movement which took political form in the American party, better known as the "Know-Nothings" because they cloaked their actions in silence. The movement arose in the big eastern cities, and its members physically attacked the Catholic churches, vilified the clergy, and beat up the immigrant faithful. All in all, as its historian noted, nativism was truly a "brass-knuckled crusade" (Beals, 1960).

The Catholic church in cities like Chicago and Milwaukee was especially visible to Protestants because it did something not done in eastern cities (Walch, 1978). The church arrived in Chicago just as that city's service institutions were building up, so there were no private social institutions to compete with this church—unlike the situation in Boston or New York. The new diocese, facing floods of immigrants, had a highly praised record of aiding them with schooling and social welfare, a record that continued through the rest of the century. In the East, however, other institutions, private and public, undertook these tasks, often competitively. Another difference in Chicago was that its Catholic immigrants arrived at the same time and in equal numbers as non-Catholics, so there was little residential segregation to resist immigrant settlement. Clearly, then, Catholic influence and involvement depended on local circumstances. To the Yankees, it was this visible operation of the Catholic church, combined with the presence of "hordes" of despised foreigners, that fueled nativism.

An economic factor operated here as well. The Irish came to build the transportation system of Illinois in the 1830s and 1840s, but in the process they sparked confrontations over working conditions, political parties, and religion (Lightner, 1973). Much of that conflict arose because the employers of the Irish were invariably American and Protestant. They provided working conditions (often dreadful) and wages (often unpaid) that soon offended the Irish. Their reaction took an organized form; it was immigrant grievances over these matters that planted the seed of later unionism (thereby giving that movement an immigrant stereotype). The Germans, on the other hand, early gained some respect because of their highly successful accomplishments in business and farming, where they were less tied to the economic will of corporations. But they, too, bore the brunt of the nativists' hatred, and they rejected Yankee Protestants' control of them in civil matters. These attacks became less violent after the Civil War, which showed the Irish and Germans could bleed and die as well as any Yankee, but the distrust and dislike still distorted relations for decades.

Regional Policy Differences in the Settlement Period

The pioneer and immigrant regularly clashed with the Yankee north over its "civilizing" efforts. In this period, there were more voters—and hence political power—in the south; the legislatures were dominated by them. Consequently, reform efforts by Yankees faced strong opposition. The period between 1855 and 1856 capped the struggle at a time when population strength was starting to tilt toward Chicago and the north. The two regions confronted one another on three major Yankee issues.

First, in the period just before the Civil War, the American states were starting to require elementary schooling. The traditional dislike of schooling in Egypt led its representatives to oppose a public-school law that, nevertheless, passed in 1855 (the Germans of St. Clair County supported it, a reflection of their own culture's respect for literature and learning). The Yankees won this one. Second, in 1855 a statewide referendum on prohibition—dear to Yankee hearts—received only 45 percent support. It lost by margins of 78 to 90 percent in southern counties, while winning by almost the same margins in northern Illinois (Winnebago County gave it 86 percent). The southerners won this one. Third, a year later, when the Republican party was emerging, southern Illinois voted heavily against it and for Democrat Stephen Douglas (his opponent, John Frémont, got only five votes in southern Jackson County); on the other hand, northern Illinois and Chicago overwhelmed Douglas (Wyman, 1984). The Yankees and GOP won this one, which permanently affected the state's political history.

These differences became fiercely focused with the issue of slavery and the onset of the Civil War. There was some secession sentiment in southern Illinois; indeed, nervous Union army commanders were stationed around Cairo early in the war. There was little love for abolitionism in Egypt and among the Irish. Both saw it as a Yankee issue, embodying the worst of their New England ways of thinking about man and God. Yankees, on the other hand, saw southern and Irish opposition to temperance as the moral stain of a backward people who would never better themselves. The rhetoric on both sides was a lot hotter than even these sentences express.

The Democratic and Whig-Republican parties provided political outlets for these culture differences. Specifically, the parties served to aggravate and institutionalize these cultural differences and their regional bases. As the two parties strengthened their bases, the electoral divisions became almost permanent, lasting to this day in rough form (Key, 1956:224–25).

In a special way, then, Illinois in its settlement period was a microcosm of the group pluralism that was to become America's hallmark. People from different countries and different regions of America came to the state at different times with different cultures. The resulting social combination was not a mix (that implies blending) and not an overlay (they were separated geographically). Rather, it was a social pluralism, that is, a system of different cultures rooted in different regions within the same political system. Illinois had a "bi-polar pluralism" in the settlement era, pitting north against south, with cultural differences along numerous dimensions. Personal contact with these differences generated group conflict that was converted into political conflict in elections and legislatures, as subsequent chapters explain. Such differences could not remain isolated, particularly in the face of the immigrant and urbanization waves after the Civil War.

Urbanization and Immigrant Waves

The social landscape of Illinois was dramatically transformed after 1865 under the bulldozing effects of people coming here and into the cities from farms and from Europe. These forces interacted dynamically with a rampant industrialism and urban-rural tensions. The result was to transform a bi-polar pluralism into a pervasive contest between Chicago and the rest of the state, which had a profound effect on Illinois culture.

The Urban Concentration

The single driving force underlying change in Illinois was an exploding urbanization in Chicago. In 1860, one in seven Illinoisans lived in the city, but by 1900 better than one in two did. By 1980, however, four of five Illinoisans lived in metropolitan areas (three of five in Chicago alone), and three of five were suburbanites (Census Bureau, 1981:7, 18). How did this enormous population shift alter social pluralism?

Urbanism and Social Control. When this period began, Illinoisans were still primarily farmers. Small towns studded here and there across the countryside were tied together by a commercial necklace of railroads. Urban life played little part in the traditionalist and Yankee cultures, except for a sense of community. But some qualities of urbanism were embraced as early as the 1850s even among southerners. For example, a typical southern town in Edgar County had developed a community leadership that was "stable, controlling most community functions apparently conscious of its role—in other words, an elite" (Alcorn, 1974:701).

Growth means bringing together more people with different cultural outlooks who will usually transform their differences into conflict. For example, in another town in the same period—Jacksonville—institutions were already developing to cope with turbulent issues stirred up by its diverse population (Doyle, 1977). As a new town, Jacksonville in the 1850s faced extensive conflict over different views about religion, nativism, temperance, and slavery. Political life was not only turbulent but downright dangerous. There were "Southerners caning Yankees, vigilante mobs chasing abolitionists, Christians squabbling over the doctrine of infant baptism, police raids on Irish grog shops, violent demonstrations to protest the Civil War . . . a Hobbesian jungle of violent discord" (Doyle, 1977:157).

The nature of conflict in Jacksonville and other cities would change over time—away from personal to institutional conflict. Typically, organizations emerged here and elsewhere to express members' views—the familiar mobilization-articulation functions of group activity in American politics. Another feature of urban life also developed—cross-cutting cleavages. Amid a scene of multiple conflicts—characteristically urban rather than rural—one could not line up against another on one issue if there were the possibility of sharing views on something else. Group coalitions then became possible. The politics of temperance mobilized the German and Irish immigrants and the working class against the Protestant middle class of whatever ethnicity. Moreover, boosterism could bridge religious and partisan divisions because all groups shared a common interest in promoting jobs and profits. In this fashion, the formation of formal institutions (e.g., parties, churches, volunteer groups) could operate to integrate a diverse population flowing in and through growing towns. If voluntary means failed to smooth over divisions, then more coercive means were available from police, schools, and laws, or by warehousing the criminals and poor. Much of this institutionalization was elite-driven, that is, it was "aimed by the native middle class against a transient, foreign-born, and deviant population" (Doyle, 1977:164). Because the foreign-born were spread throughout the state (although heavily concentrated in Chicago), this process was pervasive.

Urbanism and the Economy. Another change in the urban-rural culture of Illinois was economic as the orientation of urban life changed from agriculture to a mixed economy. Chicago, Rockford, Peoria, Springfield, and other cities most clearly demonstrated this economic diversity. But many county seats and smaller towns came to know some business activity other than just servicing farmers' needs. Some sites became one-industry towns, catering to a manufacturer of farm implements or to a mining company. As the twentieth century progressed, mixed economies became more typical of even the small towns. One study of the industrial geography of towns along the Wabash River (Cutshall, 1941) found that even a half-century ago such towns were representative of the nation between Appalachia and the Mississippi River. That is, "The life of the people is not dependent upon manufacturing, or upon mining, or agriculture, but upon a combination of these basic industries. . . . There are no true 'one-industry' towns" (Cutshall, 1941:304).

There is an important implication of this economic reorientation in town life. Growing urbanism became increasingly tied into the industrialization of American society that exploded after the Civil War and soared to ever greater heights in this century. No longer was the economy one of growing corn in Egypt and raising cows in northern Illinois. Rather, it was an economy characterized by Chicago dominating much manufacturing, middle-sized cities linking to firms elsewhere, and small towns balancing farm, realty, and small manufacturing activities. After World War II, the suburban rush created cities dependent upon the metropolitan center, not the farmland. All of these places became tied into the increasingly interdependent economy. Depressions in the 1890s, 1930s, and early 1980s—and boom times in between—affected everyone, whether urban or rural, in business or farming. The early settlement farmers could claim their independence from outsiders—they really weren't, of course, because of market prices—and their dependence only upon nature and God. But the newly urbanized population was fully dependent upon many others locally and elsewhere—even abroad. The farmers meanwhile became even more dependent upon economic and social forces outside their control. And nature and God were still uncertain influences on their work.

These urban-rural changes resulted in a unity, brought on by interdependence, but also a diversity that persists to this day. The diversity is not simply that between city and rural folk. Even among the larger cities of Illinois in the 1970s, polls and documents demonstrate great variety in their histories, populations, economies, governments, politics, and qualities of life (Johnson and Veach, 1980). It is this pervasiveness of urbanism throughout the state that changed the bi-polar pluralism of the settlement era into a "multifaceted pluralism."

The Ethnic and Racial Factor

For the native-born Americans, the real "strangers within my gate" came in a flood after the Civil War and touched almost every county in some fashion, decade after decade. The cold statistics of this experience must be matched with the life experience of the new arrivals to understand how their pervasiveness on the cultural landscape had continuing effects on the state's society.

Some propositions about ethnicity and race can be gleaned from census data (Census Bureau, 1981:18; 1975:27; Keiser, 1977:table A; Schwartz, 1959). Although a rich variety of nationalities came here, Germans dominated the immigrant groups until surpassed by Poles in 1930. The immigrants settled in every region, reaching 5 percent in the most southern—and Appalachian origin—counties in 1870. The average foreign-born percentage of the population among all counties for eighty years is shown in Figure 2–2. Moving northward from Egypt, the proportions increased, with most concentrated in cities and especially in Chicago. The foreign-born were always a minority: one in five Illinoisans in 1870 and 1890, but only about one in twelve as late as 1950. This surge and decline was mirrored in every region of the state, not simply in Chicago. The black proportion has been even smaller until quite recently. Compared to the foreign-born, blacks have been even more concentrated in one region (85 percent in the Chicago area in 1980), though small neighborhoods of blacks always existed throughout the state.

Figure 2–2. Distribution of the Foreign-Born Population of Illinois by Counties, 1870–1950

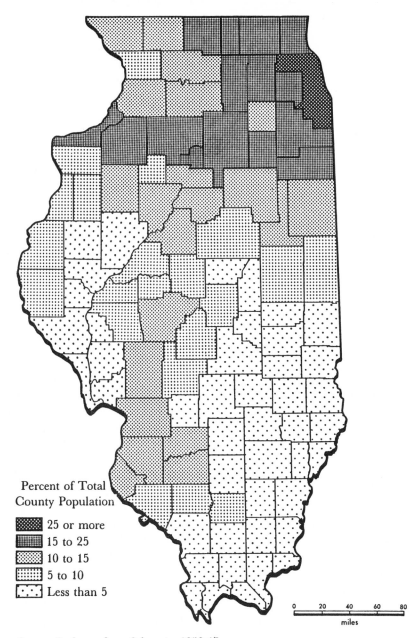

Percent of Total
County Population

25 or more
15 to 25
10 to 15
5 to 10
Less than 5

0 20 40 60 80
miles

Source: Redrawn from Schwartz, 1959:47.

Ethnicity was a key factor in the state's economy after the Civil War. While the native-born dominated all economic sectors, of course, Germans dominated all foreign-born workers in all sectors except mining (English and Welsh) and transportation-commerce and public services (Irish). Racial factors operated as well. Blacks and later Mexican-Americans were regularly used as strikebreakers (Keiser, 1972; Reisler, 1973); in Chicago, both were restricted to certain types of jobs (Pinderhughes, 1987).

This employment of the immigrant, and later black and Hispanic, set off latent contradictions between the values of the economic and cultural order. On the one hand,

> "Progress" and "growth," the two bywords of the age, demanded new people to work the land and man the factories. The universal frenzy of real estate speculation demanded an unending supply of buyers, and boosters and railroad agents encouraged immigrants to settle. [On the other hand, the values of these boosters] met a solid wall of defensive parochials who saw the increased work force as a threat to their financial security and the strange dress and customs of the foreigners as a threat to the sanctity of their cultural institutions [Keiser, 1977:8].

The very pervasiveness of the ethnic and black presence across the state meant that this contradiction could generate statewide both a social stress and a distrust of the center of all this cultural threat— Chicago. Ethnic and black alike found contact with the native-born stressful. Regional diversities in ethnicity and race bespoke different life experiences for each group, even though a common experience prevailed throughout the state as a result of dominance by the native-born. Of course, each group shared with the dominant group some common experience, such as politics and even recreation (professional baseball early forged wide cultural support for the Cardinals, Cubs, and White Sox). But there was also a history of intergroup stress; sketches of that experience for the major groups will illuminate the abstraction of terms like stress.

German Immigrants. The German experience was one of great rise and fall in influence in the state. Their dominant size has already been noted. Their numbers and politics were so powerful in the founding of the Republican party that one of Illinois' leading historians has concluded that in 1860, without the Germans, Lincoln and the GOP "would have been decisively defeated" (Cole 1922:341–42). As a consequence, German political influence was strong in the legislature for decades. As the Yankee temperance wing of the GOP grew stronger, Germans left for the Democratic party in the 1870s; that party elevated John P. Altgeld to the governorship two decades later. Apart from politics, the Germans were founders and continuing supporters of cultural institutions in the letters and music, and their contributions to commerce and agricultural were major even in the settlement era.

World War I broke their status and influence as a group when the fervid patriotism of that war submerged anything Teutonic. It tore apart their sense of being both German and American that many in this group had proudly demonstrated. Their own animosity to European Slavs (sometimes violent) and their enthusiasm for Kaiser Wilhelm's militarism backfired after America's entry. A decline in their most-favored status dropped sharply in rudimentary polls and never recovered (Holli, 1981). The patriots' reaction could even take the form of an anti-German lynching in German-dominated Madison County (Hickey, 1969). A generation later, American entry into World War II broke any German influence that remained, especially when some members were involved with the Brown Shirt (or American Nazi) party. Some of their cultural attributes have survived, however. In the mid-1980s, an anthropologist found German identity being maintained in private and public ceremonies in St. Clair County, especially in Belleville. In this area of small towns of German origin, innumerable interactions in language and behavior reflected a recognizable German/Kultur (Coggeshall, 1986).

Irish Immigrants. The Irish experience centered around the church and the political machine in urban Illinois. Especially in Chicago, their great concentration translated numbers into votes and hence into political influence. In the beginning they were viewed by the native-born as little better than blacks, namely, "white Sambos" in the slander of that era. For example, these early Irish were warned in job advertisements not to apply. In Yankee Protestant eyes, Irishism was associated collectively with the anti-Christ, while the Irish individually were seen as lazy and criminal. Viewed this way, they could be hired to dig the Illinois and Michigan Canal or lay the Illinois Central railroad, but they were also exploited in wages and working conditions everywhere across the state (Lightner, 1973).

Later, they would rise through business and politics to command great influence. From the beginning the Irish were associated with politics and always with Democratic party politics (Bogart and Thompson, 1922; Cole, 1922). They came to dominate Chicago's politics shortly after the Civil War and for over a century fought off challengers from other minority groups. When Irish ward leaders were faced with waves of Italian immigrants after 1880, they moved during succeeding decades from an attitude of contempt to friendly concern and then to acceptance of the politically ambitious—even to the replacement of Irish precinct workers. But a Chicago Irish ward leader like John Power could control the decades-long process of Italian challenges and grudging acceptance (Nelli, 1970).

In this interethnic politics, Catholicism served as a bridge for the Irish to other "hyphenated Americans," while a complex symbiotic relationship developed among machine, business, and ethnic voters. Ethnic self-interest, when mobilized, became a means of gaining a small edge in the many sectors of urban life. This process of Irish ascendance and its goals were anathema to the Protestant Yankee influence that was dominant in the middle classes; the latter saw the community in a "civic-minded" perspective opposed to special interests of narrow groups. They could not understand that "civic mindedness is enlightened self-interest for the established. For the unestablished it is unreal" (Novak, 1972:99–100). Democrats or Republicans might head the machine, but the Irish interest was always first in its members' minds, a motif which runs through Chicago's politics even today.

The Irish example typifies a more general model of urban ethnic politics in the American political system that is generated by the challenge from ethnic, would-be successors to the Irish dominance of resources. Eastern cities have most often been seen as prototypes of this model, but Chicago fully demonstrates it as well (Buenker, 1974). Only in the 1980s was Irish dominance of the Democratic party broken with the death of the last three Irish party leaders (Kelly, Kennelly, Daley) and the succession of blacks and Hispanics (Gove and Masotti, 1982; Pinderhughes, 1987). There may be a curious parallel in this succession. As an observer has noted, "More than any other group, blacks have emerged ready to contest the Irish as political players; probably more than any other group, blacks have borne an experience similar to the Irish" (Bukowski, 1987:11).

Black Immigrants. The black experience in Illinois does share some similarities with the Irish, but blacks encountered much more hatred and violence, and until recently they enjoyed far fewer resources and less public acceptance. Their presence generated statewide reactions early in Illinois history. Before the Civil War, the issue of abolition of slavery versus simply excluding all blacks from the state stirred white Illinoisans deeply; in neither situation were blacks welcome. The then-emerging Republican party of the 1850s first attracted those voters opposed to excluding slaves from the state but later attracted anti-black and nativist elements. The GOP and Lincoln retreated to a more moderate position on race, hedging their stands as his presidential campaign developed (Rozett, 1976).

Between the Civil War and World War I, signs of the black presence surfaced, both in their own culture and in the white reaction to them. Black newspapers were widespread across the state (but concentrated in the north)—a total of 190 from 1862 to the early 1970s, when 21 still operated (Belles, 1975). Black institutions were developing in the last of the nineteenth century. Their many churches were probably the strongest institution providing support to black life; the business world provided several small-scale opportunities; and the professions offered a few possibilities. An example of the last is the first successful heart operation on a fellow black performed in 1891 by Dr. Daniel H. Williams at a Chicago hospital that also provided the first nurses' training for black women (Keiser, 1977:15). But their numbers were small, and in Chicago or rural county seats they tucked themselves away in small corners of urban life.

White reaction to this small black presence was contradictory. Some reaction was deadly violent. Businesses regularly used blacks as strikebreakers, thereby inflaming an endemic white prejudice. One historian has concluded that in the pre-1900 period, "racial antagonism stemmed, to a large extent from the use of black strikebreakers" (Keiser, 1972:315). The practice existed in all regions, from Cook to Williamson counties and in all northern cities. Their presence incurred such hostility that on one occasion, in the mining areas of Williamson County in Egypt, five blacks were killed, many more were wounded, and subsequent trials of the accused whites led only to acquittals (Keiser, 1977:14; Angle, 1952). Other white violence was evident in racial lynchings, twelve occurring in just the period between 1900 and 1915. Again, this violence took place across all the regions—in Egypt (Belleville, Cairo, and East St. Louis) and in northern Illinois (Springfield and Chicago). Riots accompanied lynchings in the last three sites. In East St. Louis nearly 50 died, 16 acres were burned, and 250 buildings were destroyed. In Chicago in 1919, the most famous riot lasted 13 days and 38 persons were killed (Tingley, 1980:chapter 10).

This all-too-familiar white reaction to the black presence was contradicted by an opposing behavior—providing limited support of black needs through the white-controlled parties and legal institutions. When there were but few blacks in the Chicago area in the 1870s, one was elected Cook County commissioner and another state representative. Similarly, state laws were passed forbidding discrimination; an 1874 statute barred school discrimination and another in 1885 banned discrimination in public and private facilities. They were not enforced, however, so little progress was made during most of this century.

Chicago became the most segregated city in America, while East St. Louis ran a close second. Concentration of numbers did not produce equivalent payoffs from the public and private sectors. One study found that those who were poor white and ethnic got more from the social system than those who were poor and black; while blacks and immigrant Italians and Poles began the century poor and with low status, in following decades the immigrant groups advanced further in social institutions or won larger returns from public and private sectors than did the blacks (Pinderhughes, 1987). But by the early 1980s, in places where blacks concentrated, litigation and the weight of their votes provided some protection against discrimination. The election of Harold Washington as mayor in Chicago (Gove and Masotti, 1982) and litigation in 1986 and 1987, overturning forms of municipal government in Springfield, Peoria, and Danville that had regularly diluted black voting strength, were important political advances for all blacks, not just a few fortunate individuals. But in deepest Egypt, blacks in Cairo—after riots in the late 1960s and despite slow efforts to integrate schools and city government—were "in miles and culture . . . closer to Jackson, Mississippi, than to Chicago" (*Washington Post Weekly*, April 6, 1987:6).

Other Immigrants. These sketches do not cover the range of ethnic experiences in Illinois. Their rich variety of particularism is spotted across the state. The English in the southeast (Edwards County) were a bastion of Republicanism amid a sea of Democratic votes in 1880 as well as in 1948 (Key, 1956:225). Bulgarians and Greeks built an enclave in Granite City but left for "home" in 1912 in large numbers to fight in the first Balkan war (Cassens, 1985). The Hispanic influx into the state did not begin after 1970, but rather in the 1920s. Recruited for cheap-labor jobs that Europeans could no longer fill under new immigration law, these first-wave Mexican-Americans often were used as strikebreakers and were ignored by the Catholic church, the political parties, and other social institutions (Reisler, 1973). A half-century later, their growing numbers in Illinois (5.6 percent), with most (91.3 percent) located in Chicago, brought them increasing attention and political influence (Census Bureau, 1981:29).

The Impact of Ethnicity and Race. The conflict among ethnic and racial groups sketched above is striking because it took place across the state, not just in Chicago. Throughout the state, there were race riots and anti-German hysteria. The census data reported earlier indicate a foreign-born presence in every major region from 1870 to 1950. Cross-regional pervasiveness of ethnicity and race has produced three results. First, it created a multifaceted social pluralism within Illinois after the Civil War that replaced the bi-polar pluralism of the settlement era. Second, it provided the native-born of all regions with a continuing experience and attitudinal socialization in nativism and racial prejudice. Third, the pervasiveness of these attitudes could be easily focused upon the citadel of such group differences—Chicago.

These factors arising from immigrant and racial conditions need to be joined to the urban-rural conditions explored in the previous section to understand Illinois regionalism during the 125 years after the Civil War. Most simply, the less urban and more native-born citizens had the same regional location, while the more urban and less native-born had a separate location. As a result of both urban and ethnic-racial influences, state politics crystallized into a Chicago versus downstate contest, with downstate regions (whatever their earlier origins) uniting in hostility toward these cultural differences. The possibility exists that these regions held other attitudes in common, as we shall shortly examine.

In all societies the political system's essential role is to regulate conflict among its groups with their differing values and policy preferences. How that system operates—that is, its politics—is shaped by the nature of these groups' demands and how the system and its politics are perceived and valued by its citizens. What, then, were the political dimensions of the kind of multifaceted pluralism described?

Politics and Social Pluralism

This review of forces underlying regionalism in Illinois makes the point that an increasingly diverse pluralism created both common and distinct qualities in the state's culture. All the groups—the Yankee culture of northern Illinois, the southern culture of Egypt, Irish and East Europeans concentrated in Chicago, and blacks located in Chicago and East St. Louis—created regional bastions for their interests and values. No region was uniform, however. Within each regional bastion, ethnic fought ethnic—or the blacks—and labor fought management; the local political and social systems provided forums for such conflict. In conflict between these regional bastions, however, the state electoral system and the legislature provided arenas for impressing particularistic group values upon the state's political system. In time, this increasing pluralism of groups and voters shifted the center of political gravity to northern Illinois. How was all this manifested in the electoral behavior and political culture of the state?

Elections and Regional Residues

Voting patterns over time tell us much about the presence and continuity of regional differences; historical voting behavior indicates regional persistence. In the 1870s, party identification told much less about how one voted than did religious preference. For example, in towns like Geneseo over 90 percent of the Protestant denominations voted Republican in 1877, while 90 percent of the Catholics voted Democratic. Religion was relevant to voting in several ways. It produced different moral views (pietistic or revivalist versus liturgical or ritualistic), it provided an in-group solidarity that reinforced uniformity of action, and it could work actively in issue controversies as they arose (Jensen, 1970).

Nevertheless, regional influences operated because opposing religions settled predominantly in the north or south. In this process, political parties could aggravate and institutionalize such regional differences. In the elections of 1864, 1880, and 1900, one analyst of the county returns found "no change in the basic geographic distribution of the vote" (Keiser, 1977:74). Northern Illinois (especially Winnebago, Boon, McHenry, DeKalb, Kendall, and DuPage counties, the center of the Yankee, liturgical cultures) was heavily and consistently Republican. In southern Illinois (below a line running from Hancock to Clark counties), Democrats won 50 to 60 percent of all elections; some of these counties had huge Democratic majorities (Pope, Massac, and Pulaski), while others swung between the parties (St. Clair, Jackson, and Clay). A closer factor analysis of different offices confirms this regional distinction in the 1896 vote for William Jennings Bryan; his vote correlated (r = .58) with the region's population origins in Appalachia (noted for its pietistic religion) versus New England (with its liturgical religion) (MacRae, 1960:680). These regional distinctions did not vanish over time. V. O. Key, Jr. (1956:223–26) noted in comparing county maps how different the two regions were in two elections as widely separated as 1880 and 1948. In his words, "residues of traditional voting" existed even in the modern era (1956:224), which means that political regionalism persisted also.

Types of Political Cultures

This history suggests that the differing "political cultures" Daniel Elazar (1972) found for the nation exist within these regions as well. Political culture refers to citizens' perceptions about government's purpose, officials in government, and the way government is practiced. Rooted in the colonies and spread across the country, three distinctive political cultures were found in differing population streams.

Citizens with a moralist culture see politics as a process for realizing goals for the common good. Politics is a process in which all citizens should participate, elections are a healthy means for selecting some leaders (and merit systems for selecting others), and all leaders should be accountable for their use of authority. This culture was rooted in New England's ethnic and religious groups and spread across northern America; it was deeply reflected in the Scandinavian settlement west of the Great Lakes.

In a traditionalistic culture, the citizens view politics as a process for maintaining the social and economic power of an elite (usually based in agriculture). Politics is a process which limits popular participation in elections and governing, avoids party competition, bends political authority to the interests of elites, and distrusts the merit claims of bureaucracy. When tradition dominates the political system, a concept like "progress" has little importance. This culture was rooted in the deep South and spread to the Southwest and up the lower Midwest.

In an individualist culture, citizens see politics as a process that works much like the marketplace. By combining with others in parties, one should pursue personal interests regardless of public values. This view denies that there is any general interest, that merit is desirable in public administration, or that honesty in elections and public services is important. Rather, private interest, patronage, and corrupt use of authority should be pursued by those with political power, namely, those who control votes. This culture was rooted in the Mid-Atlantic states and spread to the big cities there and then later across the Midwest.

Political Cultures in Illinois

Some evidence suggests that these subcultures have existed in Illinois (see Elazar, 1972:107, for the location of the various subcultures). Elazar (1970) studied fifteen "cities on the prairie" in this state (all the major ones except Chicago) as well as cities elsewhere. He found that the individualistic culture dominates Illinois; politics is treated like the marketplace so that group needs can be satisfied by obtaining public resources through the mechanism of the political party and its typical bargaining. Elazar concluded, "Politics in Illinois came early to be centered on personal influence, patronage, distribution of federal and later state benefits, and the availability of economic gain of those who were professionally committed to politics as their 'business'" (1970:286).

Elazar found the presence of the other two cultures in the pioneer-Yankee distinction explored earlier—moralist in the north and traditionalist in the south. In the south, disparagement of government, opposition to progress, and rejection of government interference in private life fit well this culture described earlier. These viewpoints were reinforced by the Germans east of St. Louis. Elazar also found a moralist culture in the northern counties, dominated by Yankees and later Scandinavians with their views of a political commonwealth arising out of a new moral order. They were particularly important as the reform element in state politics, seeking local option structures, free public education, and so on. But these reforms actually changed very little the state's dominant individualism; indeed, by raising the possibilities of a better order, moralists may have contributed to popular cynicism about the political system.

The importance of cultural origins was highlighted when Elazar found that Illinois cities with different cultures showed the effects of the three political cultures as recently as the 1960s. For example, as one might expect, in 1960 there was more schooling achieved in moralist than in traditionalist cities; the percent completing high school in Moline was double that in East St. Louis (1970:273). Similar and modern distinctions emerged among these northern and southern cities in such matters as providing planning services and handling crimes like drinking, gambling, and prostitution (1970:226–27, 272–80).

But the overall pattern of the state still emphasizes a dominant individualist culture. That dominance came about through a nineteenth-century compromise between its advocates and the moralists that pertains even today. In this compromise:

> The individualistic political culture retained and even increased its dominance over the state as a whole, with a few traditionalist survivals and moralist increments built in. . . . At the same time, the various civil communities were tacitly given the option of remaining largely outside the state political culture and maintaining a culture—traditionalist or moralist—of their own choosing. [The] Yankee leadership [would] take advantage of the option offered them and develop reasonable auton-

omous civil communities within the areas of the state which they dominated [e.g., Moline and Rockford]. Of course, the civil communities which exercised their option gave up the possibility of forging good connections with the state political system as a whole . . . and [have] frequently suffered for it [Elazar, 1970:288–89].

Implications for Regionalism Today

We have shown that, from the time of the early settlers, cultural differences existed in Illinois that affected the politics and policies of the state's different regions. Cultural differences, thus, have great implication for understanding how the political system regulates social conflict—its traditional role in all societies. This political task became even greater when earlier and simpler regional differences gave way to such variety that social pluralism best described what confronted government. These differences arose in the economic, urban-rural, and minorities' bases of life. A political culture dominated by a market orientation to government resulted. Although two other kinds of culture existed in the northern and southern regions, the dominant individualist culture permeated even these regions.

Regional distinctions of ideas became increasingly weakened, however, because Illinoisans no longer stayed in their regions and screened out hostile ideas. This breaching of regional walls arose from a number of sources during this century and particularly since World War II. There developed what Richard Jensen's bicentennial history of the state termed "the equalitarian thrust in the most modern ethic" (1978:173).

The influences weakening the regional bases of conflict in Illinois are like those at work in other states. Some of these changes came from influences, either inside or outside the state, working upon its citizens. For example, more education produces citizens more aware of what happens elsewhere in the state and more likely to seek allies elsewhere. State law not only facilitated this spread of education by funds and broad goals, but it also stimulated it directly by mandating school consolidation (from 12,000 elementary districts in 1942 to 600 in 1978) and professionalization. Schooling now came from "strangers who heeded the advice of professors in Chicago and Champaign rather than the wisdom of the crossroads service station" (Jensen, 1978:157–58). Standardization of other local public services also occurred because of increasing state control of policies; this meant less sharp disparities in what the state did for its citizens. In time, too, nationalizing rules of behavior emanated from Washington through statute and litigation. The result was a web of intergovernmental relations (Glendening and Reeves, 1984). This brought more even federal services and, in the case of constitutional liberties, more even treatment of how government protected its citizens across the state.

Changes came not simply from currents moving into the state but also from the people themselves moving in or out of it. Greater geographical mobility was spurred by world wars and an increasingly interdependent economy. Military mobilization and the search for jobs during depressions and boom-times would take youths from both southern Williamson and northern Winnebago counties (whether white or black) to where they were needed in the state and nation. A national network of groups would form to articulate, mobilize, and focus special interests within the political parties and policy-making organs. Persons similarly influenced in differently located places would share common needs and interests and would turn to government to promote and protect these. Ultimately, the media would project all of these changes into every home, thereby giving a sense of what not only the state, but the nation and world were like. Backwoods farmers near Shawneetown, where fields were first trod by buckskin pioneers, now have microwave receivers beamed to the heavens. They have finally joined the global village.

REFERENCES

Alcorn, Richard. 1974. "Leadership and Stability in Mid-Nineteenth Century America: A Case Study of an Illinois Town." *Journal of the Illinois Historical Society* 61:685–702.

Angle, Paul. 1952. *Bloody Williamson*. New York: Knopf.

Beals, Carlton. 1960. *The Brass-Knuckled Crusade*. New York: Hastings.

Belles, A. Gilbert. 1975. "The Black Press in Illinois." *Journal of the Illinois Historical Society* 68:344–52.

Bogart, Ernest L., and Charles M. Thompson. 1922. *The Centennial History of Illinois*. Vol. 4, *The Industrial State, 1870–1893*. Chicago: A. C. McClurg.

Briggs, Harold. 1952. "Folklore of Southern Illinois." *Southern Folklore* 16:207–17.

Buenker, John. 1974. "Dynamics of Chicago Ethnic Politics, 1900–1930." *Journal of the Illinois Historical Society* 67:173–99.

Bukowski, Douglas. 1987. "Chicago and the Politics of the Past." *Chicago Tribune*, February 26.

Cassens, David. 1985. "The First Balkan War and Its Impact on the Bulgarians and Greeks of Southwestern Illinois." *East European Quarterly* 19:69–74.

Census Bureau. 1975. *Historical Statistics of the United States, Part 1*. Washington, D.C.: Government Printing Office.

————. 1981. *General Population Characteristics, Illinois.* Washington, D.C.: Government Printing Office.

Coggeshall, John. 1986. " 'One of Those Intangibles': The Manifestation of Ethnic Identity in Southwestern Illinois." *Journal of American Folklore* 99:177–207.

Cole, Arthur. 1922. *The Era of the Civil War, 1848–1870,* Vol. 3. Chicago: A. C. McClurg.

Cutshall, William. 1941. "Industrial Geography of the Lower Wabash Valley." *Economic Geography* 17:297–307.

Demos, John. 1986. *Past, Present, and Personal.* New York: Oxford University Press.

Doyle, Don. 1977. "Social Theory and New Communities in Nineteenth-Century America." *Western Historical Quarterly* 8:151–65.

Elazar, Daniel. 1970. *Cities of the Prairie.* New York: Basic Books.

————. 1972. *American Federalism,* 2d ed. New York: Crowell.

Geography, Department of. 1958–63. *Atlas of Illinois Resources,* Vols. 1–6. Urbana: University of Illinois.

Glendening, Parris, and Marvis Reeves. 1984. *Pragmatic Federalism,* 2d ed. Pacific Palisades, Calif.: Palisades.

Gove, Samuel, and Louis Masotti. 1982. *After Daley.* Urbana: University of Illinois Press.

Hickey, Donald. 1969. "The Prager Affair: A Study in Wartime Hysteria." *Journal of the Illinois Historical Society* 62:117–34.

Holli, Melvin. 1981. "Teuton versus Slav: The Great War Sinks Chicago's German Kultur." *Ethnicity* 8:406–51.

Jensen, Richard. 1970. "The Religious and Occupation Roots of Party Identification." *Civil War History* 16:325–43.

————. 1978. *Illinois, A Bicentennial History.* New York: Norton.

Johnson, Daniel, and Rebecca Veach. 1980. *The Middle-size Cities of Illinois.* Springfield, Ill.: Sangamon State University.

Keiser, John. 1972. "Black Strikebreakers and Racism in Illinois, 1865–1900." *Journal of the Illinois Historical Society* 65:313–26.

————. 1977. *Building for the Centuries: Illinois, 1865 to 1898.* Urbana: University of Illinois Press.

Key, V. O., Jr. 1956. *American State Politics.* New York: Knopf.

Lightner, David. 1973. "Construction Labor on the Illinois Central Railroad." *Journal of the Illinois Historical Society* 66:258–301.

MacRae, Duncan. 1960. "Critical Elections in Illinois: 1888–1958." *American Political Science Review* 54:669–83.

Nelli, Humbert. 1970. "John Power and the Italians: Politics in a Chicago Ward, 1896–1921." *Journal of American History* 57:67–84.

Novak, Michael. 1972. *The Rise of the Unmeltable Ethnics.* New York: Macmillan.

Pinderhughes, Dianne. 1987. *Race and Ethnicity in Chicago Politics.* Urbana: University of Illinois Press.

Pooley, William. 1968. *The Settlement of Illinois from 1830 to 1850.* Ann Arbor, Mich.: University Microfilms.

Power, Richard. 1953. *Planting Corn Belt Culture.* Indianapolis: Indiana Historical Society.

Raines, Edgar, Jr. 1985. "The Ku Klux Klan in Illinois, 1867–1875." *Journal of the Illinois Historical Society* 78:17–44.

Reisler, Mark. 1973. "The Mexican Immigrant in the Chicago Area during the 1920s." *Journal of the Illinois Historical Society* 66:144–58.

Rozett, John. 1976. "Racism and Republican Emergence in Illinois, 1848–1860: A Reevaluation of Republican Negrophobia." *Civil War History* 22:101–15.

Schwartz, Carroll. 1959. *Distribution of the Foreign-born Population of Illinois 1870–1950.* M.A. thesis, Department of Geography, Southern Illinois University.

Smith, Grace. 1941. "Folklore from 'Egypt.' " *Journal of American Folklore* 54:48–59.

Sweet, William. 1939. *Religion on the American Frontier: The Congregationalists,* Vol. 3. Chicago: University of Chicago Press.

Tingley, Donald. 1980. *The Structuring of a State.* Urbana: University of Illinois Press.

Walch, Timothy. 1978. "Catholic Social Institutions and Urban Development: The View from Nineteenth-Century Chicago and Milwaukee." *Catholic Historical Review* 64:16–32.

Wyman, Mark. 1984. *Immigrants in the Valley.* Chicago: Nelson Hall.

The Evolution of Regional Economic Differences within Illinois, 1818–1950

3

Jeremy Atack

Even a cursory examination of the historical data on Illinois' development reveals marked regional disparities at any point in time and marked shifts in the relative status of the different regions over time. When extensive settlement began in Illinois at the start of the nineteenth century, growth was concentrated in the south. It spread slowly northward as Illinois agriculture blossomed in the wheat boom of the 1850s. Eventually, it became concentrated in northern Illinois, especially in the Chicago area, as manufacturing and commerce became the chief engines of growth. In the process, the southern part of the state in particular did not share equally in the benefits of the growth and development of Illinois. I argue that this pattern of regional development within the state reflected trends in the Midwest and in the nation with respect to such factors as sectoral and industrial growth as well as ethnic and cultural differences. These were then compounded by the influence of changing forms and costs of transportation. This approach to regional development follows that proposed by Perloff, Dunn, Lampard, and Muth (1960). It emphasizes the spread of population and the development of agriculture and manufacturing in relation to the transportation network and its improvement. Services, however, receive little attention because the collection of statistics was erratic, incomplete, and inconsistent during most of the period under consideration.

Since 1818, Illinois has undergone tremendous economic change. At the start of the nineteenth century, the territory was an isolated frontier wilderness with a widely scattered population that lived close to the margin of subsistence through a mixture of hunting, herding, and self-sufficient agriculture. By 1950, it was the fourth most populous state with the second highest median family income in the country.[1] Growth took place not only extensively (that is, more was produced in absolute terms) but also intensively (that is, more was produced per person). As a result, there was considerable structural and sectoral reallocation both within and between the different regions in the state. Whereas in 1840, Illinois ranked eighteenth of twenty-six states in industrial production and about eighth in agricultural commodities, by 1950, it ranked second or third among the states in industrial value-added and fourth in the value of agricultural products sold.[2] The benefits of this growth were not, however, distributed evenly among the citizenry in different parts of Illinois. In 1959, for example, per capita personal income by county in Illinois ranged from $3,429 in DuPage County to $901 in Pope. Moreover, the top five counties in per capita personal income were all in the northern part of the state, clustered around the Chicago area, whereas the five poorest counties on this measure were all in the southern tip of the state (U.S. Department of Commerce, 1975).

This chapter examines the changing position of Illinois within the context of national development and then focuses on growth-initiating factors within the state at the regional level. It emphasizes those aggregates for which long series of roughly comparable data can be constructed—population, agricultural output, and manufacturing output. These data are used to examine the extent to which regions of Illinois shared in overall growth and how the relative positions of the regions shifted.[3] In addition, the data cast light upon the extent to which regional growth or decline may be attributable to industry composition or within industry shifts in location. Last, the relative advantages of the individual regions with respect to location vis-à-vis input and output markets and external economies of scale are discussed.

Development of Illinois within the National Economy

Population

Figure 3–1 provides an overview of Illinois' economy relative to that of the entire United States from territorial times to 1950. From 1810 to 1870, Illinois' population was growing more rapidly than that of the country as a whole; consequently, the proportion of Illinois' population to total U.S. population was increasing over this period. This rapid population growth reflected both high rates of natural increase and high rates of in-migration. Fertility was especially high among the farm population. In 1860, for example, the child-woman ratio

Figure 3–1. Illinois' Population, Manufacturing, and Agriculture Relative to the Rest of the Nation, 1810–1950

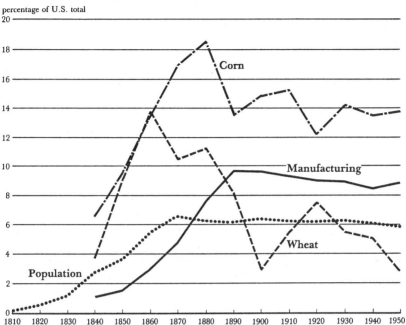

Sources: Data from U.S. Census Office, census data, and *Statistical Abstract of the United States,* various years.

among Illinois farm families was estimated to be 1,637 per thousand women or more than 60 percent higher than among the comparable population in the Northeast.[4] On the other hand, the fertility rate among the non-farm rural population was somewhat lower and approximately the same as in the East (Atack and Bateman, 1987). According to Richard Easterlin (1976), this higher fertility rate among the farm population reflected the availability of agricultural land for settlement. Land availability also had an impact on in-migration since it lured those who wanted to become farmers. Those whose ambitions lay in other directions were attracted to Illinois by the higher wages that resulted from the relative scarcity of wage labor when cheap land was available (see, for example, Turner, 1920; Fogel and Rutner, 1972).

During the 1870s, Illinois' share of total population dipped sharply from 6.6 percent in 1870 to 6.1 percent in 1880 as settlement farther west took off. Thereafter, its share remained fairly stable, with a slight recovery in the 1890s and the loss of that gain during the following decades until 1930. Beginning in 1930, Illinois' share of the population began to erode even further. By 1950, Illinois' share of total population had fallen to about 5.8 percent.

Agriculture

Illinois' relative share of both manufacturing output and the production of its two important agricultural crops indicates a pronounced shift in Illinois' economic activities over time (Figure 3–1). When the first economic data were collected by the Census Office in 1840, they showed that Illinois was a predominantly agricultural state, but one that had already moved beyond simple self-sufficiency. In that year, Illinois farmers produced 4 percent of the nation's wheat crop and 7 percent of its corn, though Illinois had only 3 percent of the U.S. population. On the other hand, the extent of its manufacturing activity, measured by the proportion of total manufacturing capital invested in the state, was only one-third of Illinois' population share. Thereafter, Illinois' share of the nation's wheat crop grew faster than population until 1860, when it reached almost 14 percent of the nation's production, as a result of high foreign demand for American wheat. Indeed, in 1860, Illinois was the leading wheat producer in the country. With the development of both the southern winter wheat and the northern spring wheat belts, the locus of wheat moved west of Illinois, and Illinois' share declined, falling below its share of population in 1900 and again since 1930. Illinois' share of corn output continued growing until 1880, when it reached over 18 percent of the nation's output.

Manufacturing

In contrast to the statewide pattern of agricultural development, manufacturing activity in Illinois expanded no faster than its population until 1870. Nevertheless, Illinois' share of total U.S. manufacturing was still increasing because it was growing faster than the national average. After 1870, the pace of industrial expansion sped up and exceeded the rate of growth of population in the state, which by then was slowing to the national average.

Prior to 1870, manufacturing development was extensive rather than intensive and was dominated by agriculturally related industries. In 1860, for example, except for machinery production, which ranked ninth in terms of output value, Illinois' ten leading industries were dependent upon agriculture either for inputs, as in the case of flour milling, or as the major consumer, as in the case of agricultural im-

Table 3–1. Ten Leading Industries in Illinois, 1860–1920 (value of output in millions of dollars)

Rank	1860	Rank	1890
1	Flour milling (20.6)	1	Meat packing (200.4)
2	Liquor distilling (4.3)	2	Liquor distilling (52.0)
3	Meat packing (4.0)	3	Machinery (38.9)
4	Lumber milling (2.5)	4	Flour milling (38.0)
5	Agricultural implements (2.5)	5	Iron and steel (37.1)
6	Malt liquors (1.5)	6	Clothing (33.6)
7	Wagons and carriages (1.3)	7	Agricultural implements (24.6)
8	Boots and shoes (1.1)	8	Lumber milling (20.5)
9	Machinery (1.1)	9	Carpentering (20.4)
10	Printing (0.8)	10	Printing (17.3)

Rank	1920
1	Meat packing (1,284.1)
2	Machinery (235.4)
3	Clothing (197.6)
4	Iron and steel (173.3)
5	Agricultural implements (128.3)
6	Railroad cars (125.2)
7	Electrical machinery (119.5)
8	Flour milling (116.6)
9	Printing (110.9)
10	Processed foods (94.2)

Sources: Federal Censuses of Manufacturing, 1860: U.S. Department of the Interior, Census Office, *Eighth Census*, Vol. 3, Manufacturers of the United States in 1860 (Washington, D.C.: GPO, 1865), pp. 111–13. 1890: U.S. Department of the Interior, Census Office, *Eleventh Census*, Vol. 6, Part I, Report on Manufacturing Industries in the United States (Washington, D.C.: GPO, 1895), pp. 386–97. 1920: U.S. Department of Commerce, Bureau of the Census, *Fourteenth Census*, Vol. 9, Manufactures, 1919 (Washington, D.C.: GPO, 1923), pp. 348–59.

plements or wagons and carriages (Table 3–1). By 1890, malt liquors, wagons and carriages, and boots and shoes were no longer among the ten largest industries in Illinois by output; they had been replaced by iron and steel, clothing, and carpentering. Meat packing replaced flour milling as Illinois' leading industry. Indeed, the meat packers, concentrated in Chicago, produced output worth more than all the other top ten industries combined. Flour milling, by contrast, was in relative decline. Thirty years later, meat packing remained the preeminent industry in the state, but other industries—most notably machinery and clothing, but also iron and steel—had grown relatively faster. Flour milling, on the other hand, continued its relative decline. There were also three new industries among the top ten in 1920. Processed foods just made the list, but railroad cars moved from eleventh to sixth over the period. More dramatic was the rise in the manufacture of electrical machinery, a relatively new industry in a field that was to expand even more rapidly in the 1920s. Its emergence as a major industry in Illinois is indicative of the continued ability of the state to attract new industries despite the relative decline of its industrial sector after 1890.

Illinois' share of total U.S. manufacturing peaked in 1890 at almost 10 percent of the nation's output compared with its 6 percent share of total population. Thereafter, Illinois' share of manufacturing generally drifted lower. Beginning in 1940, however, there were signs of a slight resurgence in manufacturing activity despite a declining share of population.

In 1860, manufacturing plants in every industry were scattered across the length and breadth of the state, in rural as well as urban areas. Firms tended to be small because their markets were small and dispersed. The upsurge in manufacturing after 1870, however, was accompanied by the relocation of Illinois industry from rural to urban areas, especially the Chicago area. It also marked a switch from extensive to intensive development. In the process, manufacturing in Illinois moved from the simple processing of agricultural commodities—designed as much to reduce weight and permit shipping longer distances as to meet local consumption needs—to a much more diversified manufacturing, meeting the needs of industry and urban consumers as much as the agricultural sector. In 1860, Chicago accounted for perhaps 23 percent of Illinois' manufacturing output. By 1880, Chicago's share was 60 percent; by the next census in 1890, Chicago generated 73 percent of the state's manufacturing output and was the second leading manufacturing center in the country after New York City.[5] Thereafter, its share tended to drift lower, falling to about 67 percent in 1920.[6]

Development within Illinois

Population and Settlement

On the day that Illinois became a state, its population amounted to perhaps 35,000 and was concentrated in two areas in the south on opposite sides of the state. In southwestern Illinois, white settlements in the fertile agricultural bottomlands around Kaskaskia and Cahokia had displaced the Indian population from what had been their home for millennia. In the eastern part of the state, people had settled in the vicinity of the salines in Gallatin County (Pease, 1922). Both areas had locational advantages because they were situated at breaks in river transportation between the Mississippi and Missouri and the Ohio and the Wabash rivers. At the beginning of the nineteenth century, these rivers also served as gateways to Illinois for immigrants and trade and represented the only feasible means of transportation in the Illinois wilderness.

Using the Census Bureau definition of a frontier region as anywhere population density was under six persons per square mile, more than three-quarters of the state was unsettled in 1820. Counties beyond those adjacent to water transportation lay at or beyond the frontier (Figure 3–2). In the years that followed, population flooded into Illinois. In 1820, the three federal land offices in Illinois at Shawneetown, Kaskaskia, and Edwardsville registered only 6,699 acres of public-land sales.[7] The next year, partially as a result of the liberalization of land-sale terms through the Land Act of 1820 and the opening of two new offices in Vandalia and Palestine, sales surged to over 50,000 acres, more than half through the Edwardsville office. In 1823, the opening of yet another land office in Springfield further boosted sales and settlement. Land sales throughout the 1820s, however, remained modest compared with the levels reached in the following decade.

The distribution of population in 1830 (Figure 3–3) shows population pushing northward in Illinois along the major rivers. However, except for some settlement around Galena in extreme northwestern Illinois, northern Illinois and east-central Illinois were virtually unpopulated by white settlers in 1830. By 1840, the picture was radically different (Figure 3–4). Population had moved into almost all Illinois counties. Except for Champaign, Ford, Iroquois, southern Kankakee, and Livingston counties, all counties had at least two persons per square mile. Moreover, outside the prairie lands of central and northern Illinois and Jasper and Effingham counties in the south, settlement had moved beyond the frontier stage. Some relatively dense, if isolated, pockets of settlement existed in northern Illinois around Rock Island, Galena, Rockford, and the Chicago area. This spread of population reflected the tremendous upsurge in Illinois land sales in the mid-1830s (Figure 3–5). In 1831, almost 341,000 acres were sold, 200,000 of them through sales offices in Edwardsville and Springfield. Sales were thus still concentrated in southern Illinois and in the southern fringes of central Illinois. Sales through the newly opened land offices in Quincy and Danville were small. In 1835, the opening of

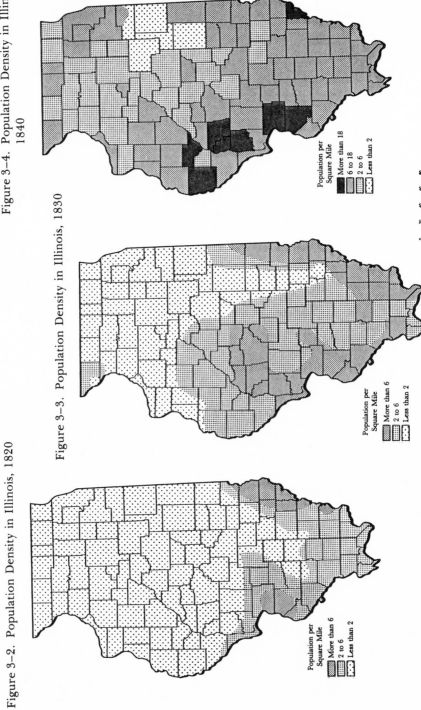

Figure 3–4. Population Density in Illinois, 1840

Figure 3–3. Population Density in Illinois, 1830

Figure 3–2. Population Density in Illinois, 1820

Population per
Square Mile

More than 18
6 to 18
2 to 6
Less than 2

0   20   40   60   80
miles

Population per
Square Mile

More than 6
2 to 6
Less than 2

Population per
Square Mile

More than 6
2 to 6
Less than 2

Sources: Redrawn from Pease, 1922:facing pp. 4, 174, and 384.

Figure 3–5. Land Sales in Illinois, 1820–39 (acres by land office)

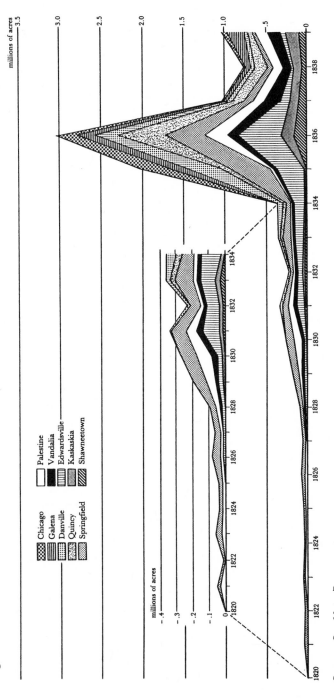

Source: See Note 7.

the last two land-sale offices in Illinois at Chicago and Galena marked the real opening of northern Illinois and the Chicago area to settlement. Sales boomed. In that year, sales topped two million acres; the next year, three million. Sales were especially heavy at those land offices in central and northern Illinois.

Many of these purchases were speculative, encouraged by state plans to underwrite an ambitious program of internal improvements, and sales plummeted in the financial panic of 1837 to 1838. However, the sales already completed had laid the foundation for settlement in the northern half of the state. Although transportation still favored the southern half of the state (Figure 3–6), a network of roads now crisscrossed northern and west-central Illinois.

The settlement opportunities in northern Illinois and improvements in transportation led settlers to enter from the east via central and northern Indiana and from the north via the Great Lakes. The ethnic and cultural background of these settlers was different from that of the settlers who had entered from the south via the Mississippi and Ohio rivers or from Kentucky or southern Indiana. Most of the northern settlers came from northeastern states, especially New York, Ohio, and Pennsylvania, or abroad. Those who settled the southern half of the state were generally southerners from Kentucky, Tennessee, North Carolina, and Virginia, who migrated there by river (Figure 3–7). In large part, this pattern seems to be explained by the similarities between the migrants' place of birth and where they settled, including the soil, terrain, vegetation, and climate. These similarities maximized the value of the migrants' human capital (Steckel, 1983).

The settlers from the South and those from the East were quite different. Lois Kimball Mathews described the difference very clearly:

> Many of the Southerners . . . were poor; they had been unable to hold slaves in the South by reason of their poverty, and had come into the Northwest Territory not only to better their condition, but also to avoid a system of which they did not disapprove in principle, but found unpleasant on account of the social distinctions it produced. Others had turned their faces Illinois-ward, even after the passage of the Missouri Compromise; but that measure diverted Southern emigration very markedly . . . leaving northern Illinois for the New Yorkers and New Englanders. Most of these later emigrants were wealthy farmers, enterprising merchants, millers, and manufacturers who built mills, churches, schoolhouses, cities, and made roads and bridges with astonishing public spirit; so that the southern part of the state, though it was many years older in point of settlement, was noticeably behind in

Figure 3–6. Roads, Canals, and Railroads in Illinois, 1840

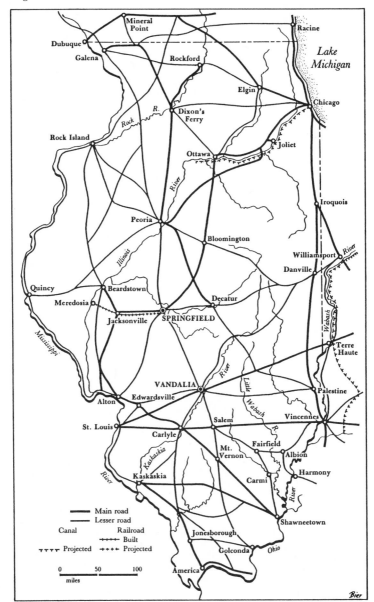

Source: Adapted from Buley, 1950:facing p. 446.

Figure 3–7. State of Birth of Largest Native
Migrant Group in 1850

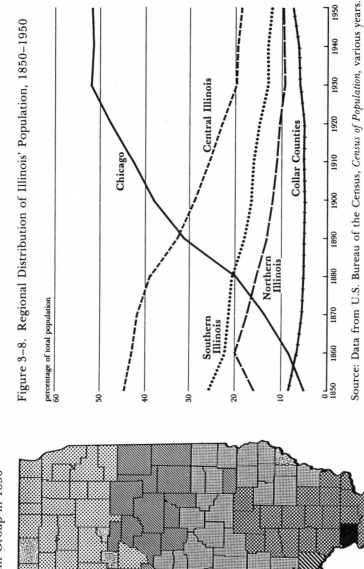

Figure 3–8. Regional Distribution of Illinois' Population, 1850–1950

New York
Ohio
Pennsylvania
Kentucky
New Jersey
Tennessee
South Carolina
North Carolina

Source: Based on 1850 census data in author's files.

Source: Data from U.S. Bureau of the Census, *Census of Population*, various years.

point of wealth and evidences of public spirit and prosperity [Mathews, 1909:208–9].

Their motivations for settling were quite different, as well. The southerners were refugees pushed out of the South by resource competition from the richer slaveowners (see, for example, Phillips, 1906:789–816). Vermont migrants, on the other hand, had "a longing for good land— fat land and flat land, to be had for a song all over the West," and northerners, in general, moved to take advantage of the superior profit opportunities in a rapidly expanding state (Stilwell, 1937:229; see also Gates, 1960).

The relatively rapid growth of the northern half of Illinois in this period can be seen in the concentration of Illinois' major urban areas. In 1850, Illinois had only ten incorporated cities—Chicago, Alton, Springfield, Beardstown, Pekin, Quincy, Peoria, Bloomington, Galena, and Rock Island—all but one of which were in central or northern Illinois (U.S. Census Office, 1853:703–17). Central Illinois was home to the largest proportion of Illinois' population, almost 45 percent; southern Illinois with 26 percent of the state's population was second. Chicago at the time had but 5 percent (Figure 3–8).

During the ensuing decade, there was another tremendous surge in population so that by 1860 only a few counties in southern and central Illinois had population densities under 20 persons per square mile (Figure 3–9). Since such a population density could be achieved even in an agrarian county with one farm family per quarter-section (160 acres), it seems likely that these counties still had extensive tracts of unsettled land. Along the Illinois River and the shores of Lake Michigan, however, the population was 30 per square mile, and in some cases more than 50. In Cook County, the growth of Chicago had pushed the population density to over 155 persons per square mile.

From 1860 until 1930, each downstate region's share of population declined, while Chicago grew (Figure 3–8). As a result, Chicago in the 1920s contained more than half the state's population. Sometime before 1900 Illinois ceased to be a predominantly rural state, and by 1930 more than three-quarters of the state's population lived in urban areas.[8] As urban Illinois—especially Chicago—grew, the largest loser in relative terms was central Illinois. By 1930, its share had fallen to less than 20 percent of Illinois' population.

The onset of the Great Depression, however, marked an abrupt pause, even a reversal, in Chicago's relative growth. Indeed, for the first time in more than a century, the proportion of rural population

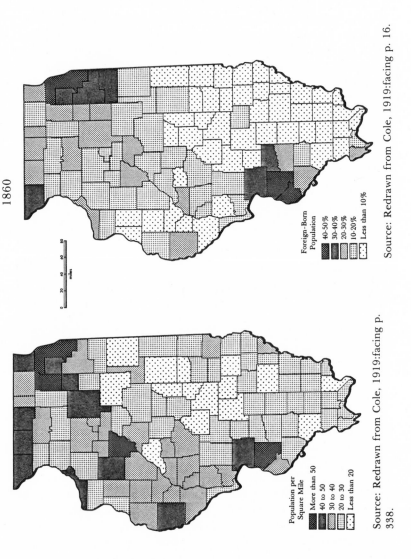

Figure 3–9. Population Density in Illinois, 1860

Figure 3–10. Density of Immigrant Settlement in Illinois Relative to Native-Born, 1860

Population per Square Mile
More than 50
40 to 50
30 to 40
20 to 30
Less than 20

Foreign-Born Population
40-50%
30-40%
20-30%
10-20%
Less than 10%

miles
0 20 40 60 80

Source: Redrawn from Cole, 1919:facing p. 338.

Source: Redrawn from Cole, 1919:facing p. 16.

rose. This flight to the land reflected the search for a means of subsistence in the face of a mounting economic calamity. When urban growth resumed after 1940, it generally occurred in the collar around Chicago and in northern Illinois rather than in the city of Chicago.

Urbanization further reinforced the ethnic and cultural differences between regions, particularly between southern Illinois (outside of the East St. Louis area) and the rest of the state. All urban areas attracted large immigrant populations, and the clustering of particular immigrant groups in neighborhoods created isolated, homogeneous communities with a unique ethnic character (Figure 3–10). Urban workers tended to be wage laborers, many of whom were refugees from unrest and revolutionary protest in Europe. In the wake of the suppression of the 1848 revolutions in Germany, for example, waves of German immigrants flocked to America. Many settled in Illinois. They tended to form militant labor unions to press for their collective demands, while the rural population remained more isolated, independent, and conservative.

Agriculture

Data on the value of agricultural production (current prices) are unavailable before 1870. Prior to that date, therefore, I have used production of the two most important cash grain crops, wheat and corn, as proxies for agricultural production. These data show that central Illinois was the premier agricultural region in the state as early as 1850. Indeed, central Illinois itself would have ranked as the fifth largest wheat producer in the nation and the second largest producer of corn by 1860 (U.S. Census Office, 1864:184–85). The export boom that had caused the rapid rise in the market price of wheat dissipated, however, in the early 1860s as prices fell and as new, better-suited wheat-growing areas farther west opened to settlement. As a result, wheat production fell in every region of Illinois, except in the south, where it expanded one and a half times.

Foreign demand was not, however, the only external source of demand for Illinois' agricultural produce. According to Douglass North, the Midwest's development in general and Illinois' in particular depended upon the export of surplus agricultural commodities to the South. The income thus earned enabled Illinois farmers to buy eastern manufactured goods, particularly textiles, thereby creating a market for the South's cotton crop. In this trade, Illinois was strategically located; its proximity to the market gave it a considerable cost advantage over other competing midwestern states. With the development of more direct east-west transport routes (see below), midwestern farmers also increasingly displaced eastern farmers in producing cereal for East Coast consumption (North, 1966; see also Schmidt, 1939; Fishlow, 1961; Hutchinson and Williamson, 1971).

In 1870, central Illinois accounted for more than half of the state's agricultural output by value (Figure 3-11). This share grew until 1920, peaking at almost 57 percent, but since then it has drifted irregularly downward. Agricultural production in the Chicago area (Chicago proper and the collar), on the other hand, was very small and has remained so, fluctuating in a fairly narrow band around 2 percent in the case of Chicago and 7 percent for the collar region. Northern Illinois' share also remained relatively stable until 1910, when it began to grow. This trend was interrupted by the Great Depression but resumed after 1940. Agricultural production in southern Illinois, by contrast, fell relative to the rest of the state from 1870 to 1930; thereafter, the region's share stabilized somewhat.

The data in Figure 3-11 also show another interesting phenomenon. In both central and southern Illinois, shares of agricultural production fell during the 1920s and rose in the 1930s, whereas in northern Illinois and in the collar around Chicago, production shares rose in the 1920s and fell in the 1930s. This pattern perhaps reflects the differential effect of price declines, particularly in grains, during the 1920s from their peak in May 1920, and the effect of federal price supports for these same commodities during the 1930s.

Estimates of the per capita value of agricultural production can be made beginning in 1870 (Figure 3-12). Agricultural production in the Chicago area contributed only $11.52 per person in 1870, and it then declined to a low of only 68 cents per person in 1930. It has since risen but remains negligible; therefore, agricultural production in Chicago is ignored in the discussion that follows. The other four regions had approximately the same value of agricultural production per person in 1870. Estimates ranged from $78.25 in southern Illinois to $100.31 in the central region. The value of agricultural commodity production per person then fell for the next two decades in the long-term, secular price decline that began after the Civil War.[9] The effects of falling prices on farm income were exacerbated because the price elasticity of demand for agricultural commodities was low and because the prices of agricultural commodities fell faster than those for all goods and services, increasing the wedge in the farm sector and reducing real farm income. Prices began to rise again after 1896, and the value of farm income per person subsequently rebounded in all regions except the collar region around Chicago, where it continued falling until 1910.

Figure 3–11. Regional Distribution of Illinois' Agricultural Production, 1870–1950

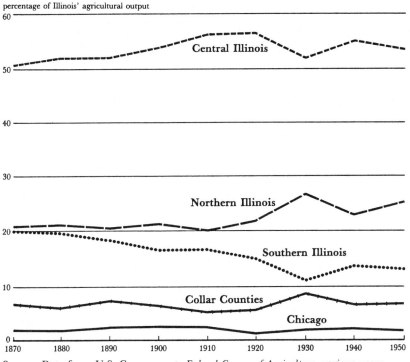

Source: Data from U.S. Government, *Federal Census of Agriculture,* various years.

Figure 3–12. Value of Agricultural Output per Person in Illinois by Region, 1870–1950

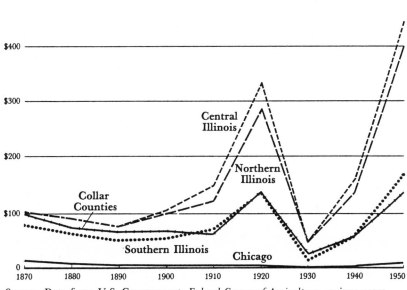

Source: Data from U.S. Government, *Federal Census of Agriculture,* various years.

All of the regions show the same cyclical fluctuations in the value of agricultural production per person. Experiences were similar across the regions through 1890, after which they diverged. Per capita income in southern Illinois and in the collar region showed smaller cyclical fluctuations than in northern and central Illinois, but levels were only one-third to one-half of those realized in the latter regions. This situation was particularly serious for southern Illinois because the region's greater involvement in manufacture failed to make up the difference completely.

Manufacturing

County data on manufacturing output are not available before 1860 and could not be located for 1910 or 1950.[10] As a result, the statistics on manufacturing trends are more limited than those for population and agriculture. Nevertheless, there are enough observations for us to trace the general regional pattern and how this changed over time.

Manufacturing in Chicago grew even more rapidly than its population through 1890. Between 1860 and 1870, for example, Chicago's population grew 143 percent while manufacturing expanded 583 percent. As a result, Chicago's share of state manufacturing output increased rapidly from 1860 to 1890, when it reached a plateau at a little over 70 percent (Figure 3–13). Chicago's relative gain, however, came at the expense of northern, central, and southern Illinois, whose shares declined. The relative decline in downstate manufacturing shares was particularly acute in central Illinois. In 1860, it produced more output than Chicago but roles were reversed by 1870. Indeed, until 1920, manufacturing in central Illinois continued to expand more slowly than in the rest of the state so its share of the total continued to fall. Since then it has been growing slightly more rapidly. Southern Illinois, by contrast, increased its share of state manufacturing output between 1890 and 1920. Indeed, it is tempting to suggest that central Illinois' losses during this period were southern Illinois' gains and vice versa since 1920. Manufacturing in the collar region around Chicago, on the other hand, grew at approximately the same rate as in the state as a whole. As a result, its share of state manufacturing output only fluctuated within two percentage points throughout the entire period.

Per capita estimates of manufacturing output in 1860 (Figure 3–14) show all regions except Chicago at approximately the same level, around $20 per person. Output in Chicago was much higher, $94 per person. All of the regions tended to diverge after 1860, and by 1940 the regions fell into three groups. Per capita manufacturing

Figure 3–13. Regional Distribution of Illinois' Manufacturing Output, 1860–1940

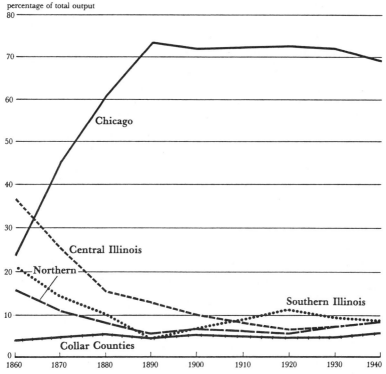

percentage of total output

Source: Data from U.S. Government, *Federal Census of Manufactures,* various years.

Figure 3–14. Value of Manufacturing Output per Person in Illinois by Region, 1860–1940

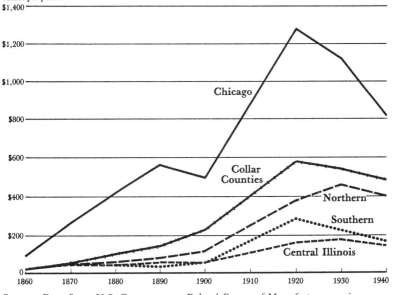

dollars per person

Source: Data from U.S. Government, *Federal Census of Manufactures,* various years.

output in Chicago was highest at over $800, or about double that in the collar around Chicago and northern Illinois. Output in those regions was more than double that in the central and southern parts of the state.

Early growth was most rapid in the collar region around Chicago; per capita production grew eightfold between 1860 and 1890. The graph, however, is dominated by the absolute gains in manufacturing output per capita by Chicago residents. While their output expanded a little more than fivefold over the period, their income gain was $467 per person. Northern Illinois experienced a fourfold increase over the period. Growth in central Illinois was much slower, increasing less than two and a halffold, but even this was much better than the poor 56 percent growth in southern Illinois. The relatively poor performance of southern Illinois in manufacturing output per person during this period reflects the poor performance of its manufacturing sector, which actually shrank between 1880 and 1890, rather than a sharp influx of population. Indeed, had its population growth been closer to the state's average, the problem would have been much more serious.

Chicago's per capita manufacturing output fell 12 percent between 1890 and 1900; it was the only region to exhibit such a movement as trends in the other four regions remained essentially unbroken until 1900. Two historical explanations for Chicago's experience in this decade suggest themselves. First, this decline coincides with a rise in labor militancy in Chicago, exemplified by the Pullman strike in 1894. This may have temporarily discouraged some plants from locating or expanding there. Second, there was a major economic depression in the mid-1890s; however, since the rest of Illinois was apparently untouched, this explanation must depend upon the particular mix of industry in Chicago.

Beginning in 1900, manufacturing output per person in all regions increased sharply. Again, the greatest absolute change was in Chicago, where per capita output rose almost $800; the greatest relative change was in northern Illinois, where income per capita more than tripled. In 1920, manufacturing output per person peaked in three of the regions — Chicago, the collar, and southern Illinois. In the south, this situation reflected the absolute contraction of the manufacturing sector, whereas in Chicago and vicinity, the sector simply expanded less rapidly than the population. In northern and central Illinois, on the other hand, the manufacturing sector continued to experience strong growth until the onset of the Great Depression.

Figure 3–15. Commodity Production per Person in Illinois by Region, 1870–1940

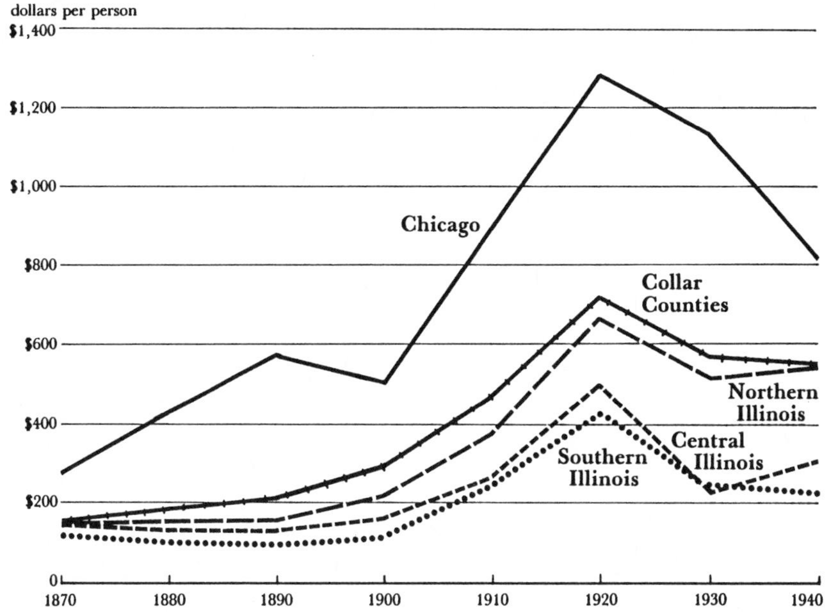

dollars per person

Sources: Data from U.S. Government, *Federal Census of Agriculture* and *Federal Census of Manufactures*, various years.

Commodity Production per Person

Estimates of regional agricultural and manufacturing output can be aggregated to provide an estimate of regional commodity production per person (Figure 3–15). Aggregation had an insignificant impact upon the Chicago region, which was far and away the wealthiest region throughout the period. The other regions remained paired—the collar with northern Illinois and central Illinois with southern Illinois—at markedly different commodity production levels. However, aggregation of manufacturing and agricultural output generally reduced the relative income disparities between regions outside Chicago that were suggested by Figures 3–12 and 3–14. Furthermore, whereas all regions experienced a cyclical downturn in per capita commodity income during the 1920s, commodity production per person outside of Chicago tended to grow during the 1930s as a result of the recovery of agriculture.

Figure 3–15 also points to one particularly significant and alarming trend in Illinois. In general, factor mobility within small geographic areas, particularly a state, tends to be higher than between more widely separated areas because information costs, risk, and uncertainty are lower. Since resources flow toward their highest valued uses and increases in supply tend to drive down prices while reductions in supply raise them, factor mobility generally works in the direction of equalizing returns. Within Illinois, however, the evidence presented here shows widening interregional gaps over time. In 1870, commodity production in the state ranged from $119 in southern Illinois to $270 in Chicago, a ratio of 1:2.3. At the same time, all regions except Chicago had income levels within $40 of that in southern Illinois. In 1940, however, not only was the gap much wider in absolute and relative terms, but the dispersion of income levels had also increased. In that year, commodity production per person in Chicago topped $810 compared with less than $225 in southern Illinois, a ratio of 3.6:1. Moreover, incomes in central Illinois were over $300, and those in northern Illinois and around Chicago exceeded $525. If service income could be included, it is likely that these gaps would only widen.

Transportation and Regional Development

This raises the issue of why factor mobility has failed to equalize regional income levels. Indeed, not only are income levels not equalized but they even seem to have grown. One key factor has been the differential development of the infrastructure, particularly the transportation network, within the state. Governor J. Matteson thought transportation was the key to development in the state; in his address to the Eighteenth General Assembly, he claimed that "almost every portion of the state is now [1853], by means of the canal, the lake, and our majestic shipping, the railroads and plank-roads, rapidly being furnished with a convenient and profitable market. So central is our state, that our products go westward to the mines of California, and eastward to the cities and to Europe" (*American Statistical Annual*, 1854:209). This transport system, however, increasingly came to favor the northern half of the state, particularly the Chicago area, and limited the ability of central and southern Illinois to attract and hold industry in the competition for resources within the state.

Water

Early settlement within Illinois occurred along, or within a day's wagon ride of, the navigable rivers—particularly the Mississippi, Ohio, and

Wabash—to take advantage of the cheap transportation which these rivers afforded in a region without roads or other avenues of commerce. From there, settlements spread northward along the rivers. The attractiveness of locating along the navigable rivers was further enhanced by the expansion of steamboat traffic that offered increasingly cheap and reliable communication with the rest of the world. By the late 1820s, steamboats plied the rivers from Pittsburgh in the east, to Minneapolis in the north, and down the Mississippi to New Orleans. From there, cargo could be interchanged for shipment along the coast or overseas (Hunter, 1949). When Illinois became a state, it cost perhaps $1.00 to ship 100 pounds of freight to New Orleans and $6.00 to receive a like shipment from New Orleans. By 1850, productivity gains and competition had driven these rates down to 50 cents each way (Hunter, 1949). Traffic expanded rapidly. In 1822, 6 steamboats served St. Louis and Galena; by 1828 Galena recorded 99 arrivals, and by the 1840s more than 300 steamboats docked in the average year (Schockel, 1917–18; Petersen, 1937; Hunter, 1949). Commerce within the state also grew with the introduction of steamboats on the Illinois River in the late 1820s. By 1836, Beardstown recorded 225 arrivals, and in the twelve months beginning July 1, 1841, Peoria received 432 steamboats. Of these, 143 arrived from Peru and 11 more from other upstream locations. The balance arrived from destinations outside the Illinois River, primarily St. Louis (259) but as far away as Pittsburgh and New Orleans (Hunter, 1949:46). By the early 1850s, the commerce of the Illinois River was put at over $42 million, and in 1852, 1,608 steamboats berthed in Peoria (*American Statistical Annual*, 1854:210).

The same basic technology of steam navigation applied so successfully to the western rivers also appeared on the Great Lakes, where traffic was also increasing as a result of the Erie Canal, which provided the gateway to the East Coast. Before the Illinois and Michigan Canal and the growth of Chicago, however, there was little traffic on Lake Michigan. In 1836, the commerce of the port of Chicago was estimated at $325,203 in imports, with exports of only $1,000. By 1840, imports were worth $562,106, but exports had jumped to $228,635; by the mid-1840s, imports were in excess of $2 million, while exports exceeded $1 million. In 1851, imports totaling $24,416,211 were recorded, while exports were put at $5,511,656. Most of this commerce was domestic, but the port also cleared fourteen foreign vessels (*American Statistical Annual*, 1854:215).

The growth of traffic on the Illinois River first spurred settlement in Chicago, contrary to the popular myth that the railroad made the city. Indeed, located some twenty miles north of the southern end of Lake Michigan, Chicago was anything but conveniently located for the railroads, particularly the east-west lines that were forced to veer northward from their principal axis. Chicago owes its early growth to the low portage—often flooded in wet weather between the lake and the Des Plaines River. This portage is clearly marked on the earliest maps of Illinois, and it formed the nucleus around which Chicago grew.

The portage also held the promise of an easy, inexpensive, all-water transport link between the Great Lakes and the western rivers. The project, the Illinois and Michigan Canal, formed the key to the state's ambitious scheme of internal improvements in the late 1830s, but extensive logrolling was required in order to secure passage through the state legislature. Plans soon called for state financed construction of a railroad from the southern terminus of the canal to the confluence of the Ohio and Mississippi, a railroad from Quincy to the Wabash and Erie Canal being built in Indiana, and improvements to the Illinois and Wabash rivers (see, for example, Pease, 1922:194–215).

By these schemes, southern Illinois hoped to recapture some of the ground then being lost to the northern part of the state. John Logan, the state representative for Jackson County, spoke enthusiastically of ocean-going vessels from the West Indies unloading their cargoes at Cairo for shipment north by the only year-round transportation possible—the railroad (Pease, 1922:219). Jealousies and mistrust, however, led to the requirement of simultaneous construction of all projects, severely straining finances and limiting progress. The failure of these schemes in the financial panic of the late 1830s brought ruin to the state, and the special tax bill of 1841 was used as an argument by neighboring states to attract Illinois emigrants to their borders (Pease, 1922:233).

Even as late as 1850, the impact of water transportation on settlement densities was apparent. The only counties where population density exceeded 22.5 persons per square mile were those adjacent to the navigable rivers, the Illinois and Michigan Canal, or Lake Michigan. The most noticeable exception to this rule was Kane County, where a railroad to Chicago had been constructed.

Railroads

Completion of the Illinois and Michigan Canal gave a decisive boost to Chicago. By 1850, Chicago had a population of 43,385, making it the largest city in Illinois. As the terminus of the canal and with substantial lake shipping, Chicago had an established trade that the railroads hoped to tap, syphoning off the high value-to-weight freight. In this, they were successful. In 1852, for example, the railroads carried about 67 percent of the wheat and 40 percent of the flour shipped to Chicago, but only 22 percent of the corn; the canal carried only 15 percent of the wheat, 2 percent of the flour, but more than 67 percent of the less valuable corn (*American Statistical Annual,* 1854:209).

Railroads were systematically built the length and breadth of the state during the 1850s. The internal improvements of the 1850s differed from those of the 1830s, when many projects seem to have been much more speculative or motivated by purely political considerations. Of the total railroad miles built in the state by the end of 1853, more than 60 percent were in the eleven leading wheat counties and the eight largest corn-producing counties in 1850, even though these counties comprised less than one-fourth of the area of the state (Fishlow, 1965:173, 205–36). Population increased sharply in those areas served by railroads between 1850 and 1861 (North, 1966:147–49).

By 1860, railroad mileage in Illinois totaled 2,799 miles. This opening up of the state through improved transportation in the 1850s had a marked impact on agricultural production. Farms in these areas served by good transportation increasingly developed commercial, more specialized agriculture with large surpluses that could only be shipped by rail, barge, or steamboat. This growing commercial orientation of farming was reflected in the differential rates of increases in farmland values (Fishlow, 1965; Atack and Bateman, 1987). By 1860, there were only five Illinois counties that were neither on a navigable river or canal nor served by a railroad—Franklin, Johnson, Williamson, Hamilton, and Saline, all in southern Illinois. In these counties, land was worth only 41 percent of the average for the state as a whole.[11] Not only did the very provision of cheaper, improved transportation stimulate commercialization, but the railroads, particularly the Illinois Central, played a leading role in actively promoting settlement in Illinois. The Illinois Central stimulated commercial agriculture, especially on the prairie, which hitherto had been shunned by settlers, by providing an outlet for surplus produce, a cheap source of drainage tile, and the active promotion of settlement both at home and abroad (Gates, 1934).

Although not all parts of the state could be served by the rivers, river traffic remained the railroads' serious competitor throughout the 1850s. External events finally tipped the scales in the railroads' favor. The Civil War effectively closed the Mississippi River to shipments from the Midwest to the East Coast and overseas markets during a crucial period in Illinois' development. As a result, railroads achieved ascendancy. Rail centers such as Chicago and routes east eclipsed river towns and routings such as Cairo and the routes south, which declined both relatively and absolutely. In 1869, the commerce of Cairo was some $20 million; by 1886 this had fallen to somewhat less than $8 million (U.S. Congress, 1888:515). The Chicago Board of Trade provides no similar summary measures of the trade in Chicago; however, the annual reports indicate substantial increases in physical shipments of virtually every commodity. For example, meat shipments increased from 86.7 million pounds in 1869 to 886.1 million pounds in 1886. Even in the flour-milling industry, which was in relative decline, shipments increased from 2.8 million barrels to 6.4 million over the period (Chicago Board of Trade, 1869, 1888).

By the 1890s, continued expansion of the rail network kept Illinois at the forefront of the states in total railroad mileage — 10,315 miles, or 18 miles of road per 100 square miles of territory and 36 miles per 10,000 inhabitants. Perhaps even more significant, 85 percent of all lands in the state were within five miles of a railroad, 11.5 percent lay between five and ten miles from the nearest line, and only 1 percent lay more than fifteen miles away. None was farther than twenty miles from a railroad (Railroad and Warehouse Commission, 1894:31).

Roads

The survey provisions of the Land Ordinances of 1785 provided for public rights-of-way at section and township boundaries (that is, every mile and every six miles). Few roads in Illinois, however, were more than earthen tracks, deeply rutted and all but impassable in wet weather. At various times, the state legislature provided grants-in-aid for road construction (as in 1823 when it appropriated $8,000 to build roads radiating from Vandalia in Fayette County), but no serious effort was made to improve road transportation because it was viewed more as a local than a state concern (Pease, 1922:42).

With the revival of interest in railroad construction in Illinois in the late 1840s and early 1850s came renewed interest in road improvement. Particular importance was attached to plank roads (constructed of wooden planks laid upon the earth to provide a durable, resilient surface), and the state passed enabling legislation for the general incorporation of plank-road associations to facilitate construction. These roads often functioned as a means of getting goods to (and from) the railhead, and hundreds were built with the savings of thousands of investors. Stock in a road from Chicago to the Will

County line, for example, was quickly snapped up, with $53,000 stock subscribed at the end of the first day of sale. In part this reflected investor optimism about the potential, and in some cases actual, return. The northwestern road from Chicago toward Elgin, for example, accumulated tolls sufficient to pay expenses plus 42 percent dividends after only six months of partial operation. By mid-1851, approximately 600 miles of roads had been built or surveyed, representing an investment of about a million dollars, but virtually all were in the northern half of the state.[12]

In 1871, after the adoption of the new state constitution, a standing house committee on roads, highways, and bridges was appointed; a new road law passed the following year to provide for district care and superintendence of the state's roads. This legislation was subsequently repealed, revised, and reenacted a number of times. In times of falling agricultural prices, with the farmers caught in a wedge between prices they paid and those they were paid, there was often little sentiment for increased local taxes to pay for road improvement. Nevertheless, legislation was passed in 1883 to provide for special county taxes for the construction of "hard roads." This was the first legislation providing for permanent roads at public expense; unfortunately, there are no data on the extent of roads so constructed (Bogart and Thompson, 1922:354–62).

Road improvement in the twentieth century was attendant upon the coming of the automobile, which was less able to cope with mud and deeply rutted roads than the horse-drawn wagon. Also, World War I brought about the realization at the federal level that poor roads had both strategic and economic costs. As a result, all main roads were soon paved; efforts since then have focused on upgrading the weight limits on bridges and increasing the capacity of roads by widening them, removing hazards such as sharp corners, limiting access, and bypassing town and city business districts. Even the most cursory perusal of a road map reveals that road density is greater in the northern than in the southern half of the state. As a result, not only are market distances greater in the southern region, but user costs per mile also tend to be higher.

The Costs of Transportation

The transportation improvements discussed above had a dramatic impact on the costs of shipping goods, thereby raising the price received by producers while simultaneously lowering the price paid by consumers. In the beginning of the nineteenth century, overland wagon transport cost perhaps 30 to 70 cents per ton-mile depending upon the terrain, either at the upper end in wooded and mountainous areas crisscrossed by steams, such as in southern Illinois, or at the lower end, where there were no natural impediments as in the prairies (Taylor, 1951:133).

By mid-century, freight rates for wagon transportation had been reduced to perhaps 15 to 20 cents per ton-mile. Costs by river or canal were much lower. Rates on the Illinois River were about 1.2 cents per ton-mile, those on the Mississippi, only .6 cents per ton-mile. At the same time, charges on the Illinois and Michigan Canal averaged 1.4 cents per ton-mile, while railroads such as the Western Railroad charged 2.5 cents per ton-mile between Buffalo and Chicago (Taylor, 1951:442; see also North, 1965). Transport costs thus fell to as little as 1 percent of their levels at the beginning of the century.

This had a profound effect on the area over which commodities could be profitably marketed. According to Clarence Danhof, transport costs generally could not constitute more than about 20 percent of the market price of a commodity before its market attractiveness was substantially impaired (1979:127–91). Based on this rule, commodities, especially relatively low-valued agricultural commodities such as corn, had virtually no market beyond the farmgate early in the nineteenth century. By mid-century, the market for surplus wheat was limited to perhaps 40 miles and surplus corn to perhaps 20 miles if carried by wagon, but wheat could be carried as far as 1,000 miles or corn 500 miles if shipped on the Mississippi River. By the end of the century, railroad rates had fallen to about the same level as the river rates of mid-century (.83 cents per ton-mile), though given the different ways in which the rates were computed, the real differences between water and rail were substantially less.[13]

Historical Regional Differences and the Political Process

The growing economic regional inequalities within the state as it developed created political tensions between disparate constituencies. These differences were then magnified by the ethnic and cultural prejudices of the various groups which had settled the different regions. Historically, these political tensions were often between the manufacturing and commerce interests, on the one hand, and agriculture, on the other. As time passed, however, this division became virtually identical with tensions between Chicago and "downstate."

Consider, for example, the effect of the spread of railroads westward from Chicago. Whereas those roads to the East served the interests of Illinois farmers by providing a cheaper and more convenient means of exporting surplus agriculture products to urban East Coast markets or overseas, the western roads brought a flood of even cheaper agricultural commodities from the newly developing states farther west, adversely affecting the markets for Illinois farmers. Chicago, however, benefitted from the increased commerce, and manufacturers gained easy access to a new group of potential customers.

The conflict between agriculture and manufacturing and commerce generally reflected the different economic circumstances in which the sectors found themselves. Agriculture was perfectly competitive, while there were barriers to entering manufacturing and commerce. As a result, resources denied entry into the monopolistic sectors flooded into agriculture, driving down the relative rate of return. Theodore Saloutos wrote, "Perhaps no development of the nineteenth century brought greater disappointment to the American farmers than did their failure to realize the prosperity that they had expected from industrialism" (1948:156). Lack of control over their economic destiny thus led farmers to seek political solutions to their problems and needs. Those solutions almost invariably adversely affected the rest of the economy and hence did not go unchallenged.

This search for a political solution to an economic problem is clearly shown by the events following the Civil War. Illinois farmers played a leading role in these events. Encouraged by inflation and wartime scarcity, agriculture in Illinois became even more commercially oriented. Farmers increasingly specialized in a narrower range of crops, especially corn, and assumed more debt through mechanization and land purchases in a speculative market. Agricultural profits, driven by rising commodity prices, were high. For example, corn, which in 1859 brought only 50 cents per bushel (Norton and Wilson, 1930), was selling for 78 cents per bushel by 1867 (U.S. Department of Commerce, 1975). As a result, demand for land was high, and considerable speculative capital gains were made.

By 1870, however, corn prices collapsed to 52 cents per bushel, falling to 31 cents in 1878, before bottoming out at 21 cents in 1896 (U.S. Department of Commerce, 1975). Those farmers who had expanded and assumed debts in the expectation of continued high prices were caught by this collapse. Although declining prices were not confined to agriculture, prices declined further and faster in that sector than in others. As a result, the real income of farmers declined, and many faced a cash-flow crisis due to the service burden of their debt (Saloutos, 1948).

The sectoral response to the farm crisis was political. Farmers joined the National Grange of the Patrons of Husbandry and became a potent force pushing for relief from their economic distress. So successful was this movement in Illinois that they captured the state legislature and passed laws establishing the Illinois Commerce Commission with regulatory oversight of railroad rates and practices, warehouses, and grain elevators. This legislation, confirmed by the U.S. Supreme Court in *Munn v. Illinois* (94 U.S. 113), established the right of governments to regulate any business that was "clothed with the public interest." It was, however, inimical to business, especially the warehousing, elevator, and railroad operations, such as the Joint Executive Committee in the Chicago area.

Other political parties also captured the farmers' hearts, notably the Greenback party and the Populist party. These had the liberalization of the money supply as one of their major policy goals. Restricted monetary growth was the leading cause of the deflation that was in large part responsible for the plight of the farmer, but it was favored by commercial interests and manufacturers interested in "sound money" and the resumption of currency convertibility into gold.

Conclusion

Regional differences in Illinois are not a recent phenomenon. They have existed from the start of settlement in the state, although they tended to be relatively smaller then than now. They were also the opposite of those today. In the early nineteenth century, the southern half of the state was the richest and the most developed. By the middle of the nineteenth century, however, the regional balance shifted northward with the opening of northern routes for settlement. This introduced a different class of settlers, who had different ethnic and cultural backgrounds and different motivations for settling in the state. The transition then accelerated with the growth of Chicago and the concentration of manufacturing and commerce in the area at a break in transportation between river, canal, and lake enroute to the richest market in America, the East Coast. Indeed, I argue that the availability and cost of transportation and location vis-à-vis markets were decisive factors favoring development in the northern half of the state.

Commodity production was dominated by manufacturing output, and Chicago dominated the other regions from as early as 1870. Divergence among the downstate regions did not, however, really appear until the end of the nineteenth century and especially during the first twenty years of this century. By 1940, per capita commodity production in the area around Chicago and in northern Illinois was about double that in the central and southern Illinois. Central Illinois seems to have performed marginally better than southern Illinois because of its greater agricultural productivity.

At the same time that the regional data show wide variation between the different regions of Illinois, the county-by-county data show even greater variability within the separate regions. This was especially true in southern and central Illinois, where commodity output per person in 1940 varied by a factor of 28 to 1 between Madison and Hardin counties and 12 to 1 between Tazewell and Fulton. Even in northern Illinois, where the range was the smallest in 1940, the variation in commodity output per person was over 3 to 1 between residents of Stephenson and Jo Daviess counties. Nor are the results for 1940 unusual. The ranges were even greater in 1930. Furthermore, the inclusion of service income is unlikely to narrow them. Indeed, it may even widen the differences since wealthier areas with higher densities of manufacturing and agricultural output have a higher demand for services, if only because of the income elasticity.

NOTES

1. U.S. Department of Commerce, 1975:297. In terms of average per capita income payments to individuals, Illinois would have ranked sixth in 1950. See U.S. Department of Commerce, 1952:258.

2. U.S. Census Office, 1841:358, 364; agricultural rank based upon wheat and corn production, industrial rank based upon capital invested in manufacturing. Illinois and Ohio switch places in manufacturing value-added between 1949 and 1950; Illinois ranks second based on the 1949 data, and third on the 1950 data, but the margins of error are such that these rankings might be reversed. See U.S. Department of Commerce, 1952:782, 601.

3. These data are available from the Bureau of Economic and Business Research, University of Illinois, 1206 South Sixth Street, Champaign, Ill. 61820.

4. See Atack and Bateman, 1987:table 4.1. The child-woman ratio is defined as children under 10 per thousand women aged 16–44.

5. The movement of industrial activity from the countryside and small towns to the city was sufficiently marked that in 1890 the Census produced a separate report on urban industry. See U.S. Department of Interior, Census Office, 1895.

6. Cook County's share remained more or less constant at 73 percent.

7. These and the land-sale figures that follow are taken from House Executive Documents, U.S. Serial Set 206, 21 Cong., 2d sess., No. 2, "Report of the Commissioner of the General Land Office": 72-73; House Executive Documents, U.S. Serial Set 271, 23 Cong., 2d sess., No. 3, "Report from the Secretary of the Treasury": 93; House Executive Documents, U.S. Serial

Set 286, 24 Cong., 1st sess., No. 5, "Operations of Land Offices—1834 and 1835": 11; House Executive Documents, U.S. Serial Set 301, 24 Cong., 2d sess., No. 6, "Annual Report—Commissioner of the General Land Office": 9; House Executive Documents, U.S. Serial Set 383, 26 Cong., 2d sess., No. 38, "Annual Report—Commissioner of the General Land Office": 10; Senate Public Documents, U.S. Serial Set 238, 23 Cong., 1st sess., No. 9, "Report of the Secretary of the Treasury": 60; Senate Public Documents, U.S. Serial Set 314, 25 Cong., 2d sess., No. 11, "Report of the Secretary of the Treasury": 13; Senate Public Documents, U.S. Serial Set 338, 25 Cong., 3d sess., No. 17, "Report of the Secretary of the Treasury": 8; Senate Public Documents, U.S. Serial Set 355, 26 Cong., 1st sess., No. 21, "Report of the Secretary of the Treasury": 13.

8. U.S. Department of Commerce, 1975:27. Urban areas are defined as communities with populations of 2,500 or more.

9. See, for example, the Warren-Pearson price index in U.S. Department of Commerce, 1975:200–207.

10. County data do not seem to have been published in 1910, and the 1950 volumes are currently unavailable.

11. U.S. Census Office, 1864; estimate based on the average cash value of farm per acre (improved and unimproved).

12. This paragraph is based upon Cole, 1919:28. Cole explicitly mentions roads from Chicago, Florence, Beardstown, Macomb, Pekin, Bloomington, Peoria, LaSalle, Peru, and Ottawa. None in the south is mentioned.

13. Allowance must be made, for example, for the greater speed of the railraod and the insurance protection provided as part of the rail tariff. See Railroad and Warehouse Commission, 1894:36.

REFERENCES

American Statistical Annual for the Year 1854. 1854. New York: J. H. Colton.

Atack, Jeremy, and Fred Bateman. 1987. *To Their Won Soil: Agriculture in the Antebellum North.* Ames: Iowa State University Press.

Bogart, Ernest L., and Charles M. Thompson. 1922. *The Centennial History of Illinois.* Vol. 4, *The Industrial State, 1870–1893.* Chicago: A. C. McClurg.

Buley, R. C. 1950. *The Old Northwest: Pioneer Period, 1815–1840,* Vol. 1. Bloomington: Indiana University Press.

Chicago Board of Trade. 1869. *Annual Statement of the Trade and Commerce of Chicago for 1869.* Chicago: Horton and Leonard.

———. 1888. *Annual Statement of the Trade and Commerce of Chicago for 1887.* Chicago: Knight and Leonard.

Cole, Arthur C. 1919. *The Centennial History of Illinois.* Vol. 3, *The Era of the Civil War, 1848–1870.* Springfield: Illinois Centennial Commission.

Danhof, Clarence H. 1979. "The Farm Enterprise: The Northern United States, 1820–1860s." *Research in Economic History* 4:127–91.

Easterlin, Richard A. 1976. "Population Change and Farm Settlement in the Northern United States." *Journal of Economic History* 371 (March):45–75.

Fishlow, Albert. 1961. "Antebellum Interregional Trade Reconsidered." *American Economic Review* 54 (May):352–64.

———. 1965. *American Railroads and the Transformation of the Antebellum Economy.* Cambridge, Mass.: Harvard University Press.

Fogel, Robert W., and Jack Rutner. 1972. "The Efficiency Effects of Federal Land Policy, 1850–1900: A Report of Some Provisional Findings." In William O. Aydelotte (ed.), *The Dimension of Quantitative Research in History.* Princeton, N.J.: Princeton University Press.

Gates, Paul W. 1934. *The Illinois Central Railroad and Its Colonization Work.* Cambridge, Mass.: Harvard University Press.

———. 1960. *The Farmer's Age: Agriculture, 1815–1860.* White Plaines, New York: Holt, Rinehart, and Winston.

Hunter, Louis C. 1949. *Steamboats on the Western Rivers.* Cambridge, Mass.: Harvard University Press.

Hutchinson, William K., and Samuel H. Williamson. 1971. "The Self Sufficiency of the Antebellum South: Estimates of the Food Supply." *Journal of Economic History* 31 (September):591–609.

Mathews, Lois Kimball. 1909. *The Expansion of New England.* Boston: Houghton Mifflin.

North, Douglass Cecil. 1965. "The Role of Transportation in the Economic Development of North America." In *Les grandes voies maritimes dans le monde XV–XIX xiecles.* Paris: SEVPEN.

———. 1966. *Economic Growth of the United States, 1790–1860.* New York: Prentice-Hall.

Norton, J. L., and B. B. Wilson. 1930. "Prices of Illinois Farm Products from 1866 to 1929." *University of Illinois Agricultural Experiment Station Bulletin 351.* Urbana: University of Illinois.

Pease, Theodore C. 1922. "The Frontier State, 1818–1848." In *The Centennial History of Illinois,* Vol. 2. Chicago: A. C. McClurg.

Perloff, Harvey S., Edgar S. Dunn, Jr., Eric E. Lampard, and Richard F. Muth. 1960. *Regions, Resources, and Economic Growth.* Baltimore: The Johns Hopkins University Press for Resources for the Future.

Petersen, William J. 1937. *Steamboating on the Upper Mississippi.* Iowa City: Torch Press for the State Historical Society of Iowa.

Phillips, U. B. 1906. "The Origin and Growth of the Southern Black Belt." *American Historical Review* 11:789–816.

Railroad and Warehouse Commission. 1894. *Twenty-third Annual Report of the Railroad and Warehouse Commission of Illinois.* Springfield: Rocker.

Saloutos, Theodore. 1948. "The Agriculture Problem and Nineteenth Century Industrialism." *Agricultural History* 22:156.

Schmidt, Louis B. 1939. "Internal Commerce and the Development of a National Economy before 1860." *Journal of Political Economy* 47 (December):799–822.

Schockel, B. H. 1917–18. "Settlement and Development of the Lead and Fine Mining Region of the Driftless Area with Special Emphasis upon Jo Daviess County, Illinois." *Mississippi Valley Historical Review* 4:181–85.

Steckel, Richard H. 1983. "The Economic Foundations of East-West Migration during the Nineteenth Century." *Explorations in Economic History* 20 (January):14–36.

Stilwell, Lewis D. 1937. "Migration from Vermont (1776–1860)." *Proceedings of the Vermont Historical Society* 52:63–246.

Taylor, George Rogers. 1951. *The Transportation Revolution, 1815–1860.* New York: Holt, Rinehart, and Winston.

Turner, Frederick Jackson. 1920. *The Frontier in American History.* New York: Henry Hold.

U.S. Census Office. 1841. *Sixth Census: Compendium of the Enumeration of Inhabitants and Statistics of the United States.* Washington, D.C.: Blair and Rives.

———. 1853. *The Seventh Census of the United States.* Washington, D.C.: Robert Armstrong.

———. 1864. *Eighth Census: Agriculture of the United States in 1860.* Washington, D.C.: Government Printing Office.

U.S. Congress. House. 1888. *Report on the Internal Commerce of the United States, Part II.* 50th Cong., 1st sess., H. Executive Doc. 20, Serial 2552.

U.S. Department of Commerce. 1952. *Statistical Abstract of the United States.* Washington, D.C.: Government Printing Office.

———. 1975. *Historical Statistics of the United States from Colonial Times to 1970.* Washington, D.C.: Government Printing Office, Series G219.

U.S. Department of Interior. Census Office. 1895. *Eleventh Census: Report on Manufacturing Industries, Statistics on Cities.* Washington, D.C.: Government Printing Office.

U.S. Government. 1870–1950. *Federal Census of Agriculture.* Washington, D.C.: Government Printing Office.

U.S. Government. 1850–1950. *Federal Census of Manufactures.* Washington, D.C.: Government Printing Office.

The Politics of Regionalism, Nineteenth-Century Style

4

Robert Sutton

The careful—and even the casual—observer of the Illinois scene will almost certainly be attuned to the classic Chicago-downstate dichotomy which has clearly dominated Illinois politics for the bulk of this century. Not only has this been true in fact, but it has even been encouraged in theory (perhaps unwittingly and certainly unwisely) by such semiofficial slogans as "Just outside Chicago there's a state called Illinois."[1]

The stark contrasts between metropolitan Chicago and rural Illinois are only the most recent and certainly the most pervasive of a long history of regional stresses and strains which characterized nineteenth-century Illinois. Almost from the day it was admitted to the Union in 1818, the Prairie State has felt the "pull and haul" of regional interests and pressures. In the nineteenth century the issues were frequently economic in nature, and they were reflected, as were social and constitutional issues, in the political activity of the young state. Such diverse subjects as slavery versus anti-slavery, canals versus railroads, county government versus townships, free schools versus subscription-based education have a strange and unreal ring to twentieth-century ears, and yet they demanded and received an enormous amount of attention from nineteenth-century Illinoisans (Federal Writer's Project for the State of Illinois, 1947; also Hutton, 1946).

Two factors are most discernible in shaping the direction and growth of the early state: one is strictly geographic in character and the other is heavily influenced by geography. The size, shape, and location of Illinois virtually dictated regional (and uneven) development. The great length of Illinois (380 miles from north to south) when contrasted with its widest point (205 miles) may not attract immediate attention; but to be told that northern Illinois is the same latitude as Boston, Massachusetts, while Cairo, at the southern tip, shares a latitudinal level with Richmond, Virginia, almost always elicits surprise if not disbelief at first hearing.

The wide latitudinal range of Illinois and the existing avenues of transportation leading to the Prairie State dictated the early pattern of white settlement. The deep protrusion of Illinois into the upper South and the well-developed river system in that part of the country encouraged the movement of people from Virginia and the Carolinas through Tennessee and Kentucky into southern Illinois. For those who chose to come overland, the widely used trail through the Cumberland Gap and across the Kentucky bluegrass had its own advantages. By contrast, there were no readily available access routes into northern Illinois, and that region languished for several decades. Thus it was that Illinois at the time of statehood reflected a definite southern flavor (Barnhart, 1953:chapters 9, 13, 14; Power, 1953:1–3, 5–56).

I

Before beginning an examination of the regional tensions which strained the young state, it would be well to discuss an earlier congressional decision reached at the time of statehood which shaped the destiny of Illinois from that day to this. It has to do with the permanent boundaries for Illinois, and one must look back to the Ordinance of 1787, enacted by the Congress of the Confederation for the details (Commager, 1968:754–56).

The Ordinance of 1787, which applied to the territory north and west of the Ohio River (the "Old Northwest" in American parlance), ordained that not less than three nor more than five states should be formed from the region. It further suggested appropriate boundaries for the prospective states — regardless of whether their number should be three, four, or five. Since the ultimate decision was to create five states, the 1787 law directed that the upper tier of states (Michigan and Wisconsin) be separated from the lower tier (Ohio, Indiana, and Illinois) by a line beginning at the Mississippi River and "drawn through the southerly bend or extreme of Lake Michigan." The proposed boundary would extend eastward to Lake Erie. Had this arrangement prevailed, neither Illinois nor Indiana would have had any frontage on Lake Michigan (article five of the Ordinance of 1787; also Buley, 1951). Congress, however, retained the power to adjust the boundaries of the new states and did so in every case. Ohio benefitted from a very slight adjustment in its northern boundary, which enabled it to retain the valuable harbor that became Toledo. When Indiana was prepared to enter the Union (1816), its promoters recognized the potential advantage which frontage on Lake Michigan would afford. Consequently, it recommended and Congress approved a ten-mile northerly extension of the Indiana border where it rests today.

When Illinois petitioned for statehood two years later, a similar arrangement prevailed. The Enabling Act of January 23, 1818, proposed a ten-mile northward extension of the Illinois border, and in that form the legislation went before Congress. Nathanial Pope, territorial delegate from Illinois and one of the truly forgotten heroes of Illinois history, offered an amendment to the Illinois Enabling Act extending Illinois' northern border an additional forty-one miles to latitude 42°30'. This audacious move on Pope's part fixed the boundary between Illinois and Wisconsin approximately fifty-one miles north of the original ordinance line (Buck, 1917: 224–25; Brown, 1844: 351–53).

Pope's amendment added to Illinois a significant area of nearly 8,000 square miles, including all or parts of sixteen of its present most populous and prosperous counties. Without it, Chicago, Rockford, and other northern Illinois cities would be in Wisconsin, and the Prairie State, deprived of nearly 80 percent of its present population, would be greatly reduced in stature and influence. Once the admission of Illinois was assured, Pope reported his success to friends back home in an enthusiastic and remarkably prophetic letter, in which he said: "We may say with truth, that we will enter upon a state government with better prospects than any state ever did—the best soil in the world, a mild climate, a large state, with the most ample funds to educate every child in the state; however poor, a man may well hope to see his child rise to the need of this mighty nation, if he have talents and virtue. Our Avenues for navigation are towards the east and the west, the north and the south" (Buck, 1917:310–17; Sutton, 1968:1–3).

II

Who would ever suspect that Illinois would have had a serious flirtation with the institution of slavery? Yet the very first issue which agitated and distracted the infant state was over that very subject. Admitted to the Union as a free state in 1818, Illinois felt restrained and manipulated by article six of the Ordinance of 1787, which declared that "neither slavery nor involuntary servitude" could exist in the territory. The trouble was that slavery already existed in Illinois, having been introduced by the French in the 1720s while they were in control of the region. The number of slaves was never large, but their presence was continuous, confirmed in law first by the French, later by the English, and finally by Virginia before it surrendered its western land claims to the central government. One would have assumed that the unequivocal statement found in article six of the Ordinance and incorporated into the first Illinois constitution would have settled the matter once and for all, but it did not (Harris, 1904; see also Davidson and Stuve, 1874:309–27).

The ambiguity of the situation was pointed up by the fact that the first Illinois constitution, which declared that "neither slavery nor involuntary servitude shall hereafter be introduced into this state," failed to deal with the presence of slaves already there. Arthur St. Clair, first governor of the Northwest Territory, further confused the situation by ruling that slaves already present could remain without interference from local authorities (Pease, 1918:72–76; Davidson and Stuve, 1874:312–17; Ford, 1854:51–52).

It was against this background that some of the leading figures in early Illinois, many of whom were slaveholders (including Ninian Edwards, territorial governor and one of the first U.S. senators from Illinois), began to agitate for the legislation of slavery within the state. Their position was strengthened by the guarantee, also contained in the Northwest Ordinance, that new states would be admitted "on an equal footing with the original States," and was further fed by the feeling that Illinois would be at a disadvantage economically as the westward flow of settlers passed it by in the search for territory where the institution of slavery would be welcome. Notice the extent to which a southern frame of mind dominated the thinking in early Illinois.

The surprising election of an anti-slavery Virginian, only recently removed to Illinois, as second governor of the state in 1822 brought matters to a head. When Governor Edward Coles made it clear that he intended to enforce the anti-slavery provisions of the constitution, the pro-slavery forces went into action. With clear majorities in both houses of the General Assembly, they were able to ram through, with the necessary two-thirds vote, a resolution calling for a new constitutional convention. What followed was a sharp and corrosive eighteen-month campaign before the people, since the public would have to approve or reject the proposed call for a new convention. It is not clear to this day whether the pro-conventionists had limited or unlimited slavery in mind, but they used every possible argument to persuade the public that slavery was an object well worth embracing.

Naturally, the anti-conventionists, led by Governor Coles, were equally resourceful and even more energetic in their response. This bitter verbal contest, continuing until the next general election in August, 1824, reveals the extent of the regional disagreement already present in frontier Illinois (Babcock, 1854:52–55).

By no stretch of the imagination could the outcome be called an anticlimax, even though the results of the balloting were not nearly as close as had been anticipated. The pro-slavery party was overwhelmed, the anti-convention forces vindicated. Of the 11,612 votes cast (8,606 had been cast at the gubernatorial election only two years before), 6,640 or 57 percent opposed the calling of a convention to legalize slavery in Illinois, while 4,972 or 43 percent favored it. The Prairie State continued to be numbered among the free states of the Union (Pease, 1923:27).

The extent of the victory of the anti-slavery forces came as something of a surprise—especially to the convention forces. They probably suffered from a degree of overconfidence, undoubtedly fed by their overwhelming majorities in the General Assembly. They certainly failed to gauge accurately the temper of public opinion. They also failed to recognize or take into account the subtle demographic changes already at work in Illinois. In the few short years since statehood, Illinois was already beginning to experience that fantastic population growth which would continue throughout the nineteenth century.[2]

The Illinois state census of 1825 returned a total of 72,817 inhabitants, almost double the population reported at the time of statehood. Much of this growth occurred in the middle counties and in the more distant western counties of the state as settlement, encouraged and abetted by steamboats on the western waters, pushed up the Illinois River valley. Represented in this sizeable pool of newcomers were non-slaveholding southerners, "Yankees" from New England and the East, and the multiple-moving neighbors from the region in between. Obviously, little sentiment for slavery would be found in any of these groups, and no one should have been surprised at the electoral outcome. The pro-slavery forces showed their greatest strength in the deep southern river counties opposite the slave states of Kentucky and Missouri—Gallatin County returned an 82 percent majority for the convention; Jefferson County, 70 percent; and Pope County, 69 percent. The issue was a toss-up in the transitional counties which separated the southern counties from the rapidly growing central counties. In these central counties the anti-slavery forces ran up majorities which stagger the imagination—Pike County, 90 percent;

Morgan County, 91 percent; and Edgar County, across the state on the Indiana border, 99 percent (Pease, 1923:27–29).

Following the spirited contest of 1823–24, the slavery issue disappeared from Illinois politics but the problem did not go away. The ambivalent situation of slaves living in Illinois remained; long-term indenture contracts still prevailed, and it would be another twenty-five years before the courts would find the entire indenture system illegal. The state's vicious Black Code, dating back to territorial days and reenacted as late as 1853, was not finally repealed until very near the end of the Civil War (Watkins, 1963:495–507; Sutton, 1968:1–4).

III

The years following the admission of Illinois to the Union saw a revolution in the nation's political life. During the so-called "era of good feelings," the complete triumph of Thomas Jefferson and his successors for the moment put an end to bipartisan politics. In Illinois the political game revolved around the ambitions of political leaders, the rivalries of political cliques, and the adaptation of political measures to the special interests of a section or region. For at least two decades after statehood, political parties as we understand them today were totally absent from the Illinois scene.

It was the arrival of the colossal figure of Andrew Jackson on the national political scene which changed all of this. For the first time political party organization, depending upon discipline and strict party loyalty, became a factor in the nation's political life. The Age of Jackson was no figment of the imagination. Party formation was slower in the western states however; as late as 1840, the alignments in Ohio, Indiana, and Illinois, which emerged during the presidential election of that year, bore only a vague resemblance to party contests (Chambers and Burnham, 1967:100–101; Howard, 1972:138–43).

In the meanwhile, local politics often reflected the ambitions and concerns of specific regions of the state. Just as the internal improvements debate was beginning to heat up, the General Assembly found it necessary to take time out to discuss the relocation of the state capital. The first General Assembly had located the capital in the wilderness of Vandalia for twenty years in the hope that the state would profit greatly from the sale of town lots and from the resultant speculation in the fertile lands of the Kaskaskia River basin. But the rosy plans had not been realized. Vandalia had not prospered and speculation on town lots speculation had been a failure. Once it had been determined that the General Assembly, and not a board of commissioners, would make the decision about the location of the state capital, a popular referendum was provided for to test the wishes of the voters. Among the aspirants were Jacksonville, Springfield, Alton, Vandalia, Peoria, and a town, as yet unnamed, to be located at the geographical center of the state. Each location had its strong boosters as well as its harsh detractors. In the referendum of 1834, Alton was favored but by a narrow margin only (Baringer, 1949; Angle, 1935; see also, Pease, 1918).

The final decision did not come until 1837. In the midst of the tumultuous tenth General Assembly session, Alton preferred to trade its numerical advantage for economic ones, and Springfield emerged as the successful candidate. Sangamon County was then the most populous county in the state, and the Sangamon delegation in the General Assembly was both strong and well disciplined. Known as the "long nine" (because of their above-average height) and including Abraham Lincoln in their ranks, they proved to be very effective at legislative logrolling and behind-the-scenes maneuvering. On June 20, 1839, Governor Thomas Carlin issued the necessary proclamation removing the state capital to Springfield.[3]

IV

The decade of the 1830s embraces both personalities and events which make it the most momentous epoch in the early history of Illinois. These were the years which witnessed the tragic Black Hawk War; the rise of Chicago, first chartered as a village in 1833 and then as a city with 4,000 people in 1837; the murder of Elijah Parish Lovejoy, martyred for his defense of freedom of speech and press; and the budding of the political careers of two of its most celebrated adopted sons, Stephen A. Douglas, born in Vermont, and Abraham Lincoln from Kentucky. These years also included the first example of state-wide economic planning on the part of Illinois, which, unfortunately, became the supreme example of regional politics run riot in the Prairie State (Sutton, 1965:34–40; Davidson and Stuve, 1874:427–53).

Illinois leaders from the very first had been conscious of the need for improving transportation facilities within the state. Usually sub-sumed under the general heading of "internal improvements," this subject received more attention than any other during the 1830s. Geographically, nature had dealt kindly with the Prairie State. With a relatively flat terrain, no mountains or other severe physical obsta-cles, and a varied and stimulating climate, the region was attractive almost from the day it was first observed by European explorers. Long before Illinois was a state, its crossroads setting was understood by those who were familiar with its geography (see, for example, Krenkel, 1958).

No outside event in the early history of the republic had a greater impact upon Illinois than New York State's completion of the Erie Canal in 1825. The effect can be stated in two ways: theoretical and practical. So great was the success of the Erie Canal that it became almost immediately a model which other states were anxious to copy. This was particularly true in Illinois, as it was in the other new states of the West, and it did not matter that the population patterns, the traffic potential, or the level of economic development in the new states could not match that of the Empire State. A great deal of interest was expressed in the possibility of connecting the Great Lakes to the state's river system. In fact, the first French explorers to visit Illinois, Louis Jolliet and Father Jacques Marquette, had suggested a canal from Lake Michigan to the Illinois River, which of course would mean access to the Gulf of Mexico by way of the Mississippi River. The success of the Erie Canal further reinforced the movement for the Illinois and Michigan Canal, and a federal land grant to Illinois of nearly 300,000 acres in 1827 gave added impetus. The federal grant included the alternate sections of land five miles deep on either side of the proposed route of the canal. Work was to commence within five years and be completed in twenty.

The practical impact of the building of the Erie Canal upon Illinois was equally great.Providing as it did a satisfactory link between the Hudson River and the Great Lakes, its role in the settlement and economic development of the north-central states is almost beyond measure. So far as this state is concerned, the opening of the Erie Canal–Great Lakes transportation route inaugurated a boom period in northern Illinois that surpassed anything previously experienced in the Old Northwest. It hardly seems necessary to call attention to the effect that this development had on the growth and importance of Chicago. For the first time, northern Illinois could compete on an equal footing with central and southern Illinois (Taylor, 1951:32–36).

Interest in internal improvements reached fever pitch in the mid-1830s. Even southern Illinois got into the act. The oldest settled part of the state, where population had remained fairly static since statehood, recognized that its hegemony was threatened by what was happening in central and northern Illinois. In a remarkable demonstration of reckless courage the tenth General Assembly fashioned the Internal Improvements Act of 1837, which undertook to revolutionize Illinois' entire transportation system. In addition to the Illinois and Michigan Canal (which was incorporated into the scheme), the act proposed to build railroads, deepen rivers, and improve highways, especially with an eye to facilitating the delivery of the United States mail. To that end the General Assembly appropriated more than $10 million, which as it turned out was grossly inadequate but was sufficient to tax the credit of the state to the breaking point.

The act made a strenuous effort to provide something for everyone, and no major section or region of the state was left without one or more "improvements." In an amusing act of generosity, the legislation set aside $200,000 in a kind of grab-bag fund which was to be expended in those counties that would benefit little (or not at all) from the overall plans. It was at this point that the Sangamon County delegation used its leverage most effectively. With the issue of the location of the state capital still before the General Assembly, the "long nine," by voting for the pet projects of others and especially by nursing Alton's expanding ambition to be the commercial and economic center of the state, were able to command enough reciprocal votes to insure the state capital for Springfield.

The internal improvements program, had it been successful, would indeed have revolutionized transportation within the state of Illinois. Because of its failure, proponents of laissez-faire economics made this unfortunate experiment in state capitalism the object of their scorn and derision for years to come. It was looked upon as a kind of horrible example and a warning to those who would put the state into enterprises where private capital might better operate.

Many explanations have been offered for the failure of the program. Two deserve careful attention. The error of the legislature was a grievous one, for instead of insisting that one unit of the system be completed before another could be begun, it bowed to local pressure and jealous sectionalism by decreeing that work must begin simultaneously on all the projects. This was to insure that no city or region would gain an initial advantage over another. Apparently no one stopped to realize that in addition to inadequate funding, pioneer Illinois lacked engineering talent, manpower, and the construction materials necessary for such an enormous undertaking. Nevertheless, a considerable amount of preliminary work, such as surveying, grading, bridge and culvert building, and roadbed preparation, went on all over the state. Soon the appropriated funds were exhausted, no further credit was forthcoming, and there was very little of the finished product to be seen. For years thereafter, evidences of construction here and there around Illinois remained as embarrassing reminders of what many described as the state's "supreme folly."

The other problem was beyond the power of the General Assembly to control and is a part of the all-too-familiar boom-or-bust cycle which appears again and again in nineteenth-century America. The prosperous years of the 1830s, fed by spiraling inflation, bold speculation, and booming land prices, suddenly gave way to currency stringency and a general stagnation of business which our national history calls the Panic of 1837. Land values plunged downward, the price of grain and other food products fell sharply, and unemployment was widespread. The next five or six years found Illinois and the nation in the grip of a severe depression.[4]

When a total exhaustion of both funds and credit finally brought the internal improvements work to a standstill in 1840, Illinois could show only twenty-four miles of completed railway. Against this pitiful showing was the state debt of more than $14 million, two-thirds of which had been spent on railroad and canal construction. Throughout the 1840s the ominous shadow of this crushing debt hovered over Illinois. Not only railroad building but also work on the Illinois and Michigan Canal had to be abandoned. The sale of lands from the federal grant, which was supposed to go a long way toward financing the building of the canal, was seriously curtailed by the depression, which also dried up credit sources in both the eastern states and England.

The decade of the 1840s began in an atmosphere of depression and despair. The state's major energies were directed toward salvaging whatever was salvageable from the internal improvements nightmare of the previous decade and toward avoiding the temptation to repudiate the crushing load of debt which remained. There were clear signs of economic recovery before the mid-century point was reached, and these proved to be preliminary to another amazing period of growth and expansion in the Prairie State (Howard, 1972:237–71; Ford, 1854:445–47).

But for the moment Illinoisans were still digesting the bitter lessons they had so recently learned. A new constitution, the second in the state's history, was written in 1847 and adopted the following year. At the very moment that Illinois needed a flexible and forward-looking document to enable it to cope with the tremendous economic changes which were just ahead, the constitution makers of 1847 gave it a narrow, limited, restrictive instrument which attempted to insure that the legislative disasters of recent years would not be repeated. The General Assembly, for example, could not contract debts of more than $50,000 for the state as a whole unless the voters ratified a specific law to that effect.

Another example of the regionalism prevalent in the state and the growing influence the New England element in northern Illinois is found in the local government section of the 1848 constitution. Most of the early settlers of the state had come from the south, where the county was the unit of local government and where there was no township organization. The new settlers from the northeastern states, however, were accustomed to some form of township government, and they were successful in having a provision inserted in the new constitution permitting any county whose voters favored it to adopt the township system. This optional arrangement was continued in the 1870 constitution, and eventually 85 of Illinois' 102 counties were so subdivided. Only 17 counties, most of them in southern Illinois, retained the county system only. From a twentieth-century perspective, one might wish that Illinois had not been saddled with what often seems like a wasteful and unnecessarily overlapping system of local government. Yet this dual arrangement reflects a constitutional compromise which effectively accommodated both the early southern orientation and the more recent eastern influence in the state (Cornelius, 1972:25–44; Garvey, 1958:27, 515–16).

One last reflection of the jealous sectionalism so apparent in the early history of Illinois appears in legislation in 1849. With the growing canal and railroad influence already poised to redirect the energies of the Prairie State, the General Assembly moved to make sure that Illinois' good fortune would not be turned to the advantage of any of its neighbors. Describing the geographical position of Illinois as "one of the great natural advantages which she possesses," the legislation called upon the General Assembly to "encourage improvements that are of an internal character and advantage, and not such as are mainly intended to promote external interests" (Davidson and Stuve, 1874:565).

This ingenious effort to keep all the benefits of an expanding commerce safely (and selfishly) at home went under the euphemistic label of "state policy." Alton, still nursing ambitions to rival St. Louis and perhaps become the transportation center of the region, had been chosen to be the terminus of several projected railroads, one connecting it with Chicago and the others coming from the East. "State policy" insisted that these railroads terminate at Alton and not be extended twenty miles south to Illinoistown (today's East St. Louis) lest such an extension benefit St. Louis. Even though a bridge over the Mississippi at St. Louis was still a quarter of a century away, the Illinois legislature was determined that no economic advantage accrue to its neighbor state as a result of railroad building in Illinois (Davidson and Stuve, 1874:562–70; Moses, 1889:566–67).

V

The mid-century years provided a series of turning points which separate the "old" Illinois from the "new." Most of these were related in one way or another to the fantastic growth of Chicago and northern Illinois which occurred between 1840 and 1870.The opening of the Erie Canal–Great Lakes route for both trade and travel has already been noted. With the convenience of that commercial highway already demonstrated and with the completion of the Illinois and Michigan Canal in 1848, Chicago began the dazzling and spectacular growth that propelled it from village status in the 1830s to a teeming city of nearly 30,000 inhabitants by 1850—far and away the largest in Illinois. On the eve of the Civil War, Chicago had already passed the 100,000 mark, and in 1870, by which time it was the business and commercial leader of the Midwest and the railroad center for the entire nation, its population was pushing 300,000 (Belcher, 1947:72–89; Schnell, 1977:245–65).

The same forces which fed the fires of Chicago's fantastic growth were reflected in the agricultural and business expansion of northern Illinois. European immigration was a significant aspect of that movement, as a steady flow of newcomers responded to the pull of the distant magnet. The Irish provided many of the canal and railroad workers, while the English, German, and Scandinavian cohorts contributed not only laborers, but farmers, merchants, and professionals.[5]

The most obvious and immediate effect of the growth and expansion of northern Illinois was a total reordering of the state's political, economic, and social axes. The more rapid population growth of that section soon denied southern Illinois the political advantage it had enjoyed since statehood. Likewise, the predominantly north-south flow of trade and commerce, following the Mississippi River and its tributaries, was about to be challenged by a new east-west orientation. The initial challenge came from the Erie Canal–Great Lakes combination, but the Illinois and Michigan Canal and the new east-west rail lines, which reached Chicago and the Midwest in the 1850s, posed a much more serious threat. So long as the Mississippi River trade was dominant, southern and western Illinois held their own in the struggle for political and economic hegemony, but great changes were already under way. Even before the Civil War burst upon the nation, the pendulum of political advantage was pointing toward Chicago and northern Illinois. The war, of course, accelerated this movement; Mississippi River commerce was disrupted early in the war, never to be restored to its prewar eminence.

Meanwhile, the iron horse thrust its fiery challenge into every section of Illinois. In 1850, there were only two tiny rail lines totaling barely 100 miles operating in Illinois, one connecting Springfield, Jacksonville, and the Illinois River and the other radiating out of Chicago. Ten years later, the state could boast of almost 2,800 miles of operating railroad (surpassed only by Ohio among the states in the Union); Chicago, with eleven railroads terminating in its midst, was already the railroad center of the nation. Now for the first time, thanks to the building of the Illinois Central, the fantastically fertile fields of central and eastern Illinois were open to profitable agriculture (Belcher, 1947:183–203; Gates, 1934).

New tensions and stresses in the Prairie State created by the Civil War are too intricate and too vast to be considered in this essay. Suffice it to say, however, that the war intensified some of the old strains and created new ones not previously experienced. For example, there was a sizeable number of Confederate sympathizers, especially in southern Illinois but in other parts of the state as well. This threat seemed so great that early in the war there were suggestions that the state perhaps ought to be divided to permit the southern third to secede. This possibility might have taken on additional reality if the slave states of Kentucky and Missouri (which completely surrounded southern Illinois) had seceded from the Union. President Lincoln's successful border-state policy, which kept these states and others in the Union, greatly reduced the pressure on "Egypt" and in the end contributed mightily to the salvation of the Union (Gray, 1942:57–77; Cross, 1942; Klement, 1960).

As Chicago and northern Illinois rose to economic dominance in the Prairie State following the Civil War, they did not automatically gain political power. The long-dominant agrarian element in Illinois politics did not relinquish its control without a struggle. For the remainder of the nineteenth century and well into the twentieth, new alignments and political alliances revealed themselves in a variety of ways. Ultimately, the new shape of regional politics in Illinois was determined by the multifaceted urban-rural competition.

Growing distrust of Chicago did not surface until after the Civil War, and it was further postponed by an outpouring of shock, distress, and compassion which followed in the wake of the disastrous Chicago fire of October 7–8, 1871. Gradually, however, the twin factors of urban (and thus labor) growth and agrarian distress fueled by inflation, mechanization, and overproduction determined the agenda for the "new" Illinois (Howard, 1972:345–68).

The widening gulf between the interests of farmers, laborers, and manufacturers—coupled with continuing heavy immigration and further complicated by economic depression—produced an extremely volatile mixture. Not surprisingly, this mixture exploded in a series of savage and violent confrontations which left deep scars in Illinois. Repercussions of the widespread railroad strikes of 1877 were felt in Chicago and East St. Louis (and elsewhere), while the tragic and unnecessary Haymarket riot in 1886 revealed something of the depth of anti-labor and anti-foreign feeling. Frequent clashes between coal mine operators and miners punctuated these years, culminating in turbulent outbursts at Virden, Pana, and Braidwood. The bitter strike at Pullman in 1894, supported by the American Railway Union, threatened a national railroad tie-up. Only a court injunction and the presence of federal troops dispatched from Fort Sheridan broke the strike and sent Eugene V. Debs, its leader, to a federal penitentiary (Bruce, 1959; Shannon, 1945; David, 1936; Gutman, 1960; Hicken, 1959; Buder, 1967). An inflamed public made no distinction between anarchists, the American Railway Union, and organized labor in general, with the result that all suffered and the labor movement was set back for years.

The revolt of the farmers, stimulated by falling grain and meat prices, the high cost of new machinery, and the alleged discrimination of railroad rates, followed a much less violent pattern but had far-reaching results nevertheless. Using the Grange organizations in the 1870s and 1880s and the Populist movement of the 1890s, farmers left their mark on the social and political structures of the time even though their main target may have been the nation's economy. The regional differences of an earlier generation were largely replaced by new problems that were more likely to have their roots in class, ethnicity, religion, or occupation. The echoes of the bitter encounters of Haymarket and Pullman, of Braidwood and Virden, and of grangers and populists were clearly heard and felt in the new progressive agenda which ushered in the twentieth century.

VI

The nation as a whole entered the twentieth century on a wave of buoyant optimism. The successful conclusion of the "Splendid Little War" with Spain, the effort to project unselfish humanitarianism into the acquisition of the nation's first overseas empire, and the general return of prosperity following the dark days of the 1890s contributed to what might almost be called a new "era of good feelings." In all this Illinois shared handsomely (Freidel, 1958:938–44).

In almost every category that could be measured, Illinois had grown in a spectacular fashion during the final years of the nineteenth century. The population of Chicago had passed the one million mark, making it the second city in the nation; growing proportionally faster than the remainder of the state, Chicago soon had one-third of the population of Illinois. To quote Carl Sandburg, Chicago was, indeed,

> Hog Butcher for the World,
> Tool maker, Stacker of Wheat,
> Player with Railroads and the
> Nation's Freight Handler;
> Stormy, husky, brawling,
> City of the Big Shoulders
> [*Chicago*, 1916].

Another of the great morale builders for the Prairie State was the success of the World's Columbian Exposition held in Chicago in 1893 to celebrate the 400th anniversary of the discovery of America. Perhaps the most ambitious of world's fairs in this hemisphere, it proved to be one of the notable artistic displays of modern times. Its famous "White City" of some 150 buildings assembled on the shore of Lake Michigan (in what is now Jackson Park) drew 27.5 million people (Wagenknecht, 1964:6–12).

Once into the twentieth century, it becomes increasingly difficult to identify and isolate problems and issues which were peculiar to Illinois. The old regional and sectional antagonisms prevalent in the nineteenth century had all but disappeared, to be replaced by a single, overriding concern that still lies at the heart of Illinois politics. Ultimately, the new shape of regional politics in Illinois was determined by the growing urban-rural tensions, which is really another way of describing the Chicago-downstate bitterness.

Perhaps the urban-rural competition was natural and inevitable, but it was certainly fueled by a number of unfortunate (and even avoidable) circumstances. A case in point has to do with the legislative districts from which senators and representatives were elected to the Illinois General Assembly. The 1870 Illinois constitution was a distinct improvement over its predecessors and provided, as most constitutions do, for periodic redistricting to reflect population changes within the state. Article IV, Section 6 of the constitution reads: "The General Assembly shall apportion the State every ten years, beginning with the year one thousand eight hundred and seventy one . . . " (Verlie, 1919:111). The constitutional mandate was followed faithfully from 1871 through 1901, each successive decennial redistricting reflecting the growing population and shifting concentration of citizen voters within the state. After the census of 1910, however, it appeared that a majority of the legislators would soon be elected from Chicago and Cook County. Not willing to face this reality, the General Assembly, after numerous rancorous discussions, simply refused to carry out its constitutional mandate.

The long dominant rural, village, and small city combination which reflected downstate conditions did not give up easily or gracefully. The result was that as Chicago and northern Illinois rose to population and economic dominance, political power did not automatically shift with them. This situation prevailed beyond the mid-century point and became one of the festering sores which exacerbated Chicago-down-state relations throughout the century (Kenney, 1970:123–24; Steiner and Gove, 1960:84–87; Murphy, 1964:6–7).

The new stresses and strains in the Illinois social and political fabric revealed themselves in a variety of ways. One example was the conflict between William Hale Thompson, the flamboyant mayor of Chicago elected in 1915, and Governor Frank Lowden. Though they were both Republicans, no love was lost between Mayor Thompson and Governor Lowden, so different were they in background, temperament, and political style. With the nation involved in World War I after 1917, each leader strove to demonstrate his patriotism in every conceivable way. The governor regularly inveighed against halfhearted patriots, even while praising the loyalty of Illinois' great body of German-American citizens. The Chicago situation was further complicated by a small but vocal coterie of Socialists who were basically pacifist in outlook and opposed to the Selective Service system (Hutchinson, 1957:374–81).

Mayor Thompson's decision, late in the summer of 1917, to permit anti-war demonstrators calling themselves the "People's Council of America for Democracy and Terms of Peace" to hold a public meeting in Chicago angered Governor Lowden and led to a bitter exchange between the two. Resting his case on First Amendment rights (a somewhat unusual stance for him), the mayor insisted that pacifists were law-abiding citizens and refused to deny them the right to meet in Chicago. The governor, citing his solemn duty as chief executive to maintain public order, argued that anti-war meetings could lead to riots. Frustrated in his determination to prevent the convention, Governor Lowden as a last resort dispatched the state's adjutant general with several companies of the Illinois National Guard by special train to Chicago. Fortunately, the assembly had adjourned before the troops arrived (Hutchinson, 1957:378–79).

In retrospect, it could be said that the mayor won the battle, but the governor won the war. The public and press overwhelmingly approved the governor's stand, and for a while the mayor appeared to have been left "twisting gently in the breeze." The encounter not only contributed to the estrangement between Lowden and Thompson, but it also illustrated the deepening disenchantment between state and city. This drift was continued and intensified by the tragic Chicago Race Riot of 1919. The week of violence, which coincided with a streetcar strike in the Windy City, only ended when Mayor Thompson, in spite of his previous differences with the governor, asked Lowden to send in Illinois National Guard troops (Lewis and Smith, 1929:388–95; Hutchinson, 1957:404–6).

Perhaps the most extreme and certainly the most disappointing demonstration of the new pattern of regional bitterness was revealed in connection with the Great Depression of the 1930s. The decade of the 1920s, often identified in American history as a "prosperity decade," had not been easy years for Illinoisans. In Illinois, the national phenomenon of severe pockets of depression in the midst of general prosperity was clearly illustrated. Coal mining, which had been one of the state's major employers since the 1890s, experienced strikes and violence in the wake of falling prices and wages. Violent confrontations between rival unions only intensified the difficulties (Soule, 1968:107–26; Young, 1947:313–30). Agriculture likewise suffered from overproduction and falling prices. On top of that, severe and recurrent droughts and widespread flooding of the Mississippi River system added to the general distress. The Illinois economy was not in good shape when the worldwide depression struck in 1929. Soon business stagnation and paralyzing unemployment in manufacturing activities combined with the continuing crisis in farming and mining to produce widespread suffering.

As was true in most states of the nation, Illinois state revenues were simply not sufficient to meet the increased cost of public welfare and emergency relief. Peculiarities in the revenue article of the 1870 constitution appeared to make a state income tax impossible, and the general property tax at both the local and state levels had been stretched about as far as it could go (Kenney, 1970; Fisher, 1960, 1969). Governor Henry Horner believed, correctly, that only by means of a sales tax could the state pay its share of the relief load and still meet other governmental expenses. After strenuous political and constitutional maneuvering, a retailer's occupational tax of 2 percent (the official name for the Illinois sales tax) was enacted and the state property tax (not to be confused with the local property tax) was suspended (Howard, 1972:506–8; Littlewood, 1969:109–13).

This was an important step in the right direction, but even then state revenues were inadequate for the unprecedented demands of the time. At the depth of the depression, nearly a million and a half Illinois citizens were unemployed, and the federal government was pouring as much relief money into Illinois as it was into New York and Pennsylvania combined (Maurer, 1968:120–32). By 1935, Harry Hopkins, the federal relief administrator, was threatening to shut off federal funds unless the state of Illinois agreed to bear a larger share of the welfare burden. Governor Horner and Chicago Mayor Edward J. Kelly agreed to a 1 percent increase in the state's sales tax (bringing it to 3 percent), but the General Assembly dug in its heels and refused to enact the necessary legislation. Hopkins shut off federal funds and a months-long stalemate ensued (Littlewood, 1969:114–17).

The misery created by the Great Depression was felt in every corner of the state. Though the urban areas and the coal mining counties of southern Illinois probably were most severely affected, every county found it necessary to apply for relief funds to feed, clothe, and house its needy. Nothing illustrates better the widening gulf and the deepening distrust between Chicago/Cook County and the downstate areas than does the crisis over emergency relief. More than is apparently true today, the rural areas and small towns in Illinois refused to accept Chicago's suffering as their own, and as vigorously as they knew how they resisted being taxed to pay for solutions to the city's ills. There were times when it seemed as if the one goal of downstate Democratic and Republican leaders alike was to thwart the ambitions of the Windy City and suppress the power of the Chicago political machine. And this was possible, thanks to the unbalanced nature of representation in the General Assembly as a result of years of failure to reapportion the state in line with decennial census figures (Steiner and Gove, 1960:2–9; Kenney, 1970:119–26).

Finally, with the state's poor and needy caught as innocent pawns in the political tug-of-war, the General Assembly did approve the increase in the sales tax and the relief crisis in Illinois was eased (Littlewood, 1969:118–19). But the legacy of bitterness and distrust between urban and rural areas remained and only gradually dissipated.

VII

Strange as it may sound, World War II had a soothing effect on Illinois regional differences. The decision in the late 1930s to rearm the nation in the face of the Fascist threat to world peace and security revived American business and industry. The outbreak of World War II in September, 1939, stimulated production in every area and hastened national economic recovery. The rapid rise in employment and the resultant decline in the relief rolls greatly reduced welfare costs in Illinois. The widespread urban suffering associated with depression and unemployment was no longer a political issue in the Prairie State (Maurer, 1968:130–32; Watters, 1951:504–8).

Once this nation was drawn into World War II, following the attack upon Pearl Harbor in December, 1941, all local and petty issues were rapidly put aside. Every means were seized upon to support the war effort as President Roosevelt announced that "Dr. New Deal" had given way to "Dr. Win the War!" It would be naive to believe that the old animosities have all disappeared or that the recurrent hostilities have all been laid aside. But enormous changes have taken place in the intervening decades. Population shifts and reapportionment reforms, forced upon Illinois by decisions of the Supreme Court of the United States, have combined to produce a new balance of political power in the state. Instead of the classic Chicago-downstate dichotomy, the new sectional reality involves Chicago, the suburban "collar counties" around Cook County, and the remainder of the state. Perhaps it would not be too much to say that the public interest in Illinois today is a kind of common denominator hammered out by the interplay of these powerful regional forces.

NOTES

1. This slogan appeared in a number of Department of Tourism brochures in the late 1970s (see Gove and Masotti, 1982:203–4).

2. There is no way of knowing to this day whether the defeat of the convention forces was a result of more effective campaigning and the superior arguments of the anti-slavery party, or whether it was simply an example of demography in action.

3. The exciting story of the decision to move the state capital to Springfield can be followed in the pages of the *Sangamo Journal* (Springfield, Illinois), copies of which are available (on microfilm) in the Illinois State Historical Library, Old State Capitol, Springfield.

4. Krenkel (1958:chapters 7, 8, and 9) elaborates upon all these points, Howard (1972:193–212) provides a useful summary, and Ford (1854:186–87) offers an interesting contemporary view.

5. Wyman (1984) presents a fascinating study exploring the social and cultural impact of midwestern immigration.

REFERENCES

Angle, P. M. 1935. *Here I Have Lived: A History of Lincoln's Springfield, 1821–1865.* Springfield: Abraham Lincoln Association.

Babcock, R., ed. 1854. *Forty Years of Pioneer Life: Memoir of John Mason Peck, D.D.* Philadelphia: American Baptist Publication Society.

Baringer, W. E. 1949. *Lincoln's Vandalia: A Pioneer Portrait.* New Brunswick: Rutgers University Press.

Barnhart, J. D. 1953. *Valley of Democracy: The Frontier versus the Plantation in the Ohio Valley, 1775–1818.* Bloomington: Indiana University Press.

Belcher, W. W. 1947. *The Economic Rivalry between St. Louis and Chicago, 1850–1880.* New York: AMS Press.

Brown, H. 1844. *The History of Illinois from Its First Discovery and Settlement to the Present Time.* New York: J. Winchester, New World Press.

Bruce, R. V. 1959. *1877: Year of Violence.* Indianapolis: Bobbs-Merrill Company, Inc.

Buck, S. J. 1917. *Illinois in 1818.* Springfield: Illinois Centennial Commission.

Buder, S. 1967. *Pullman: An Experiment in Industrial Order and Community Planning, 1880–1930.* New York: Oxford University Press.

Buley, R. C. 1951. *The Old Northwest: Pioneer Period, 1815–1840,* Vol. 1. Bloomington: Indiana University Press.

Chambers, W., and W. Burnham, eds. 1967. *The American Party Systems: Stages of Political Development.* New York: Oxford University Press.

Commager, H. S., ed. 1968. *Documents of American History,* Vol. 1. 8th ed. New York: Appleton-Century-Crofts.

Cornelius, J. 1972. *Constitution Making in Illinois.* Urbana: University of Illinois Press.

Cross, J. W. 1942. *Divided Loyalties in Southern Illinois during the Civil War.* Ph.D. dissertation, University of Illinois.

David, H. 1936. *The History of the Haymarket Affair: A Study in the American Social-Revolutionary and Labor Movements.* New York: Farrar and Rinehart, Inc.

Davidson, A., and P. Stuve. 1874. *A Complete History of Illinois from 1673 to 1873.* Springfield: Illinois Journal Company.

Federal Writer's Project for the State of Illinois. 1947. *Illinois: A Descriptive and Historical Guide.* Chicago: A. C. McClurg and Company.

Fisher, Glenn W. 1960. *Financing Illinois Government.* Urbana: University of Illinois Press.

———. 1969. *Taxes and Politics.* Urbana: University of Illinois Press.

Ford, T. 1854. *A History of Illinois from Its Commencement as a State in 1818 to 1847.* Chicago: S. C. Griggs.

Freidel, F. B. 1958. *The Splendid Little War.* Boston: Little, Brown and Company.

Garvey, N. F. 1958. *The Government and Administration of Illinois.* New York: Thomas Y. Crowell Company.

Gates, P. W. 1934. *The Illinois Central Railroad and Its Colonization Work.* Cambridge: Harvard University Press.

Gove, S. K., and L. H. Masotti. 1982. *After Daley: Chicago Politics in Transition.* Urbana: University of Illinois Press.

Gray, W. 1942. *The Hidden Civil War: The Story of the Copperheads.* New York: Viking Press.

Gutman, H. G. 1960. "The Braidwood Lockout of 1874." *Journal of the Illinois State Historical Society* 53 (Spring):5–28.

Harris, N. D. 1904. *The History of Negro Servitude in Illinois, and of the Slavery Agitation in That State, 1719–1864.* Chicago: A. C. McClurg and Company.

Hicken, V. 1959. "The Virden and Pane Mine Wars of 1898." *Journal of the Illinois State Historical Society* 52 (Summer):263–78.

Howard, R. P. 1972. *Illinois: A History of the Prairie State.* Grand Rapids, Mich.: William B. Eerdmans Publishing Company.

Hutchinson, W. T. 1957. *Lowden of Illinois: The Life of Frank O. Lowden,* Vols. 1 and 2. Chicago: University of Chicago Press.

Hutton, D. G. 1946. *Midwest at Noon.* Chicago: University of Chicago Press.

Kenney, D. 1970. *Basic Illinois Government: A Systematic Explanation.* Carbondale: Southern Illinois University Press.

Klement, F. L. 1960. *The Copperheads in the Middle West.* Chicago: University of Chicago Press.

Krenkel, J. H. 1958. *Illinois Internal Improvements, 1818–1848.* Cedar Rapids, Iowa: Torch Press.

Lewis, L., and H. J. Smith. 1929. *Chicago: The History of Its Reputation.* New York: Harcourt, Brace and Company.

Littlewood, T. 1969. *Horner of Illinois.* Evanston: Northwestern University Press.

Maurer, D. J. 1968. "Unemployment in Illinois during the Great Depression." In D. F. Tingley (ed.), *Essays in Illinois History.* Carbondale: Southern Illinois University Press.

Moses, J. 1889. *Illinois Historical and Statistical,* Vol. 2. Chicago: Fergus Printing Company.

Murphy, J. T. 1964. "Population, Politics and Redistricting." *Illinois Business Review* 21(3):6–7.

Pease, T. C. 1918. *The Frontier State, 1818–1848.* Springfield: Illinois Centennial Commission.

———, ed. 1923. *Illinois Election Returns.* Springfield: Illinois Centennial Commission.

Power, R. L. 1953. *Planting Cornbelt Culture.* Indianapolis: Bobbs-Merrill Company, Inc.

Schnell, J. C. 1977. "Chicago versus St. Louis: A Reassessment of the Great Rivalry." *Missouri Historical Review* 71 (April):245–65.

Shannon, F. A. 1945. *The Farmers' Last Frontier: Agriculture, 1860–1897.* New York: Farrar and Rinehart.

Soule, G. 1968. *Prosperity Decade: From War to Depression, 1917–1929.* New York: Harper and Row.

Steiner, G. Y., and S. Gove. 1960. *Legislative Politics in Illinois.* Urbana: University of Illinois Press.

Sutton, R. M. 1965. "Illinois' Year of Decision, 1837." *Journal of the Illinois State Historical Society* 58 (Spring):34–40.

———. 1968. "The Inauguration of Shadrach Bond as First Governor of Illinois." In R. M. Sutton (ed.), *A History of Illinois in Paintings.* Urbana: University of Illinois Press.

Taylor, G. R. 1951. *The Transportation Revolution, 1815–1860.* New York: Rinehart and Company, Inc.

Verlie, E. J. 1919. *Illinois Constitution.* Vol. 13, *Collections of the Illinois State Historical Library.* Springfield: Illinois State Historical Library.

Wagenknecht, E. 1964. *Chicago.* Norman: University of Oklahoma Press.

Watkins, S. C., Sr. 1963. "Some of Early Illinois' Free Negroes." *Journal of the Illinois State Historical Society* 56 (Autumn):495–507.

Watters, M. 1951. *Illinois in the Second World War: The Productive Front.* Springfield: Illinois State Historical Library.

Wyman, M. 1984. *Immigrants in the Valley: Irish, Germans, and Americans in the Upper Mississippi County, 1830–1860.* Chicago: Nelson-Hall.

Young, D. M. 1947. "Origins of the Progressive Mine Workers of America." *Journal of the Illinois State Historical Society* 40 (September):313–30.

PART III

Regionalism in Contemporary Illinois: The Rise of the Metropolitan Collar

Regional Demographic Trends in Illinois, 1950–85   5

Cheng H. Chiang and Ann Geraci

American public policy, at both the national and state levels, has frequently been concerned with social and economic inequalities among regions, and numerous government programs have had among their goals the reduction or elimination of such differences. Appropriate regional policy formation requires not only the recognition of variation in social and economic well-being among regions, but also an understanding of the forces which influence such variation. Population growth and demographic trends are among the important factors which affect the relative well-being of regions; variations in these trends have contributed to regional disparities, not only at the national level, but also within Illinois.

It is well known that wide variations in population growth trends have existed among Illinois' regions for the past thirty-five years. Suburban Cook County and the collar counties have experienced very rapid growth—largely at the expense of Chicago, which experienced rapid decline—while northern, central, and southern Illinois all grew at a very slow pace. These variations in growth rates among regions were, in large part, the result of uneven interregional migration flows. Variations in birth and death rates have contributed to disparities in regional growth rates, but variations in migration rates have been the main cause of regional differences in population growth. Very high rates of net in-migration in the 1950s and 1960s contributed to the rapid population growth of suburban Cook County and the collar counties, while high rates of net out-migration through the 1970s contributed to rapid population decline in Chicago.

It is less well known that these population growth and migration patterns of Illinois' various regions have not been constant over the thirty-five-year period between 1950 and 1985. Upon close examination, a picture emerges of the various regions moving through different stages of "boom-bust" growth cycles, which are driven largely by migration. Suburban Cook County and the collar counties have moved from a "boom" stage of the 1950s and 1960s to a stage of stabilization in the 1970s and 1980s—a period of substantially slower growth, coinciding with slower net in-migration. Chicago, on the other hand, appears to be moving from a "bust" stage, which peaked in the 1970s with a population loss of nearly 11 percent, toward stabilization in the 1980s—a period of significantly smaller population loss and slower net out-migration. Northern, central, and southern Illinois appear to be moving from a stage of stabilization to one of slow decline in the 1980s. For northern and central Illinois, record high rates of net out-migration in the 1980s are associated with overall population losses occurring for the first time in the thirty-five-year period, while southern Illinois' virtual lack of growth currently is associated with the highest rate of net out-migration for the region since the 1950s. Overall, the growth trends of Illinois' various regions have tended to converge somewhat; in the 1980s, the variation among regions in terms of population growth rates is far narrower than in the 1950s and 1960s.

In regard to demographic and socio-economic characteristics, it is generally known that, compared to all other regions of the state, suburban Cook County and the collar counties have tended to have the highest proportion of youth, the highest levels of educational attainment, and the highest income levels. Again, interregional migration flows, particularly in the 1950s and 1960s, have probably contributed in part to regional demographic and socio-economic diversity in Illinois, since migrants tend to be younger, more highly educated, and have higher incomes than non-migrants.

However, while Illinois' regions have been and continue to be diverse, the gap among regions in terms of some characteristics, particularly education attainment and income, has narrowed since the 1950s. This would suggest that some unknown factors may be operating to narrow these gaps; it may also be that, as interregional migration flows have slowed, the impact of migration on the demographic and socio-economic composition of regions may have lessened.

While some convergence in population trends and characteristics among Illinois' regions may be occurring, disparities do exist among regions, and certain regions have undergone dramatic change. In particular, Chicago by most any measure has suffered serious decline, which may be slow to reverse. Northern, central, and southern Illinois may be at the threshold of a similar decline, which may be difficult to avert.

The relationship of population growth, migration, and demographic/socio-economic composition examined in this chapter gives rise to a number of regional policy issues. First, it is widely held that population growth is desirable, while population decline is not; regional policy makers must judge whether there are disadvantages to growth which outweigh the advantages or, conversely, whether there are advantages to population decline which outweigh the disadvantages. Second, regional policy makers must determine when regional diversity in terms of demographic and socio-economic characteristics poses a genuine problem and when it does not. Finally, given the impact of migration on regional population growth and composition, what, if anything, should be done to influence regional migration trends?

While demographic change for the state as a whole has been well documented (see, for example, Chiang and Kolhauser, 1982, 1983), change at the regional level has been given little attention. This chapter explores the relationship of population growth, migration, and demographic/socio-economic composition for Illinois' regions to provide information necessary for regional policy formation on issues such as those outlined above.

Regional Population Growth and Components of Change

Between 1950 and 1985, the population of Illinois grew 32 percent, from 8.7 million to 11.5 million. Illinois' regions, however, did not share equally in this growth. Some regions experienced growth five or six times as fast as the state in general, while others experienced growth only half as rapid or an absolute decline, as shown in Figure 5–1. Suburban Cook County and the collar counties experienced meteoric growth over the same period; between 1950 and 1985, the population of suburban Cook County grew by 162 percent, from .9 to 2.3 million, and that of the collar counties grew 195 percent, from .7 to 2.0 million. Northern, central, and southern Illinois all grew comparatively slowly over the thirty-five-year period, ranging from 34 percent for northern Illinois to 14 percent for southern Illinois. The population of Chicago declined by 18 percent between 1950 and 1985, from 3.6 to 3.0 million, partially reflecting the toll of suburbanization.

As a result of these disparate growth patterns, dramatic shifts in the regional distribution of Illinois' population occurred, as shown in

Figure 5–1. Regional Population Growth, 1950–85

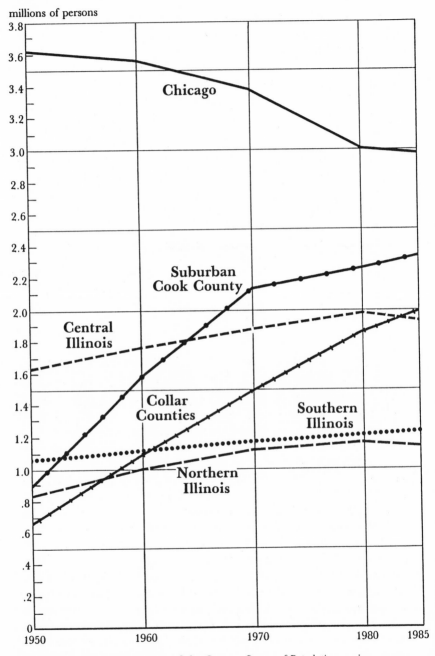

Sources: Data from U.S. Bureau of the Census, *Census of Population*, various years, and Illinois Department of Health, unpublished data.

Figure 5–2. Regional Distribution of Illinois' Population, 1950 and 1985

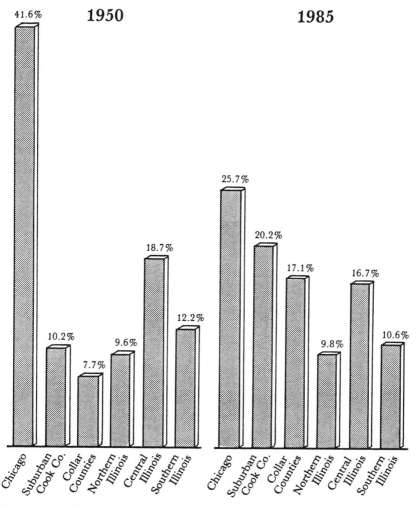

Sources: Data from U.S. Bureau of the Census, *Census of Population,* various years, and Illinois Department of Public Health, unpublished data.

Figure 5–2. Chicago, while still ranking first among all regions in population size, now comprises only 26 percent of the state's total population, compared to 42 percent in 1950. On the other hand, suburban Cook County's share of the state population nearly doubled over the thirty-five-year period, to 20 percent in 1985, and that of the collar counties more than doubled, to 17 percent. Northern Illinois' share of the state population remained about the same, while that of central and southern Illinois declined slightly over the thirty-five-year period.

Two factors determine regional population growth or decline: natural increase, which is simply the difference between births and deaths; and net migration, which equals the difference between gross in-migration and gross out-migration. Variation among Illinois' regions in the rate of natural increase, as shown in Table 5–1, partially explains the regional variation in overall growth rates. The collar counties, the fastest growing region, have consistently had the highest rate of natural increase among all regions since the 1950s. Northern, central, and southern Illinois, the slow growth regions, have generally had the lowest rates of natural increase (although since the 1970s, suburban Cook County has had a lower rate than northern Illinois).

The explanation for the high rate of natural increase in the collar counties is that this region has consistently had the second highest birth rate (surpassed only by Chicago) and, simultaneously, the lowest death rate of all regions. On the other hand, the low rates of natural increase for northern, central, and southern Illinois are due to the fact that these regions have generally had the lowest birth rates and the highest death rates of all regions (again, with the exception of Chicago in the case of death rates). These regional variations in birth and death rates — and, hence, rates of natural increase — are related to regional variations in demographic composition, particularly age and racial composition, which are discussed in the following section.

However, net migration is more important than natural increase in explaining variations in overall growth rates among Illinois' regions, especially from 1950 through 1980. For the decade of the 1950s, for example, the rate of natural increase for Illinois' regions varied less, from 11.6 to 16.1, than did the rate of net migration, which ranged from −12.9 to +45.9, as shown in Table 5–1. This remained the case through the 1970s, when the rate of natural increase ranged from 4.0 to 9.5, while the rate of net migration ranged from −16.4 to +12.9.

The rapid population growth of suburban Cook County and the collar counties between 1950 and 1985, therefore, is largely explained by the high rates of net in-migration these regions experienced, particularly in the 1950s and 1960s. Similarly, the rapid population decline in Chicago was the result of high rates of net out-migration, which peaked during the 1970s. Finally, the slow population growth of northern, central, and southern Illinois over the thirty-five-year period is associated with rather low rates of net migration (in or out).

However, the population growth trends of Illinois' various regions have fluctuated greatly over the thirty-five-year period, as shown in

Table 5–1. Vital Rates and Net Migration Rates by Region, 1950–85
(per 1,000 mid-period population)

Region	Average Annual Crude Birth Rate	Average Annual Crude Death Rate	Average Annual Rate of Natural Increase	Net Migration Rate[c]
1950–60[a]				
Chicago	24.3	11.6	12.7	−12.9
Suburban Cook	23.3	7.5	15.8	+45.9
Collar counties	24.2	8.1	16.1	+34.6
Northern Illinois	23.8	9.9	13.9	+2.5
Central Illinois	22.4	10.8	11.6	−3.8
Southern Illinois	22.6	10.8	11.8	−6.9
1960–70[a]				
Chicago	22.3	12.2	10.1	−13.6
Suburban Cook	20.0	7.5	12.5	+17.3
Collar counties	20.4	7.2	13.2	+17.7
Northern Illinois	20.1	9.6	10.5	+.1
Central Illinois	18.3	10.8	7.5	−1.4
Southern Illinois	18.5	11.4	7.1	−2.3
1970–1980[b]				
Chicago	17.9	10.9	7.0	−16.4
Suburban Cook	14.0	8.2	5.8	−.1
Collar counties	16.0	6.5	9.5	+12.9
Northern Illinois	15.5	9.0	6.5	−2.5
Central Illinois	15.2	10.0	5.2	−.1
Southern Illinois	15.1	11.1	4.0	−.1
1980–1985[a]				
Chicago	18.4	10.0	8.4	−5.4
Suburban Cook	14.0	8.0	6.0	+.2
Collar counties	16.5	6.3	10.2	+1.2
Northern Illinois	15.1	8.8	6.3	−5.0
Central Illinois	14.8	9.4	5.4	−4.9
Southern Illinois	15.1	10.6	4.5	−1.7

[a] Births and deaths from U.S. Bureau of the Census, *Census of Population,* 1960, 1970, 1980, and *Current Population Reports,* Series P-23, June, 1986, and Illinois Department of Public Health, *Vital Statistics, Illinois.* Net migration is derived residually.
[b] Provisional estimates, subject to revision.
[c] Net migration rate equals net migration divided by closed population (base-year population plus natural increase) multiplied by 100.

Table 5–2. Percent Regional Population Growth, 1950–85

Region	1950–60	1960–70	1970–80	1980–85
Chicago	−1.9	−5.1	−10.8	−1.2
Suburban Cook	+77.9	+34.5	+5.8	+3.4
Collar counties	+63.1	+35.7	+24.9	+6.8
Northern Illinois	+18.1	+11.2	+4.0	−1.9
Central Illinois	+7.9	+6.3	+5.2	−2.3
Southern Illinois	+4.3	+4.8	+4.1	+.7

Sources: U.S. Bureau of the Census, *Census of Population*, 1960, 1970, 1980, and Illinois Department of Public Health (unpublished).

Table 5–2. These regional population growth trends suggest that the various regions are moving through different stages of "boom-bust" growth cycles, which are driven by changing levels of net migration. A "boom" stage is defined here as population growth in which net in-migration exceeds natural increase, and a "bust" stage as population loss in which net out-migration completely offsets natural increase. A stage of "stabilization" is population growth in which natural increase either exceeds net in-migration or is not totally offset by net out-migration.

From this perspective, then, suburban Cook County and the collar counties have moved from a boom stage of the 1950s and 1960s to one of stabilization in the 1970s and 1980s. From 1950 to 1960, nearly .5 million of the close to .7 million population increase for Suburban Cook County and nearly .3 million of the over .4 million increase for the collar counties was the result of net in-migration. The remainder was due to natural increase, as shown in Figures 5–3 and 5–4. Similarly, from 1960 to 1970, slightly over .3 million of the .5 million increase for suburban Cook County and over .2 million of the nearly .4 million increase for the collar counties resulted from net in-migration. The subsequent slowing of population growth, or stabilization, in the 1970s and 1980s coincided with far lower rates of net in-migration than those of prior decades.

On the other hand, Chicago appears to be moving from a bust stage, which peaked in the 1970s, toward one of stabilization in the 1980s. Chicago lost over .5 million population in each of the decades of the 1950s and 1960s and nearly .6 million in the 1970s through net out-migration, far offsetting natural increase and resulting in overall population losses, as shown in Figure 5–5. In the 1980s, while net out-migration continues to exceed natural increase somewhat, the rate is far slower than in the 1970s, suggesting a move toward population stabilization.

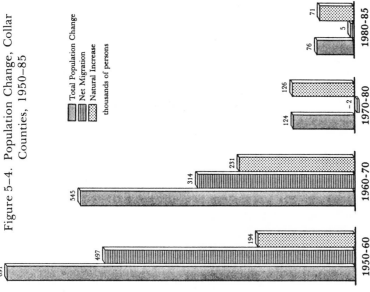

Figure 5–3. Population Change, Suburban Cook, 1950–85

Total Population Change
Net Migration
Natural Increase
thousands of persons

1950-60
422
280
142

1960-70
390
223
167

1970-80
369
212
157

1980-85
126
23
103

Sources: Data from U.S. Bureau of the Census, *Current Population Reports*, various years, and Illinois Department of Public Health, *Vital Statistics, Illinois* and unpublished data, various years. Net migration is derived residually and does not reflect the 1970 undercount.

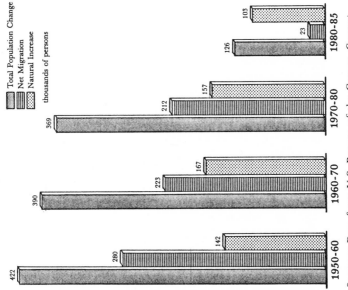

Figure 5–4. Population Change, Collar Counties, 1950–85

Total Population Change
Net Migraion
Natural Increase
thousands of persons

1950-60
691
497
194

1960-70
545
314
231

1970-80
124
126
-2

1980-85
76
71
5

Sources: Data from U.S. Bureau of the Census, *Current Population Reports*, various years, and Illinois Department of Public Health, *Vital Statistics, Illinois* and unpublished data, various years. Net migration is derived residually and does not reflect the 1970 undercount.

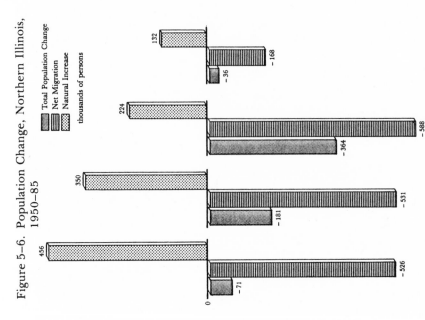

Figure 5–6. Population Change, Northern Illinois, 1950–85

Total Population Change
Net Migration
Natural Increase

thousands of persons

1950-60 **1960-70** **1970-80** **1980-85**

Sources: Data from U.S. Bureau of the Census, *Current Population Reports*, various years, and Illinois Department of Public Health, *Vital Statistics, Illinois* and unpublished data, various years. Net migration is derived residually and does not reflect the 1970 undercount.

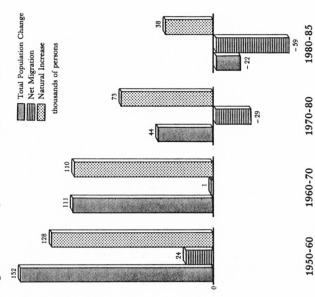

Figure 5–5. Population Change, Chicago, 1950–85

Total Population Change
Net Migration
Natural Increase

thousands of persons

1950-60 **1960-70** **1970-80** **1980-85**

Sources: Data from U.S. Bureau of the Census, *Current Population Reports*, various years, and Illinois Department of Public Health, *Vital Statistics, Illinois* and unpublished data, various years. Net migration is derived residually and does not reflect the 1970 undercount.

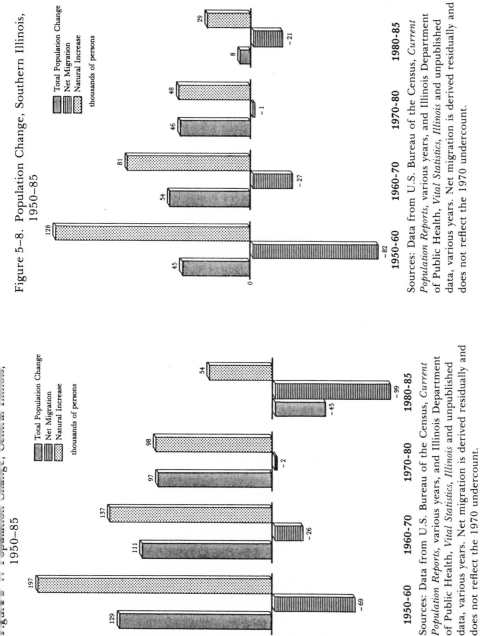

Figure 5–8. Population Change, Southern Illinois, 1950–85

Total Population Change
Net Migration
Natural Increase

thousands of persons

1950-60   1960-70   1970-80   1980-85

Sources: Data from U.S. Bureau of the Census, *Current Population Reports*, various years, and Illinois Department of Public Health, *Vital Statistics, Illinois* and unpublished data, various years. Net migration is derived residually and does not reflect the 1970 undercount.

1950–85

Total Population Change
Net Migration
Natural Increase

thousands of persons

1950-60   1960-70   1970-80   1980-85

Sources: Data from U.S. Bureau of the Census, *Current Population Reports*, various years, and Illinois Department of Public Health, *Vital Statistics, Illinois* and unpublished data, various years. Net migration is derived residually and does not reflect the 1970 undercount.

Northern, central, and southern Illinois appear to be moving from a stage of stabilization toward a bust stage in the 1980s. For northern and central Illinois, net out-migration in the 1980s has more than offset natural increase, resulting in overall population losses; for southern Illinois, net out-migration has nearly offset natural increase, resulting in virtually no growth, as shown in Figures 5–6 to 5–8.

As net migration levels have declined for most regions in recent years, however, the regions have tended to converge in terms of population growth trends, with the range of regional growth rates far narrower in the 1980s than in earlier decades. Nonetheless, the variations in historical migration patterns of Illinois' regions have had profound effects in diversifying overall growth trends of the regions. These migration patterns have also contributed to the diversity of Illinois' regions in terms of demographic and socio-economic characteristics.

Demographic and Socio-Economic Diversity of Regions

Illinois' regions have always been diverse in terms of demographic and socio-economic characteristics. In terms of some characteristics, however, the gaps between regions have narrowed somewhat over the period between 1950 and 1985. Nonetheless, to the extent that the regions remain diverse, there also may be important differences in future growth trends, economic development potential, and the demand for governmental services.

As discussed earlier, regional population growth is determined by fertility and mortality, as well as migration. The crude birth and death rates of a region are affected by the basic demographic characteristics of that region, including age and racial composition, since birth and death rates are known to vary by age and race. Variations among regions in terms of age and racial composition thus largely explain regional variations in crude birth and death rates. The age and racial composition of a region also influences the socio-economic characteristics of that region, including educational attainment, labor force participation, and income, so that regional variations in age and racial composition also help explain variations in terms of these socio-economic characteristics. Finally, as discussed in a later section, migration also can affect the demographic and socio-economic characteristics of a region, since migrants tend to be selective in terms of such characteristics, so that variations between regions in terms of migration also helps explain regional demographic and socio-economic variation.

The regional variations in birth and death rates, and therefore natural increase, discussed earlier are probably related in large part to regional variations in age composition. The low crude death rates of the collar counties and suburban Cook County over the thirty-five-year period are probably partly related to the fact that these regions have generally had the smallest proportion of elderly (population aged sixty-five and over) among all regions (with the exception of suburban Cook County since 1980). Conversely, the high crude death rates of northern, central, and southern Illinois are likely related to the fact that these regions have generally had the highest proportion of elderly. In 1980, for example, the proportion of elderly in southern Illinois was 13.9 percent, nearly double that of the collar counties, 7.6 percent, as shown in Figure 5–9. The collar counties and, until 1980, suburban Cook County have also had the highest proportion of youth (population under age eighteen) among all regions, reflecting the high crude birth rates discussed earlier.

Racial composition can also affect a region's birth and death rates. Since 1950, Chicago has had by far the highest proportion of blacks among all regions. In 1950, nearly 14 percent of the city's population was black, while the proportion of blacks for other regions ranged from 6.3 percent in southern Illinois to 1.6 percent in northern Illinois. The proportion of blacks increased in all regions between 1950 and 1980, but in Chicago it nearly tripled, while in most other regions it roughly doubled. In 1980 nearly 40 percent of Chicago's population was black, while for all other regions the proportion ranged from 9.1 percent (southern Illinois) to 4.3 percent (central Illinois), as shown in Figure 5–10.

The racial composition of Chicago probably explains in part both the city's high crude birth rates and high crude death rates, because non-whites are known to have generally higher birth and death rates than whites. Since 1950, Chicago has had the highest crude birth rate of all regions and the highest or second highest crude death rate, as shown in Table 5–1.

In addition to affecting population growth, age and racial composition can also influence socio-economic characteristics of regions, including educational attainment and labor force participation. Age composition can affect both the overall level of educational attainment and the total labor force participation rate of a region. Older adults (aged sixty-five and over), for example, tend generally to have lower levels of educational attainment and lower labor force participation rates than younger adults do. Racial composition can also influence educational attainment in that whites tend to have higher levels of educational attainment than non-whites. (For example, 1980 Census

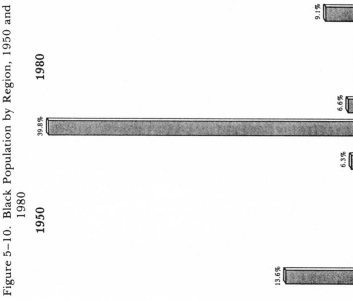

Figure 5-9. Population Aged 65 and Over by Region, 1950 and 1980

1950

Chicago 7.6%
Suburban Cook Co. 7.2%
Collar Counties 7.8%
Northern Illinois 10.0%
Central Illinois 10.7%
Southern Illinois 9.9%

1980

Chicago 11.4%
Suburban Cook Co. 10.2%
Collar Counties 7.6%
Northern Illinois 11.6%
Central Illinois 12.7%
Southern Illinois 13.9%

Source: Data from U.S. Bureau of the Census, *Census of Population*, various years.

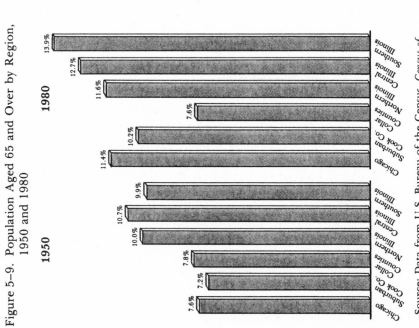

Figure 5-10. Black Population by Region, 1950 and 1980

1950

Chicago 13.6%
Suburban Cook Co. 3.2%
Collar Counties 2.2%
Northern Illinois 1.6%
Central Illinois 1.8%
Southern Illinois 6.3%

1980

Chicago 39.8%
Suburban Cook Co. 6.6%
Collar Counties 4.4%
Northern Illinois 4.6%
Central Illinois 4.3%
Southern Illinois 9.1%

Source: Data from U.S. Bureau of the Census, *Census of Population*, various years.

Table 5-3. Per Capita Income, 1959–83

Region	1959 P.C.I.	1959 Rank	1969 P.C.I.	1969 Rank	1979 P.C.I.	1979 Rank	1983 P.C.I.	1983 Rank
Chicago	$2,293	3	$3,420	3	$6,933	5	$8,971	5
Suburban Cook	2,848	1	4,381	1	9,961	1	12,715	1
Collar counties	2,394	2	3,955	2	9,503	2	11,957	2
Northern Illinois	1,859	4	3,146	4	7,654	3	9,399	3
Central Illinois	1,765	5	3,048	5	7,411	4	9,348	4
Southern Illinois	1,616	6	2,714	6	6,621	6	8,521	6

Sources: U.S. Bureau of the Census, *Census of Population*, 1960, 1970, and 1980, and *Current Population Reports, Series P-25*, June, 1986.

data show that in Illinois 68.7 percent of whites aged twenty-five and over were high school graduates, compared with 54.7 percent of non-whites.)

In turn, educational attainment and labor force participation influence a region's economic well-being, a common measure of which is income. Rather large variations in income levels across Illinois' regions historically appear to be related in part to regional differences in educational attainment and labor force participation.

Since 1959, suburban Cook County and the collar counties have consistently had the highest per capita income levels of all regions in the state. These two regions have also generally had the highest levels of educational attainment, in terms of both high school and college graduates, and the highest labor force participation rates of all regions. (See Tables 5–3 through 5–5.) In contrast, northern, central, and southern Illinois have consistently had the lowest per capita income levels of all regions since 1959 (with two important exceptions: since 1979, Chicago's rank among regions has been fifth, while northern Illinois has moved up to third). These regions have also generally had the lowest labor force participation rates and the lowest levels of educational attainment (although in the case of educational attainment, central Illinois is an important exception; since 1960, central Illinois has ranked third among all regions in terms of both high school and college graduates, although in terms of per capita income it has ranked fifth and, more recently, fourth). The lack of a perfect correlation between regional per capita income and these socio-economic characteristics is explained by regional differences in wage rates and industry mix. To the extent that industry mix affects the propensity to participate in the labor force (see, for example, Bowen and

Table 5–4. Educational Attainment of the Population Aged 25 and Over, 1950–80 (percent)

Region	1950				1960				1970				1980			
	H.S.	Rank	Coll.	Rank	H.S.	Rank	Coll.	Rank	H.S.	Rank	Coll.	Rank	H.S.	Rank	Coll.	Rank
Chicago	33.9	3	5.7	3	35.2	5	6.0	4	43.9	5	8.1	4	56.2	6	13.8	4
Suburban Cook	45.1	1	10.9	1	53.2	1	12.7	1	64.5	1	15.6	1	74.7	2	21.3	2
Collar counties	41.0	2	8.0	2	50.0	2	10.6	2	62.6	2	14.8	2	77.1	1	22.8	1
Northern Illinois	32.9	5	4.4	5	40.1	4	5.5	5	53.1	4	7.8	5	66.9	4	11.9	5
Central Illinois	33.7	4	5.3	4	41.4	3	6.6	3	53.8	3	9.2	3	67.8	3	14.1	3
Southern Illinois	22.5	6	3.0	6	29.9	6	4.0	6	42.7	6	6.2	6	58.2	5	10.1	6

Source: U.S. Bureau of the Census, *Census of Population*, 1950, 1960, 1970, and 1980.

Table 5–5. Labor Force Participation, 1950–80

Region	Working-Aged Population[a]	Total Labor Force	Labor Force Participation Rate	Rank
1950				
Chicago	2,871,962	1,698,995	59.2	1
Suburban Cook	672,766	371,954	55.3	2/3
Collar counties	506,994	280,191	55.3	2/3
Northern Illinois	634,766	340,691	53.7	4
Central Illinois	1,241,637	638,117	51.4	5
Southern Illinois	799,775	399,148	49.9	6
1960				
Chicago	2,630,049	1,590,443	60.5	1
Suburban Cook	1,082,923	625,324	57.7	3
Collar counties	745,614	434,955	58.3	2
Northern Illinois	698,256	390,011	55.9	4
Central Illinois	1,266,201	680,317	53.7	5
Southern Illinois	796,087	403,497	50.7	6
1970				
Chicago	2,393,068	1,453,685	60.7	3
Suburban Cook	1,442,464	906,931	62.9	2
Collar counties	982,820	628,561	64.0	1
Northern Illinois	756,924	455,397	60.2	4
Central Illinois	1,324,717	762,068	57.5	5
Southern Illinois	816,986	437,980	53.6	6
1980				
Chicago	2,259,222	1,371,646	60.7	5
Suburban Cook	1,726,466	1,174,412	68.0	2
Collar counties	1,351,779	954,282	70.6	1
Northern Illinois	856,814	550,443	64.2	3
Central Illinois	1,499,515	926,324	61.8	4
Southern Illinois	915,629	529,318	56.8	6

[a] In 1950 and 1960, the working-aged population is the population aged 14 and over; in 1970 and 1980, it is the population aged 16 and over.

Source: U.S. Bureau of the Census, *Census of Population*, 1950, 1960, 1970, and 1980.

Finegan, 1969), a higher labor force participation rate may not necessarily mean higher per capita income.

The most important exception to the otherwise fairly stable trends in per capita income, educational attainment, and labor force participation among Illinois' regions is Chicago. Chicago's rank in terms of per capita income fell from third in 1959 and 1969 to fifth in 1979, higher only than that of southern Illinois. While historically low, the city's rank in terms of educational attainment (the proportion of high school graduates) also fell, from fifth in 1960 and 1970 to sixth in 1980. Chicago ranks lower than southern Illinois, which had historically occupied last place among all regions. More dramatic, however, was the decline in Chicago's rank in terms of labor force participation, as shown in Table 5–5. In 1960, the city had the highest labor force participation rate of all regions in the state; by 1970 the city's rank had fallen to third, and in 1980 to fifth, higher only than that of southern Illinois. Essentially, Chicago's labor force participation rate was unchanged between 1960 and 1980 (60.5 in 1960 and 60.7 in 1980), while those of other regions all increased substantially. These dramatic changes for Chicago probably reflect the impact of the large net out-migration Chicago experienced, since migration tends to be selective in terms of socio-economic characteristics, as discussed in detail in the following section.

While variation between Illinois' regions in terms of these socio-economic characteristics exists, the gap between regions in terms of some, namely per capita income and educational attainment, has narrowed since the 1950s. In 1959, the per capita income of suburban Cook County, $2,848, the highest of all regions, was 76 percent greater than that of southern Illinois, $1,616, the lowest of all regions. In contrast, in 1983 the per capita income of suburban Cook County, $12,715 (again the highest), was only 49 percent greater than that of southern Illinois, $8,521 (again the lowest). (See Table 5–3.)

In regard to educational attainment, in 1950, the proportion of high school graduates in suburban Cook County (the highest) was double that of southern Illinois (the lowest): 45.1 percent compared to 22.5 percent. In 1980, the proportion of high school graduates in the collar counties (the highest) was only one and one-third times that of Chicago (the lowest): 77.1 percent compared to 56.2 percent. Similarly, in 1950 the proportion of college graduates in suburban Cook County was more than triple that of southern Illinois: 10.9 percent compared to 3.0 percent. In 1980, the proportion in the collar counties (the highest) was only double that of southern Illinois (the lowest): 22.9 percent versus 10.1 percent. (See Table 5–4.)

The narrowing of these gaps may be the result of factors not examined in this chapter, such as changing economic trends or government policy. This narrowing may also be the result of stabilizing migration levels in recent years. Nonetheless, to the extent that the regions continue to be diverse in terms of demographic and socio-economic characteristics, they may also differ in future growth trends, economic development potential, and the demand for various gov-

Table 5–6. In, Out, and Net Migration by Region, 1975–80 (thousands)

Region	Gross In-Migration	Gross Out-Migration	Net Migration	Percent of Total Population
Chicago	298	576	−278	−9.3
Suburban Cook	429	490	−61	−2.7
Collar counties	449	347	+102	+5.5
Downstate	400	433	−33	−.8

Source: U.S. Bureau of the Census, *1980 Census of Population and Housing, Public-Use Microdata Sample.*

ernment services. Further, to the extent that uneven interregional migration flows occur in the future, Illinois' regions will be further diversified, as discussed in the following section.

The Impact of Migration

As discussed earlier, the wide variations among Illinois' regions in overall growth patterns were largely the result of regional variations in migration trends. Hence, the boom period of population growth in the 1950s and 1960s for suburban Cook County and the collar counties resulted from levels of net in-migration far greater than natural increase, while the bust period of population loss for Chicago through the 1970s resulted from net out-migration far offsetting natural increase.

In addition to affecting the overall growth of regions, migration influences the demographic and socio-economic characteristics of regions, since migrants tend to be selective in terms of such characteristics. That is, proportionately, migrants are more likely to be young, white, and of higher levels of educational attainment, labor force participation, and income than non-movers (see, for example, Bogue, 1959, 1969; Lansing and Mueller, 1967; Taeuber, 1967; Miller, 1967; Long, 1973; Ritchey, 1976; Graves, 1979). Therefore, in the long run, uneven interregional migration flows will serve to diversify regions in terms of age and racial composition, as well as other demographic and socio-economic characteristics. To demonstrate the impact of migration on Illinois' regions, detailed data for the most recent period available, 1975 to 1980, are presented below. In this discussion, northern, central, and southern Illinois are treated as one region, "downstate."

As shown in Table 5–6, from 1975 to 1980, all regions except for the collar counties experienced net out-migration. In both absolute and percentage terms, Chicago experienced the greatest net out-migration. While Chicago gained nearly 300,000 through gross in-migration, gross out-migration from the city was nearly double that, spelling a net loss of 278,000 or 9.3 percent. This loss followed a decades-long trend of net out-migration for Chicago as discussed earlier.

After more than two decades of substantial net in-migration, sub-urban Cook County's migration pattern reversed itself in the latter half of the 1970s. From 1975 to 1980, suburban Cook County recorded the second highest level of net out-migration among all regions, with a net loss of 61,000 or 2.7 percent. Downstate Illinois experienced a small net out-migration between 1975 and 1980, 33,000 or .8 percent, continuing a trend of net out-migration since the 1950s.

From 1975 to 1980, the collar counties was the only region of the state to experience net in-migration, as it had since the 1950s. While the collar counties lost nearly 350,000 through gross out-migration, gross in-migration over the five-year period exceeded this level by over 100,000 for a net gain of 5.5 percent.

In regard to interregional migration flows, perhaps the most striking finding is how little population exchange occurred between downstate and the Chicago metropolitan area. As shown in Table 5–7, of the 400,000 gross in-migrants to downstate, only 114,000 or 29 percent came from elsewhere in Illinois (intrastate migration); the vast majority came from out of state (interstate migration). The situation is even more extreme in regard to out-migration. Of the 433,000 gross out-migrants from downstate, only 76,000 or 18 percent went elsewhere within the state; the remaining 82 percent moved out of state.

For the city of Chicago, the majority of gross in-migration, two-thirds, also came from out of state. However, in the case of gross out-migration, the majority, 55 percent, went elsewhere within the state. The *net* result was that nearly 80 percent of the total net out-migration experienced by Chicago was the result of intrastate migration, moves to elsewhere within Illinois.

In the cases of suburban Cook County and the collar counties, both experienced net in-migration through intrastate migration, but net out-migration through interstate migration; that is, both gained population from elsewhere within the state, but lost population to areas outside the state. (Regarding the destination of out-of-state bound migration, see Roseman, 1984.) The *net* result of these flows, however, differed for the two regions. Suburban Cook County experienced total net out-migration of 61,000 because the loss from interstate out-

Table 5–7. Origin of Migration Flows by Region, 1975–80 (thousands)

Region	Total Migration	Intrastate Migration	Interstate Migration
Chicago			
In	298	98	200
Out	576	316	260
Net	−278	−218	−60
Suburban Cook			
In	429	281	148
Out	490	259	231
Net	−61	+22	−83
Collar counties			
In	449	261	188
Out	347	103	244
Net	+102	+158	−56
Downstate			
In	400	114	286
Out	433	76	357
Net	−33	+38	−71

Source: U.S. Bureau of the Census, *1980 Census of Population and Housing, Public Use Microdata Sample.*

migration exceeded the gain from intrastate in-migration. On the other hand, the collar counties experienced total net in-migration of 102,000, because the gain from intrastate in-migration exceeded the loss from interstate out-migration.

As shown, most of the intrastate migration between 1975 and 1980 occurred within the Chicago metropolitan area. The migration flows between the three regions, Chicago, suburban Cook County, and the collar counties, are shown in Table 5–8. Of the 288,000 out-migrants from Chicago who remained in the metropolitan area, 213,000 or 74 percent went to suburban Cook County; in return suburban Cook County sent only 63,000 to Chicago. The vast majority of out-migrants from suburban Cook County who stayed within the metropolitan area, 150,000 or 70 percent, went to the collar counties. In return, the collar counties sent only 48,000 to suburban Cook County and even fewer, only 15,000, to Chicago.

Migration data for Illinois during the period from 1975 to 1980 also show that migrants are selective in terms of age, race, and other characteristics. For example, young people constituted a far higher proportion of intercounty migrants (in and out) and interstate in-migrants than they did among "non-movers" (those residents who

Table 5-8. Migration Flows within the Chicago SMSA, 1975-80

| | From | | | |
	Chicago	Suburban Cook	Collar Counties	Total
To				
Chicago	—	63,000	15,000	78,000
Suburban Cook	211,000	—	48,000	259,000
Collar counties	77,000	150,000	—	227,000
Total	288,000	213,000	63,000	564,000

Source: U.S. Bureau of the Census, *1980 Census of Population, Public-Use Microdata Sample.*

Table 5-9. Illinois Residents in 1980 by Residence in 1975 and Age

Persons 5 and Over	Intercounty Migrants	Percent	Interstate Migrants	Percent	Non-Movers	Percent
5-19	224,393	26.2	218,867	26.4	2,371,736	26.6
20-34	412,776	48.2	404,406	48.7	2,113,007	23.7
35-49	118,404	13.8	127,102	15.3	1,595,714	17.9
50+	100,464	11.7	79,506	9.6	2,826,290	31.7
Total	856,037	100.0	829,881	100.0	8,906,747	100.0

Source: U.S. Bureau of the Census, *1980 Census of Population, Supplementary Report S1-16.*

were not intercounty migrants or interstate in-migrants). As Table 5-9 shows, 48 percent of all intercounty migrants and 49 percent of all interstate in-migrants were age 20-34, while only 24 percent of non-movers were in this age group. Conversely, older people constituted a far smaller proportion of migrants than they did of non-movers; 12 percent of intercounty migrants and 10 percent of interstate in-migrants were age 50 and over, while 32 percent of non-movers were in this age group. Therefore, a region experiencing net in-migration may end up with a relatively younger population, while a region experiencing net out-migration may end up with a relatively older population.

In regard to race, a higher proportion of intercounty migrants were white than were non-movers, 93 percent compared to 81 percent, while a lower proportion of intercounty movers were black than were non-movers, 5 percent compared to 16 percent, as shown in Table 5-10.

Migration data for Chicago also illustrate that migration is selective

Table 5–10. Illinois Residents in 1980 by Residence in 1975 and Race

Persons 5 and Over	Intercounty Migrants	Percent	Interstate Migrants	Percent	Non-Movers	Percent
White	796,733	93.1	653,189	78.7	7,217,281	81.1
Black	38,876	4.5	67,913	8.2	1,403,125	15.8
Other	20,428	2.4	108,779	13.1	286,341	3.2
Total	856,037	100.0	829,881	100.0	8,906,747	100.0

Source: U.S. Bureau of the Census, *1980 Census of Population, Supplementary Report S1-16*.

in terms of educational attainment, labor force participation, and income. Residents moving out of Chicago to the rest of the metropolitan area were better educated, had higher labor force participation rates, and had higher incomes than did residents in Chicago. As shown in Table 5–11, out-migrants from Chicago (to the balance of the metropolitan area) were far more likely to have college degrees than were Chicago residents: 43 percent for out-migrants compared to 28 percent for city residents. Out-migrants also had a higher labor force participation rate: 70.3 for out-migrants versus 60.6 for Chicago residents. Finally, the median income of out-migrants from the city was nearly 45 percent higher than that of Chicago residents: $12,252 versus $8,479.

The selectivity of migration demonstrated here thus explains, at least in part, that the high levels of educational attainment, labor force participation, and income in suburban Cook County and the collar counties were the result of the net in-migration which these regions experienced historically, while the low levels in Chicago were the result of net out-migration. Should uneven migration flows occur in the future, further diversification of the regions can be expected. However, since migration for most regions is currently stabilizing, its impact should also be declining.

Summary and Conclusion

Since 1950, Illinois' regions have moved through various stages of boom-bust population growth cycles, with a tendency toward convergence in growth trends in the 1980s, when the disparity between regions in growth rates was much smaller than in the 1950s and 1960s. While the regions continue to be diverse in terms of demographic and socio-economic characteristics, they have also tended in recent years to converge in terms of some of these characteristics.

Table 5–11. Selected Characteristics of Chicago Residents and
Out-migrants from Chicago to SMSA Balance, 1980

	Chicago Residents	Percent	Out-migrants to SMSA Balance	Percent
Age				
Persons 5+	2,775,929	100.0	286,572	100.0
5–19	725,299	26.1	65,397	22.8
20–34	794,111	28.6	114,564	40.0
35–49	453,919	16.4	49,675	17.3
50+	802,600	28.9	56,936	19.9
Race				
Persons 5+	2,775,929	100.0	286,572	100.0
White	1,438,920	51.8	228,984	79.9
Black	1,085,164	39.1	37,161	13.0
Other	251,845	9.1	20,427	7.1
Education				
Persons 5+	1,760,228	100.0	193,533	100.0
Less than 4 years high school	770,668	43.8	51,964	26.9
4 years high school	499,170	28.3	59,289	30.6
College (1 year+)	490,390	27.9	82,280	42.5
Labor Force				
Persons 16+	2,263,685	100.0	234,500	100.0
In labor force	1,372,011	60.6	164,902	70.3
Not in labor force	891,674	39.4	69,598	29.7
Median Income				
Persons 15+	8,479	—	12,252	—

Source: U.S. Bureau of the Census, *1980 Census of Population, Subject Report 2-2C.*

Migration has played a critical role both in driving regional growth cycles and in shaping the demographic and socio-economic composition of the regions.

For suburban Cook County and the collar counties, the population growth boom has ended; these regions now experience more stable population growth rates. This slowing in growth resulted from a dramatic decline in net in-migration in recent years, both for suburban Cook County, where net in-migration derived mainly from Chicago, and for the collar counties, where most in-migration came from suburban Cook County. The massive influx of migrants to these regions in earlier years, however, undoubtedly contributed to the socio-economic advantages which these regions continue to enjoy (since migration tends to be selective, as discussed earlier); since the 1950s, of all regions in the state, these two have generally had the highest levels of educational attainment, labor force participation, and income. However, as both in-migration and overall population growth have slowed, the relative advantages of these two regions have also declined. That is, the gap between these two regions and others in terms of some characteristics, namely educational attainment and income, has narrowed substantially since the 1950s.

For Chicago, the population bust appears to be ending. Overall population loss and net out-migration for the city peaked during the period from 1970 to 1980. Since 1980, while still experiencing net out-migration, Chicago's population appears to be moving toward stabilization. Its net out-migration offsets natural increase by only one and one-fourth times, compared to more than two and one-half times over the 1970s. The vast exodus of population from the city from the 1950s through the 1970s, however, dramatically changed the city's demographic and socio-economic composition. In 1980, 40 percent of Chicago's population was black, compared to 14 percent in 1950.

Regarding educational attainment, Chicago's rank among regions in the proportion of high school graduates declined from third to last between 1950 and 1980. More dramatic was the decline in the city's ranking for labor force participation, from first in 1950 and 1960 to fifth by 1980. The city's labor force participation rate remained virtually unchanged between 1960 and 1980, while those of all other regions of the state increased substantially. Probably in large part a result of these changes, Chicago's rank in terms of per capita income also fell, from third among all regions in 1959 to fifth in 1979 and 1983. As out-migration from Chicago slows, these demographic and socio-economic effects of migration should also decline.

After thirty years of relatively stable population growth, northern and central Illinois are experiencing overall population loss in the 1980s. Net out-migration more than offsets natural increase, and southern Illinois is experiencing close to zero population growth. While not resulting in overall population losses in previous decades, net out-migration from these regions since the 1950s and 1960s probably influenced the age composition of these regions, which have consistently had the highest proportion of persons aged sixty-five and over. Age composition in turn has probably influenced these regions' educational attainment and labor force participation, which have generally been the lowest of all regions (except for Chicago in recent years), and, therefore, income levels, which have also been among the lowest. While the gaps in educational attainment and income between these regions and others have narrowed somewhat over the years, should net out-migration continue at the current pace or accelerate, the differences between these regions and others in terms of demographic and socio-economic characteristics could be exacerbated.

Given the impact of migration on regional trends in population growth and demographic and socio-economic composition, various regional policy issues arise, although the solutions are not clear-cut. For example, perhaps the most fundamental regional policy issue is whether population growth is always desirable and, conversely, whether population decline is always undesirable. On the one hand, while population decline can result in such problems as slower job growth, it can also result in lower unemployment rates due to a decline in labor force size, as studies have shown (see, for example, Greenwood, 1981). Furthermore, while population growth creates jobs, it also creates increased demand for government services and, therefore, additional government revenues. On the other hand, as was shown, migration can change the demographic and socio-economic composition of a region, so that a region which experiences net out-migration may be left with a population which is relatively older, less educated, and of lower income levels. To the extent that these characteristics are related to dependency on government services, the region may simultaneously experience increased demand for such services but diminished resources with which to provide them.

While this analysis does not answer such regional policy issues, it does provide an analytical foundation on which decision making regarding regional policy in Illinois can in part be based.

REFERENCES

Bogue, D. J. 1959. "Internal Migration." In P. M. Hauser and O. D. Duncan (eds.), *The Study of Population: An Inventory and Appraisal.* Chicago: University of Chicago.

————. 1969. *Principles of Demography.* New York: Wiley.

Bowen, W. G., and T. A. Finegan. 1969. *The Economics of Labor Force Participation.* Princeton, N.J.: Princeton University Press.

Chiang, C. H., and Richard Kolhauser. 1982. "Who Are We? Illinois' Changing Population." *Illinois Issues* 8:6–8.

————. 1983. "Illinois." *American Demographics* (April):42–44.

Graves, P. E. 1979. "A Life-cycle Empirical Analysis of Migration and Climate, by Race." *Journal of Urban Economics* 6:135–47.

Greenwood, J. J. 1981. *Migration and Economic Growth in the United States.* New York: Academic Press.

Illinois Department of Public Health. *Vital Statistics, Illinois (Annual).* Springfield: Department of Public Health.

Lansing, J. B., and E. Mueller. 1967. *The Geographical Mobility of Labor.* Ann Arbor: Survey Research Center, University of Michigan.

Long, L. H. 1973. "Migration Differentials by Education and Occupation: Trends and Variations." *Demography* 10:243–58.

Miller, A. R. 1967. "The Migration of Employed Persons to and from Metropolitan Areas of the United States." *Journal of the American Statistical Association* 62:1418–32.

Roseman, C. C. 1984. "Illinois Migrants: Where They Go and Where They Come from." In *Illinois CRD Report.* Urbana: Department of Agricultural Economics, University of Illinois.

Ritchey, P. N. 1976. "Explanations of Migration." *Annual Review of Sociology* 2:363–406.

Taeuber, K. E. 1967. "The Redistribution of Farm-born Cohorts." *Rural Sociology* 32:20–36.

U.S. Bureau of the Census. 1953. *1950 Census of Population, Illinois.*

————. 1963. *1960 Census of Population, Illinois.*

————. 1973. *1970 Census of Population, Illinois.*

————. 1983. *1980 Census of Population, Illinois.*

————. 1983. *1980 Census of Population and Housing, Public-Use Microdata Sample* (data tape).

————. 1984. *1980 Census of Population, Subject Report 2-2C: Geographical Mobility for Metropolitan Areas.*

————. 1984. *1980 Census of Population, Supplementary Report S1-16: Residence in 1975 for States by Age, Sex, Race, and Spanish Origin.*

————. 1986. *Current Population Reports, Series P-23.*

————. 1986. *Current Population Reports, Series P-25.*

The Changing Economy of Metropolitan Chicago: Past, Present, and Future

6

Marcus Alexis and John F. McDonald

The economy of metropolitan Chicago has undergone enormous changes in the past forty years, especially in the relationship between the central city and the suburbs. Forty years ago the suburbs were a rather minor adjunct to the economy of the city of Chicago. Now far more jobs are located in the suburbs than in the central city; one estimate is that 55 percent of the employment in the metropolitan area is located in the suburbs. The growth of the economy of the suburbs may well be the single most significant fact in the recent economic history of Illinois.

This chapter examines these developments and then uses this examination to generate some insights into future directions for economic policy making in the metropolitan area. We begin with a brief survey of the economic history of metropolitan Chicago. This will help us better understand its current status and direction. We then turn to a more detailed review of its current economic situation, with a focus on changing employment levels and firm-relocation patterns. These trends will help us understand the challenges and problems facing the metropolitan economy, as well as form the basis for some concluding remarks on economic policy. Throughout this chapter our focus will be on the entire metropolitan area, which is normally defined as the six-county region depicted in Figure 6–1. We will treat this area as a regional economy.[1]

A Brief Economic History of Metropolitan Chicago

Chicago was founded and prospered largely because of its key location on the lake and its proximity to rich agricultural lands. It developed as a transportation center to market agricultural commodities and to

Figure 6–1. Metropolitan Chicago, 1965

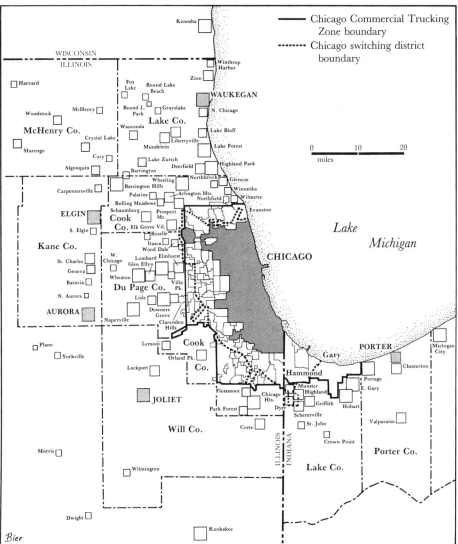

Source: Redrawn from Mayor's Committee for Economic and Cultural Development of Chicago, 1966:plate 27.

provide agricultural areas with badly needed goods and services. The announcement that the Illinois and Michigan Canal would be built caused Chicago's first real estate boom, but it was the railroad that made Chicago a major metropolitan area. The first railroad system was a regional system designed to bring agricultural products to market, which would then be shipped by water. The processing, storing, and shipping of agricultural products was, and still is, an important part of the Chicago economy. Chicago developed the massive grain elevators, the flour mills, the stockyards, the meat-packing plants, and other facilities needed for the agricultural economy of the Midwest. Chicago also developed the financial services needed to facilitate trade in agricultural commodities. The Chicago Board of Trade, insurance companies, and banks grew up around agriculture. Thus, from the beginning, the economic prosperity of the city was closely tied to neighboring economic sectors, which, in turn, prospered as a result of Chicago's development.

The regional railroad system was developed largely to foster the burgeoning trade in agricultural commodities, but it led to economic dividends. The mere construction and maintenance of the railway system required industrial development: iron and steel for rails and equipment, such as locomotives and railway cars. The regional railway system also provided the impetus for several other Chicago industries designed to provide goods to the farmers and the residents of smaller towns of the Midwest. Cyrus McCormick invented the mechanical reaper in Virginia, but he built his factory in Chicago to be able to deliver the implements to the farmers. Sears and Roebuck and Montgomery Ward located their catalog businesses in Chicago because the railway network could be used to deliver the goods. Many industries were spun off of these basic sectors—furniture, machine tools, appliances, printing and publishing, and apparel, to name just a few.

As the economy of Chicago expanded rapidly in the latter years of the nineteenth century, several critical additions were made to the transportation system and other public facilities, what economists call the infrastructure. The national railroad system linking the Chicago region to the East and the West was developed. What is not as obvious, but still very important, was the building of the extensive railway system internal to the Chicago area. This system consisted of beltway lines, switching yards, and industrial railways. By the 1890s, most of the present system was in place (see Figure 6–2). Completed in 1887, the outer line intersects the trunk lines at a distance of twenty-five to forty miles from the Loop and runs from Porter, Indiana, to Joliet, Aurora, Elgin, and Waukegan (see Figure 6–1). It provided the im-

Figure 6–2. Railroads in Metropolitan Chicago, 1967

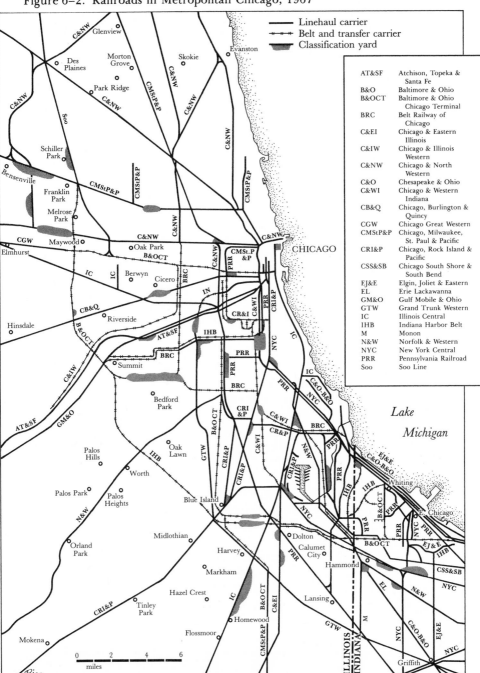

Source: Redrawn from Mayer and Wade, 1969:433.

petus for much of the early industrial growth in these cities. Well inside the outer belt line are the primary classification yards of the trunk line railways (see Figure 6–2). These yards are used to classify freight cars by inbound and outbound destinations and to assemble trains. Over the years, these rail yards have gone through a process of expansion and decentralization that many other industries have experienced. Chicago now has a series of older freight yards, which are used mainly for local interchange and switching or are abandoned. Despite this, the city remains a major connection point for east-west traffic. Conrail (Consolidated Rail Corporation), for example, switches much traffic in Chicago. A complex system of belt rail lines links the classification yards. Other belt lines provide service inside the city. Finally, there are seven railway approaches to central Chicago. At the turn of the century, a great deal of the freight moved into and out of the central area.

In addition to the railway system, the water transportation system is extensive and has been improved several times over the last century (see Figure 6–3). The Calumet River was improved in the 1870s to provide a harbor for industry. The Chicago Sanitary and Ship Canal, which reversed the flow of the Chicago River and provided a water route to Joliet, was completed in 1900 after a decade of construction work. This project required more earth excavation than the building of the Panama Canal. Subsequently, plans were made to link the Calumet River by canal with the Sanitary and Ship Canal at a point twenty-one miles southwest of the Loop. This project, called the Calumet Sag Channel, was completed in 1922. The next project linked the Sanitary and Ship Canal with the Illinois River in 1934. This inland waterway system is now known as the Gulf to Lakes Waterway. The last major development was the opening of the St. Lawrence Seaway in 1959. By 1969 the Calumet Sag Channel had been widened from 60 feet to 225 feet to handle seaway traffic.

Other important, and more obvious, parts of the transportation system so crucial to the Chicago area's economic development can be cited. The commuter railway system was largely in place by the turn of the century. The mass transit system continues to undergo extension to this day. The system of expressways was built in the 1950s and early 1960s (see Figure 6–4). Midway Airport was opened in 1927, and O'Hare Airport in 1955. In 1962 O'Hare became the world's busiest airport. Other key parts of the local infrastructure include the water-supply facilities of the Metropolitan Sanitary District, the twenty-four pipelines which carry petroleum and natural gas, and other public utilities.

Figure 6-3. Waterways in Metropolitan Chicago

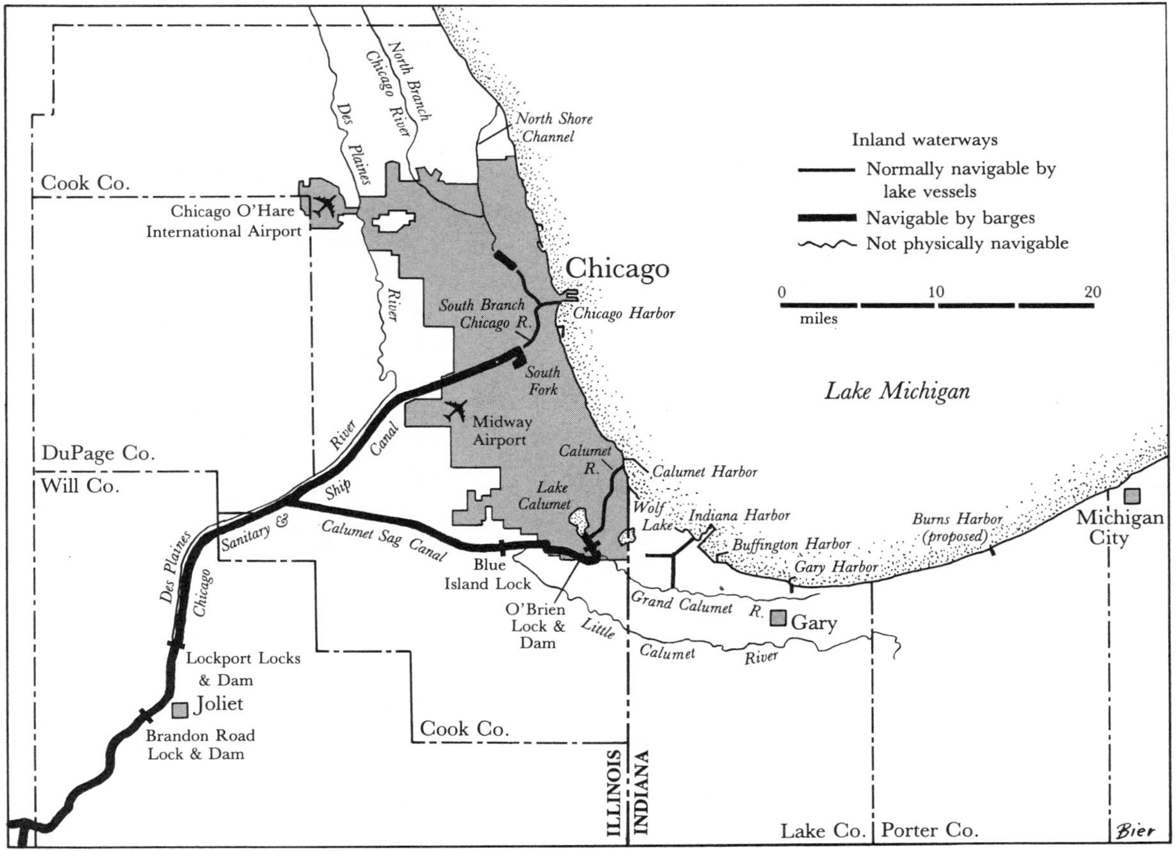

Source: Redrawn from Mayor's Committee for Economic and Cultural Development of Chicago, 1966:plate 24.

Figure 6–4. Expressway Development in Cook County

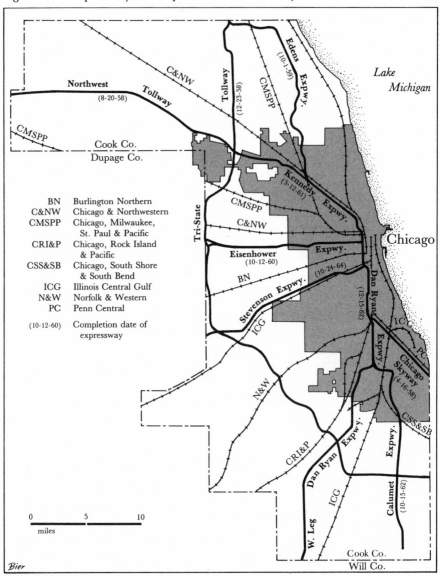

Source: Redrawn from Mayor's Council of Manpower and Economic Advisors, 1974:map 2.

This brief review of Chicago's early economic development illustrates that Chicago did not develop in a vacuum. Its key location and its proximity to a rich agricultural hinterland helped it become a primary hub of transportation in the country. Its centrality in the marketing of agricultural commodities spawned service and support industries which, in turn, attracted other industries. The spiraling economic growth of Chicago was good for both the city and the surrounding areas, which were so essential to the early stages of Chicago's economic growth. Eventually a truly impressive infrastructure was assembled that contributed mightily to Chicago's economic vitality through the early part of the twentieth century.

Economic Developments in Metropolitan Chicago since World War II

As the twentieth century progressed, the economy of Chicago encountered new challenges and opportunities. The movement of freight switched increasingly from rail to truck. Chicago adapted and became the nation's largest center for trucking. The development of refrigerated rail cars and trucks took the stockyards away from Chicago to smaller cities and towns. This was painful, but Chicago adapted and survived. Several white-collar industries found a home in Chicago's Loop: banking, financial services, insurance, real estate, government, and legal services. Major universities founded in Chicago have prospered, and the city has become a major center for medical education and research. Chicago is also a leader in cultural activities—arts, theater, music, and opera flourish. The industrial base has changed with the economy as a whole. Various light manufacturing industries (pharmaceuticals, electronics, biomedical, and environmental) supplanted heavy manufacturing as sectors of growth, and some forms of economic activity have diffused throughout the metropolitan area.

We now turn to a more rigorous and focused review of these recent economic trends, with a focus on the changing level and location of economic activity over the past forty years. We first describe two trends for each major sector of employment: total employment at the metropolitan level and shifts in the location of that employment (city and suburbs).[2] Employment figures are used for these purposes because other economic data (such as income generated by place of work, value-added in production, and gross value of output) are not available at the required level of spatial detail. We then describe in more detail the process through which the location patterns in the metropolitan area changed. Here we summarize key studies of firm

Table 6-1. Estimated Employment by Sector, Chicago and Suburbs (1000s)

	Chicago		Suburbs		SMSA	
	1947	1980	1947	1980	1947	1980
Construction	47	42	47	81	94	123
Manufacturing	668	314	189	494	857	808
Transportation, communication, and utilities	163	122	46	74	209	196
Wholesale trade	138	98	14	157	153	255
Retail trade	249	176	90	336	339	512
Finance, insurance, and real estate	93	132	26	109	119	241
Services	219	336	61	320	280	686
Government (non-military)	85	231	24	230	109	461
Other	16	8	4	10	20	18
Total wage and salary employment	1,678	1,489	501	1,811	2,180	3,299

Sources: Authors' estimates constructed from various government document sources, including Census of Manufactures, 1947; Census of Business, 1947; Hoch, 1959; U.S. Department of Commerce, Bureau of Economic Analysis, 1982.

relocation, birth, and death. These studies are arranged to provide a chronology from the 1940s to the 1970s.

Trends in Employment Levels

Table 6-1 displays estimated employment by major sector for the city and suburbs for 1947 and 1980. We see that employment in the SMSA (Standard Metropolitan Statistical Area) increased by about 51 percent over these thirty-three years, but that employment in the city *decreased* by about 11 percent. The suburbs changed from an adjunct to the economy of the city in 1947 (with 23 percent of the jobs) to a dynamic economy with 55 percent of the jobs in the SMSA in 1980. Table 6-1 also shows the sectoral shift that has taken place. There were actually fewer manufacturing jobs in the SMSA in 1980 than there were in 1947. The growth sectors in terms of employment have been government; services; finance, insurance, and real estate; and retail and wholesale trade. The largest increases in jobs were in services and government. Jobs in the city in these two sectors and in finance, insurance, and real estate increased from 1947 to 1980.

Table 6-2. Trends in Employment Growth by Sector, Chicago and Suburbs

	SMSA	City	Suburbs
Manufacturing	no growth; decline since 1978	rapid decline	rapid growth to 1978; decline since 1978
Retail trade	growth rapid growth	decline	rapid growth to 1977; growth since 1977
Wholesale trade	growth	slow decline; rapid decline since 1967	rapid growth
Construction	no growth	decline	growth
Transportation communication, and utilities	slow growth	decline	growth
Finance, insurance, and real estate	rapid growth	growth	rapid growth
Services	very rapid growth	growth	very rapid growth
Government	growth	growth	rapid growth

A characterization of the trends in each sector is shown in Table 6-2. Manufacturing employment has declined rapidly in the city (except for a brief period in the 1960s), and that decline was matched by growth in the suburbs until 1978. Since then manufacturing employment in the suburbs has declined somewhat. Employment in both retail trade and wholesale trade has declined in the city and grown in the suburbs, with the net result that the SMSA employment has grown in these sectors. Employment in the construction industry has not grown at the SMSA level; there has been decline in the city and growth in the suburbs. Similarly, the transportation, communication, and utilities sector has grown slightly at the SMSA level, with a decline in the city and growth in the suburbs. In contrast, employment in finance, insurance, and real estate and in services has grown briskly at the SMSA level. These sectors have grown rapidly in the suburbs, but they have also grown in the city. Finally, the growth in state and local government employment at the SMSA level has yielded growth in city and suburbs.

The picture that emerges from Tables 6-1 and 6-2 is that of a metropolitan economy which has shifted from primarily a center of manufacturing to a more diversified and modern urban area. The growth sectors for private employment are services; finance, insurance, and real estate; and, to a lesser extent, retail and wholesale trade. These trends are similar to the changes that have taken place in the nation as a whole, although metropolitan Chicago historically has had a greater concentration in manufacturing than has the nation.

The experience of metropolitan Chicago for most of the period since 1947 is fairly typical of the large, older metropolitan areas of northeastern United States. Norton (1979) conducted a comparative analysis of the largest U.S. cities. Chicago is in Norton's group of the twelve largest cities in 1910, which also includes New York, Philadelphia, Boston, Pittsburgh, St. Louis, San Francisco, Baltimore, Cleveland, Buffalo, Detroit, and Cincinnati. Average population growth at the SMSA level for this group of urban areas for 1950 to 1975 was 32 percent; the Chicago SMSA population grew 35 percent over this same period. Average population *decline* for this group of central cities was 21 percent from 1950 to 1975; the population of the city of Chicago declined 14 percent during this period. Employment data show a similar pattern. Average employment growth in manufacturing, retail and wholesale trade, and selected services for the group of twelve at the SMSA level was 17 percent from 1948 to 1972. The Chicago SMSA grew 21 percent in these same categories over this period. The average *decline* in the twelve central cities in these employment categories was 24 percent over this period; the decline for the city of Chicago was also 24 percent. The eighteen younger large urban areas also examined by Norton experienced more rapid employment and population growth at the SMSA level, and, with only three exceptions, experienced both employment and population growth in the central city. In contrast, all twelve of the older central cities declined in both employment and population.

A crucial finding in Norton's study is that slow growth at the SMSA level translates into decline in the central city. Norton's key empirical result can be stated briefly. Using the same employment data for 1947 to 1972 from the same thirty largest cities, Norton (1979) found that

$$J = 46.6 + 1.0M + .03L,$$

where J is the percentage change in central city employment in manufacturing, retail and wholesale trade, and selected services; M is the corresponding figure for the metropolitan area; and L is the percentage change in the land area of the central from 1950 to 1970. The R^2 for the equation is .93, and all of the estimated coefficients are highly statistically significant. This equation states that a central city which did not expand in land area and was located in a metropolitan area that did not grow would have declined in employment by 46.6 percent. An increase in the metropolitan employment growth rate of 1.0 percent would have increased the central city employment growth rate by 1.0 percent. A metropolitan area that grows slowly will have a central city that declines in absolute and relative terms; jobs will be moving from the central city to the suburbs. The experience of metropolitan Chicago fits the equation almost perfectly. For the Chicago SMSA, $M = 21$ percent for 1947 to 1972, and $L = 7$ percent, implying a predicted value for J of -25.4 percent. The actual value of J was -24 percent.

These results from Norton's study suggest that slow growth at the metropolitan level tends to exacerbate the social and political cleavages between the central city and the suburbs. The case of Chicago is typical in this sense. A declining central city that is becoming increasing black and Latino is paired with a growing suburban area that is largely white. Indeed, now only 14 percent of the students in the Chicago public schools are white. If growth at the SMSA level had been greater, the city probably would have retained more of its white population. As we emphasize at the end of this chapter, local policy should concentrate primarily on economic growth at the metropolitan level.

The available sources of data permit us to take a more detailed look over time at three major sectors—manufacturing, retail trade, and wholesale trade. Unfortunately, reliable data do not exist that give us a city suburban breakdown over time for the other employment sectors. The data are particularly incomplete in the service and government sectors.

Levels of Employment in Manufacturing. It used to be that the manufacturing sector was the largest category of employment in the metropolitan area. However, employment in the service sector now exceeds manufacturing employment. This is significant because manufacturing is usually regarded as providing most of the export sector for a local economy. Table 6–3 contains the data for manufacturing and tells a clear story. The wartime boom left the city with 668,000 manufacturing jobs in 1947, or 78 percent of the 857,000 jobs in the SMSA. From 1947 to the present, the record is one of almost continuous decline in manufacturing employment in the city. The city experienced an increase of 37,000 jobs (7 percent) from 1963 to 1967 during the boom period of the middle to late 1960s, but the long-run trend is down from 668,000 jobs in 1947 to 277,000 jobs in 1982 and 264,000 jobs in 1984. The city now has less than 40 percent of the manufacturing jobs. At the same time, manufac-

Table 6–3. Manufacturing Employment in the Chicago SMSA (1000s)

	Chicago	Suburbs	Total
1947	668	189	857
1954	615	235	849
1958	569	286	855
1963	509	352	861
1967	546	437	983
1972	430	479	909
1977	366	518	884
1982	277	468	745
	(296)	(402)	(698)
1984	(264)	(410)	(674)

Sources: Census of Manufactures (various issues). Data in parentheses are from State of Illinois, Department of Labor, 1984.

turing employment in the suburbs increased continuously until the deep recession of 1981–82. In 1977, employment in the suburbs reached 518,000 compared to 366,000 in the city. The total number of jobs (884,000) in the SMSA in 1977 was about the same as it had been throughout the late 1940s, the 1950s, and the early 1960s, but the suburbs had 59 percent of those jobs in 1977 compared to 22 percent in 1947.

The situation changed somewhat with the recession of 1981–82. Employment in the SMSA declined slightly (3 percent) from March 1977 to March 1981, but the decline from March 1981 to March 1982 was 6 percent. The decline from 1977 to 1981 took place in the city, and employment in the suburban ring remained unchanged. However, from March 1981 to March 1982, employment declined in both the city and the suburban ring (7 percent decline in the city and 5 percent decline in the ring). What is even more noteworthy is the fact that manufacturing employment in the SMSA was *less* in March 1984 than it was in March 1982. As Table 6–3 shows, employment in the city continued to decline (11 percent from 1982 to 1984), and the suburbs displayed very little recovery (only 2 percent). The national level of manufacturing employment had almost reached its ultimate recovery level by March 1984. Manufacturing employment in the nation in March 1984 was 98 percent of the level reached in 1977, and it was 92 percent of the all-time high reached in 1979. But manufacturing employment in the SMSA in 1984 was only 89 percent of the level of employment reached in 1977.

The continued decline in manufacturing employment in the SMSA is confirmed by *Employment and Earnings* (U.S. Department of Labor

Table 6–4. Paid Employees in Retail Trade, Chicago and Suburbs (1000s)

	Chicago			Suburbs	Total
	Total	CBD[a]	Rest of City		
1948	249	65[b]	184	90	339
1954	224	49[b]	174	83	307
1958	225	46	179	106	331
1963	210	40	170	143	353
1967	218	38	180	172	390
1972	193	32	161	237	430
1977	178	27	151	297	476
1982	147	20	127	308	455
	(159)	(22)	(137)	(286)	(445)
1984	(172)	(22)	(150)	(320)	(492)

[a] CBD is defined as Census Tracts 3201, 3202, 3203, 3204, 3205, and 3206. The area is bounded by the Chicago River and Roosevelt Road (1200 South).

[b] Data are reported in Meyer, Kain, and Wohl (1965:37), based on a report by the Chicago Transit Authority.

Sources: Census of Business (various issues) and Census of Retail Trade (various issues). Proprietors are not included. Data in parentheses are from State of Illinois, Department of Labor, 1984.

Bulletin) up to May 1986. A current *Employment and Earnings* report shows that manufacturing employment in the SMSA fell by 20 percent from May 1982 and by 5 percent from May 1984. Declines of this nature during a period of economic recovery and expansion are particularly alarming.

Levels of Employment in Retail and Wholesale Trade. Table 6–4 contains the data for retail trade. Employment at the SMSA level grew about 45 percent from 1948 to 1984 (339,000 to 492,000) as population grew by 37 percent from 1950 to 1980. Employment in the city was at its highest level in 1948 (249,000 jobs, 73 percent of the SMSA total). Employment in the city has declined almost continuously since then. Most of the decline took place from 1948 to 1954 and after 1967. The declines in the Chicago Central Business District (CBD) have been especially large, although the definition of the CBD used by the Census excludes the booming North Michigan Avenue area. Employment in the suburbs has grown rapidly, but only slightly more rapidly than has the suburban population. As of 1984, about 65 percent of retail employment was located in the suburbs.

These results for retail trade should come as no surprise. The development of suburban shopping centers and the decline of the

Table 6–5. Paid Employees in Wholesale Trade, Chicago and Suburbs (1000s)

	Chicago	Suburbs	Total
1947	138	14	153
1954	131	16	147
1958	132	30	162
1963	121	50	171
1967	131	68	199
1972	101	93	194
1977	91	115	206
1982	74	137	212

Sources: Census of Business (various issues) and Census of Wholesale Trade (various issues).

CBD are well-known phenomena. The shift of retailing to the suburbs stems primarily from shifts on the demand side. The movement of population to the suburbs and the increase in auto ownership stimulated the demand for retail facilities in the suburbs. The spectacular changes on the supply side, embodied in the huge emergence of modern shopping malls, probably consolidated the gains in suburban retailing into a smaller number of points.

The employment figures for wholesale trade are shown in Table 6–5. As is the case in retailing, the city dominated wholesaling in 1947, with 90 percent of metropolitan area employment. The city remained dominant until 1967 (with 66 percent of total metropolitan employment in that year), but since 1967 the wholesale trade sector has grown very little at the SMSA level (less than 7 percent from 1967 to 1982), and employment has shifted rapidly out of the city. In 1982, 65 percent of employment in wholesale trade was located in the suburbs.

Trends in Firm Relocation

Using data on employment by industry, the previous sections documented the emergence of the suburban economy over the past forty years. The purpose of this section is to describe more fully the processes through which these changes took place by examining the studies of firm relocation, the birth of firms, and the death of firms. There is a long history of such studies in the metropolitan area for the manufacturing sector. This section necessarily concentrates on that sector, even though, as we have seen, the evolution of manufacturing employment at the metropolitan level is *not* representative of all employment sectors. However, the patterns described below are probably fairly typical for an employment sector that does not grow

Table 6–6. Industrial Relocations, 1947–57

Destination	Origin						
	City of Chicago	Central Area of City	North Area of City	South Area of City	Rest of Cook County[a]	Rest of SMSA[a]	Outside of SMSA[a]
Chicago	651	421	131	99	14	5	25
Central[b]	242	196	22	24	—	—	—
North	238	131	94	13	—	—	—
South	171	94	15	62	—	—	—
Rest of Cook County	475	261	148	66	51	—	—
North	158	106	45	7	—	—	—
Central	288	145	98	45	—	—	—
South	29	10	5	14	—	—	—
Rest of SMSA	79	35	30	14	—	18	—
Outside of SMSA	37	14	18	5	—	—	—

[a] — Data not available.

[b] Area definitions: central area — 40 square miles bounded by Diversey Avenue on the north, 55th Street on the south, Western Avenue on the west, and Lake Michigan; north area — north of Madison Street in the city; south area — south of Madison Street in the city; north Cook — north of Devon Avenue, extended; south Cook — south of 87th Street; central Cook — between North Cook and South Cook.

Source: Data from City of Chicago Department of City Planning, 1961.

at the SMSA level. Unfortunately, only one study of firm relocation exists that examines non-manufacturing sectors in metropolitan Chicago. This section discusses key studies in chronological order; the studies reviewed were chosen because each is the most complete relocation study that covers a particular time period since 1947. McDonald (1984) provides a more complete survey of the many relocation studies which pertain to metropolitan Chicago.

The City of Chicago Department of City Planning (1961) completed a comprehensive study of industrial relocations from 1947 to 1957. Table 6–6 contains the basic results of this study. The largest category of relocations (651 moves) involved moves from one site in the city to another, but the next largest category (475 moves) involved moves from the city to the rest of Cook County. About 61 percent of these 475 moves were to locations in central Cook County, to suburbs such as Cicero, Franklin Park, and neighboring municipalities southeast of O'Hare Airport. Of these 475 relocations, 261 (55 percent) originated in the central area of the city. Of these 261, 145 (56 percent moved to the central area of Cook County. A number of establishments (118) moved from the city to a location outside of Cook County. In contrast, only 19 establishments moved from the suburbs to the city, while 25 moved into the city from outside the metropolitan area. In interpreting these figures, it should be remembered that in 1947 there were 10,240 manufacturing establishments in the city, 994 in the rest of Cook County, and 1,050 in the rest of the metropolitan area. Thus, during the period from 1947 to 1957, 5.8 percent of the establishments in the city moved out. One point to note is that 4.6 percent of the establishments in the city moved to the rest of Cook County, and only 1.4 percent of the establishments in the rest of Cook County moved into the city.

Another important source of change in the spatial pattern of industry is the locational choices of new firms or branch plants. During the 1947 to 1957 period, 508 new firms were established in the city, 520 in the rest of Cook County, and 271 in the rest of the metropolitan area. Thus, suburban Cook County attracted as many new establishments as did the city. Unfortunately, because the City of Chicago Department of City Planning (1961) did not investigate the establishments which went out of business during this period, a complete picture of the changes in industrial location cannot be determined.

As part of this study, Melvin (1965) conducted interviews of 45 top managers of firms that relocated in the late 1950s. Included in these interviews were 28 firms that chose a suburban location and 17 firms that chose to locate in the city. The purpose of the interviews was to discover the factors which were important to industrial decision makers in choosing a site. While Melvin's study is no more than a listing of factors that the interviewees said were important, the results are of interest as basic descriptive data. The firms that located in the suburbs have some common qualities that distinguish them from the firms selecting a site in the city. Firms choosing a suburban location were characterized by having geographically diffuse sources of input materials, suppliers, and market areas. Few downtown business contacts were needed. These firms needed a relatively large site and tended to have employment that was nonseasonal in nature. Firms which located in the city were more dependent on local suppliers and materials and had a more localized market area. Daily business contacts were more important for them, and their business tended to be more seasonal in nature so that access to an available labor pool on short notice was needed.

Through his interviews, Melvin was able to develop a set of positive and negative features for both suburban and central-city sites. The positive features of suburban sites, as of the late 1950s, fell into two categories: site conditions and transportation factors. Site conditions were favorable in suburban locations because large sites were available at relatively low cost, thereby facilitating future expansion. Also, off-street parking and loading were possible, and more attractive landscaping could be done. Access to the regional and metropolitan highway systems was important for warehousing establishments, and the regional highway system was important to production establishments. These factors were less important for office and research establishments. Access to air and rail transport was of secondary importance for suburban firms. Finally, suburban sites were closer to residential areas where managers prefer to live. The chief negative aspects of suburban sites were lack of mass transit for workers, difficulty in arranging for less-than-truckload (LTL) pickups and deliveries, isolation from business contacts, and higher utility costs.

Central-city sites had different sets of positive and negative features. Central-city sites tended to have existing buildings and facilities which could easily be converted to a desired use. Access to rail transport and mass transit was better than that for suburban sites. Central-city sites also had better LTL freight service and better access to input materials, markets, business services, and labor. Also, proximity to the parent plant was often a feature of a central-city location. On the negative side, central-city sites often lacked off-street parking and loading areas and tended to have poor local access for trucks because of narrow streets, heavy traffic, and double-parking. Most central-city sites lacked room for expansion beyond a short time horizon. Finally, central-city sites were viewed as having more problems with security and vandalism.

Factors such as tax rates, soil and drainage conditions, sewer facilities, and aspects of labor supply (available skills, available clerical workers, and available housing for workers) were considered site neutral by Melvin's interviewees.

A study conducted by the Northeastern Illinois Planning Commission (1965) is the most comprehensive study of those reviewed here. Records of the Illinois State Employment Service during March of 1955, 1959, and 1963 were used to establish employment levels and the components of employment change for thirty-eight geographic areas comprising the Chicago SMSA. The data source reputedly covered 99.4 percent of manufacturing employment. Employment changes in an area were classified as changes in establishments that did not relocate, employment in new establishments (new branch plants and new firms), employment in establishments that relocated in or out of the area, and employment in establishments that terminated. Approximately 13 percent of total employment could not be so classified.

All areas in the city lost employment during the 1955–63 period; about 131,600 manufacturing jobs were lost in all. Seven of the eight areas of the city also had negative net relocation figures. Only the Southwest Side of Chicago gained a few jobs by relocations, even as it declined in total manufacturing employment. Net relocations accounted for most of the decline near the CBD, but accounted for only a small fraction of the decline near the city limits.

The pattern presented by the data for the suburban zones is more complex. Not all of the suburban zones increased in employment; zones in the inner western suburbs (Cicero, Brookfield area, and central industrial suburbs) registered significant declines. Joliet and the rest of Will County also declined. On the other hand, all areas to the far west, northwest, and north registered increases in employment. The Chicago Heights area in the south also gained a significant number of jobs. It is interesting that the areas in northern and northwestern Cook County gained employment primarily through net relocations, while net relocations were not a large share of the total change in employment in most other suburban areas. With the exception of Oak Park, net relocations account for less than half of the increase in employment in these other suburban areas.

Data on the origins and destinations of establishment relocations can be constructed from the Northeastern Illinois Planning Commission (1965) report. In examining the results for the city, one can see the substantial volume of relocation that took place inside the city. In all, 615 establishments moved within the city. At the same time, 458 establishments moved out of the city to the suburbs; 86 percent moved to the rest of Cook County, and 14 percent to other counties in the SMSA. A total of 65 establishments moved to the city from the rest of the SMSA. The main destinations of the firms that moved out of the city were northwestern Cook County (57 firms), the northern suburbs of Cook County (160 firms), and the western suburbs of Cook County (140 firms). A relatively small number of establishments moved to southwestern and southern Cook County and to the outlying counties. Of all the suburban locations, only Cicero on the western edge of the city had more establishments move out than move in (23 versus 15).

Two studies that were completed shortly after the Northeastern Illinois Planning Commission study were partly motivated by a concern

Table 6-7. Origin and Destination of Relocating Firms, 1970-77
(Manufacturing, TCU, Retail and Wholesale Trade, and Services)

Destination	Origin			
	Cook County	Rest of SMSA[a]	Other	Total
Cook County	—	130	141	271
Rest of SMSA	757	—	43	800
Other	298	52	—	350
Total	1,055	182	184	1,421

[a] The rest of the SMSA consists of DuPage, Kane, Lake, McHenry, and Will counties in Illinois.

Source: Data from Nealon, 1978.

for economic opportunities for minority workers. Williamson (1969) examined the period from 1950 to 1959 and found that the propensity to relocate was roughly equal across all locations in the metropolitan area. However, the choice of destination was influenced positively by such factors as labor force potential, capacity of arterial streets, and the proximity of a suburb to the city. Negative factors included non-white population potential and percentage of land not available for industry. A study by Christian and Bennett (1973) examined relocation data from 1969 to 1971 and found a large number of firms had moved from the black communities on the West and South sides of the city. Thus, we find that the black communities first lost their attraction as destinations for relocating firms and later began to lose many of the firms that were already located in these areas.

A more recent study of business relocation was done by Nealon (1978). This study made use of data provided by Dun and Bradstreet for 1970 and 1977 and included firms in four categories: manufacturing; transportation, communication, and utilities (TCU); wholesale and retail trade; and services. Dun and Bradstreet maintains comprehensive files on manufacturing firms, but the quality of its data for other business sectors is less certain. Nealon presented relocation data for the aggregate of the four categories listed above, and these are shown in Table 6-7. The geographic breakdown consists of Cook County, the rest of the SMSA (DuPage, Kane, Lake, McHenry, and Will counties in Illinois), and other locations. In Table 6-7 the salient fact is the movement of 1,055 firms out of Cook County. Of this total, 757 moved to locations elsewhere in the SMSA. One can presume that most of these relocating firms originated in the city of Chicago, but there are probably numerous examples of firms that moved from

Table 6–8. Components of Cook County Employment Gains and Losses, 1970–77

	Percent Employment Gains			Percent Employment Losses		
	Births[a]	Expan- sion	In- migration	Deaths[b]	Contrac- tion	Out- migration
Manufacturing	35.9	61.3	2.8	67.4	25.6	7.0
Transportation, communication, and utilities	54.0	44.1	1.9	58.6	34.6	6.7
Wholesale and retail trade	64.8	34.5	0.7	74.6	20.4	5.0
Services	80.8	18.8	0.4	71.3	24.0	4.7
Total	60.4	38.3	1.3	66.0	27.1	6.9

[a] A birth of a firm is the appearance in the 1977 Dun and Bradstreet file of a firm that was established between 1970 and 1977 and has a new Dun's identification number.

[b] A death of a firm is the disappearance from the Dun and Bradstreet file of a firm with a particular Dun's identification number.

Source: Data from Nealon, 1978.

the older suburbs in Cook County to a site more distant from the CBD.

The more important aspect of Nealon's study is his disaggregation of the total change in employment in Cook County into its component parts. Nealon used six categories of employment change: birth of firm, expansion of existing firm, out-migration of firm, in-migration of firm, death of firm, and contraction of existing firm. Table 6–8 shows for Cook County the relative importance of the three categories of employment gain and the three categories of employment loss for employment changes. Most of the total employment gain (60 percent) consisted of firm births, although most of the employment gain in manufacturing (61 percent) came from the expansion of existing firms. In-migration accounted for only 1.3 percent of employment gains. Deaths of firms accounted for most of the employment losses in all four categories. Out-migration accounted for 6.9 percent of employment losses in the total of the four categories.

Nealon also calculated the average size (number of employees) for firms in four of the categories in Table 6–8: births, deaths, in-migration, and out-migration. The analysis showed that new firms were much smaller than firms that died. This discrepancy was particularly large in manufacturing; new firms had an average of 12 employees and firms that died had 42 employees on average. Also, firms that moved into Cook County tended to be smaller than the firms that moved out of Cook County. The average manufacturing firm that moved out of Cook County had 60 employees, while the average manufacturing firm that moved into Cook County had 45 employees. These results suggest that smaller firms found the external economies of Cook County attractive, while larger firms sought more space in the surrounding counties of the SMSA and other locations.

This brief review of relocation studies demonstrates that, since the end of World War II, there has been a marked net increase in the number of establishments that moved from the city to the suburbs. These studies also show that most *new* firms located in the suburbs. Industrial growth in the metropolitan area during this period shifted primarily to the northern, northwestern, and western suburbs. Prior to the 1950s and 1960s, these areas had not housed much industrial development. The relocators to the suburbs tended to be light manufacturers of durable goods; larger firms that relocated tended to move greater distances. As Melvin (1965) discovered, firms which located in the suburbs were seeking spacious quarters, while those firms which selected a city site sought accessibility.

For much of the postwar period, notions of accessibility tended to be bounded by the area of the Chicago Commercial Trucking Zone (CCTZ) and the expressway system (see Figures 6–1 and 6–4). But the CCTZ has been eliminated with the deregulation of the trucking industry, and there is substantial evidence to suggest that, at the present time, much of the metropolitan area outside the CBD can be regarded as a fairly homogeneous plain, at least in terms of accessibility and transportation costs. However, Williamson (1969) and Christian and Bennett (1973) found that areas within the black residential sectors of the city have failed to attract relocating firms and, since 1968, have experienced a significant out-migration of firms. Nealon (1978) placed all of the studies of firm relocation in perspective, noting that, over a seven-year period from 1970 to 1977, births and deaths of firms were the primary causes of changes in the employment level of Cook County. Nealon also noted that there was some evidence to suggest that Cook County provided positive external economies for small firms.

This last point relates to what is known as the "incubator" hypothesis, which is really three related hypotheses: (1) the births of new firms will be concentrated in certain locations characterized by the availability of external economies, (2) the survival and growth rates of new firms will vary over space, and (3) new firms that are successful and grow rapidly will relocate from the locations in which firm births are concentrated to areas that are less crowded. Given the patterns of relocation cited above, it is clear that the city historically has served as an important incubator for many of the firms that now thrive in the suburbs. In addition, Nealon's study suggests that the city is still playing the role of an incubator. However, it now appears that some areas in the suburbs are also incubators for new businesses.[3] The identification of incubator zones might be important for economic growth policy for the metropolitan area.

In any case, it is clear that the nature of the economic relationship between the city and its surrounding environs has changed dramatically over time. The city was founded to facilitate the marketing of agricultural commodities from Illinois and the rest of the Midwest; much of its later growth was due to the markets these areas provided the city in exchange for the goods and services it generated. Both sectors benefitted greatly from this symbiotic relationship. While Chicago grew into a major center of manufacturing and commerce, Chicago's burgeoning infrastructure provided a hospitable climate for aspiring entrepreneurs. Successful enterprises "born" in Chicago often moved to the accessible periphery of the metropolitan area because of changed needs. Although the city suffered a net loss as a result of these relocations, the magnitude of its loss was reduced by the ability of the suburbs to keep the relocating firms in the metropolitan area. As we have seen, this ability of the suburbs is fairly typical of suburban areas.

In the more recent past this growth pattern has changed in two ways. First, because economic growth in the Midwest has been sluggish, Chicago has moved in the direction of providing services and goods for national and international markets (e.g., futures and options exchanges, research-based products). Second, it now appears that some peripheral areas of metropolitan Chicago, such as DuPage County, are serving as incubator sites for new businesses. More details about the current situation are provided in the next section.

The Metropolitan Economy Today: Observations and Implications

What is the present status of the metropolitan economy? We think it is fair to say that the recent performance of the local economy has been disappointing in comparison to what was expected by most observers in the 1950s and 1960s. For example, the population of Illinois and metropolitan Chicago hardly increased at all from 1970 to 1980. The population of Illinois increased by less than 1.0 percent and metropolitan Chicago increased only 1.8 percent over this period; the population of the city declined by 10.6 percent as the suburban ring increased by 13.5 percent. These growth rates (declines) are much smaller (larger) than predicted by experts. For example, the projections issued by the Chicago Area Transportation Study (1959) in the early 1960s said that the population of Illinois in 1980 would be 13.8 million (rather than the actual population of 11.4 million). CATS projected a population of almost 9 million for metropolitan Chicago in 1980 (actual population — 7.1 million) and a population in the city of 3.7 million (actual population — 3.0 million). Employment projections made at the same time were also wide of the mark; CATS projected a metropolitan area (including Lake County, Indiana) employment level of 4.6 million for 1980, but actual employment turned out to be 3.4 million.

The reasons for these disappointing trends can be listed from the top down as follows: (1) national growth trends in the aggregate and by sector, (2) trends at the SMSA level, and (3) forces generating suburbanization of the metropolitan area, including changes in transportation; patterns of firm births, deaths, and relocations; and the emergence of growth poles in the suburbs.

The economic balance between city and ring in the Chicago area was strongly influenced by the growth trends at the national and SMSA levels. National growth has been less than was expected twenty-five years ago. The end of the baby boom was not foreseen, nor was the slowdown in the growth rates of GNP and labor productivity during the past fifteen years. Much the same can be said for the dramatic shift in migration patterns toward the Sun Belt. All of this has meant that the Chicago SMSA has grown much more slowly than was expected. This slow growth at the metropolitan level translated into sizeable declines in the city as the suburbs grew. If the SMSA had grown rapidly, the city would have at least experienced some modest growth. On top of these aggregate trends, there has been major sectoral shift in the national economy away from manufacturing (as a proportion of total employment) toward services; finance, insurance, and real estate; government; and retailing. Given metropolitan Chicago's historically heavy concentration in manufacturing, metropolitan Chicago actually made a rather remarkable adjustment to these national sectoral shifts. Much of this successful adjustment was due to the ability of the suburbs to hold firms that might otherwise have migrated from the state. While this ability of the suburbs to retain firms in the SMSA was generally no better than average, it clearly enhanced the economic strength of the suburbs and contributed to the overall viability of the regional economy.

The story of the modern revolution in transportation and communications need not be told here. But it is clear that this revolution generated a set of powerful forces for the suburbanization of the metropolitan area. These factors include the interstate highway system and the growth of interstate trucking (at the expense of the railroads); the expressway system; improvements in telephone service within the metropolitan area; the growth of air travel and, hence, O'Hare Airport; and improvements in electric power generation and transmission. These and other factors have greatly expanded the effective land area of the metropolitan area and have enhanced the economic viability of the outlying suburban areas. Given the underlying forces generating suburbanization of the metropolitan area, the spatial patterns of the births, deaths, and relocations of firms discussed earlier are more understandable.

While the forces of suburbanization were introducing one set of changes into the structure of Chicago's regional economy, other factors were also at work. Some of these tended to counterbalance, in the aggregate, the loss of manufacturing activity in the city. The result of these changes has been the transformation of Chicago into what some refer to as a post-industrial city.[4] Manufacturing will always be important to the regional economy, even if less important than in the past. But the dynamic sectors of the local economy now, and for the immediate future, will be in areas such as financial services, legal services, high technology and research, and retailing. It is in Chicago's financial services sector that some truly remarkable developments have occurred. The Midwest Stock Exchange is now the third largest stock exchange in the world (exceeded only by New York and Tokyo). The Chicago Board of Trade and the Chicago Board Options Exchange are dynamic centers of activity. In addition, the growth in the legal services sector in the Loop has been significant.

The metropolitan area also has a growing high technology and research sector. The I-5 corridor in DuPage County is becoming a growth pole, Illinois' version of Silicon Valley in northern California and the Route 128 corridor near Boston. This area is generating economic growth that does not appear to be connected to the city in any major way. Chicago has done well in the medical research sector; it is home to six major medical schools (including Loyola's Maywood Medical Center) and a score of research and teaching hospitals. Its retailing sector, as exemplified by the North Michigan Avenue area, Oakbrook, and others, has made Chicago a leading retail center.

O'Hare Airport has been, and is, a magnet for economic activity of many types—light manufacturing, wholesaling, transportation, finance, insurance, real estate, etc. In addition, Chicago has become a center for the production and financing of motion pictures and TV shows.

Public Policy and Economic Development

The basic message of this brief review of current developments is clear: economic conditions are ever-changing and the Chicago metropolitan economy must evolve to keep pace. Moreover, the need to adapt and evolve quickly is more important now than ever before. The Chicago area, like the rest of the nation, competes in a world economy with more formidable and aggressive competitors than in the past. In this environment, public policies fostering economic development can be crucial in maintaining the region's economic health and continued viability.

Before we proceed to discuss general policy strategies, we must first consider the factors that have important locational consequences for the employment sectors crucial to the local economy. The dynamic sectors located in and near the Loop benefit from the agglomeration of activity; many require face-to-face contact. Legal services and courts are an obvious example. Many of the quasi-legal services and regulatory activities of federal, state, and local government also require Loop locations. Traditionally, many banking and financial services required face-to-face contact and spatial agglomeration. However, the truth of this maxim is being eroded, in some instances rather quickly. Most trading at the Midwest Stock Exchange is now done via computer terminals and not by shouts and hand signals. High technology and research firms also find it beneficial to congregate near each other, although they do not appear to require the proximity of service firms located in the Loop. Such firms benefit from sharing a pool of labor, large computer facilities, and suppliers of key commodities needed in research, hence the growth of research parks in university centers. By contrast, heavy industry, such as basic steel and petroleum refining, must have a location that is convenient to the rail, water, or pipeline transportation systems.

Other employment sectors are more mobile *within* a metropolitan area. Many in the light manufacturing sector simply want a site that is accessible by truck and auto and allows them to expand. It is obvious that the comparative locational advantages once possessed by the city vis-à-vis the suburbs have all but disappeared for these industries. Apart from the Loop, the O'Hare area, the I-5 corridor, and the

Indiana Harbor area, much of the metropolitan area can be viewed as a kind of featureless plain from the standpoint of firm location. In this kind of environment, local policies (tax breaks, provision of municipal services) can have a significant impact on locational decisions by relatively mobile firms.

These are factors that primarily influence locational decisions *within* a metropolitan area. But what makes a metropolitan area attractive to firms such that they would want to move to or stay within it? As always, there are demand and supply factors. The firm must see that there is sufficient demand for its product(s) or services(s) in the area and its environs. Given the nature of modern transportation and communication, most firms have several metropolitan areas that provide it with adequate access to the sources of demand for its product. The decision then turns on supply factors. In many of the dynamic sectors of the contemporary economy, the supply side boils down to labor force and infrastructure. The Chicago area has notable features here. With its great universities and cultural attractions, Chicago has available a highly trained and educated labor force. And, as we have already emphasized, the diversity and infrastructure of metropolitan Chicago are impressive.

The advantages enjoyed by the Chicago area in this regard are the result of decades of cumulative investments in public and private capital development. Such an infrastructure would be difficult to duplicate under present conditions. Yet the metropolitan area cannot afford to become complacent or content with the status quo. It must continue to add to its infrastructure, create a healthy economic and social environment, and aggressively pursue economic growth. But in doing these things policy makers must keep in mind that the area's real competitors are outside the region, outside the state. The real economic unit is the metropolitan area; neither the city nor its suburbs are separate economic units. They are intertwined in inseparable ways. Moreover, as our brief review of the region's economic history revealed, this has always been the case. Past economic achievements have never been the result of isolated efforts of either the city or the suburbs. Moreover, what has benefitted one geographic sector has often benefitted the other.

These considerations should be kept in mind in the formulation of economic development policies. Efforts to structure localistic policies aimed simply at shifting economic activity within the metropolitan area are fruitless for the metropolitan area as a whole. They may have short-term political payoffs and narrowly based economic benefits. However, to the extent that these activities do not contribute to the overall ability of the metropolitan economy to compete in the new world economic order, they will be self-defeating in the long run.[5] The very size and complexity of the metropolitan area compound the political difficulties involved in coordinating policies affecting economic development. However, there have already been some hopeful signs of regional cooperation, including the Regional Transit Authority, the Metropolitan Sanitary District, the new state office building, the University of Illinois at Chicago, the O'Hare expansion project, the use of state police to patrol Chicago's expressways, and Cook County (rather than the city of Chicago) operation of the major hospital for indigents, the jails, and the welfare system. The region must continue to pursue these cooperative activities; at the same time, it must insure that its comparative advantages are maintained. Primary among these is the region's impressive urban infrastructure. The maintenance and judicious expansion of this infrastructure is getting more expensive, and cooperative efforts will be required for continued progress. Also, the impressive cultural features of the metropolitan area, and Chicago in particular, must be supported. These features are important for attracting and keeping the talented people who help the local economy grow. Indeed, policy makers must take care to maintain the general quality of life in the city. This will require continued vigilance because the city has lost, and probably will continue to lose, both jobs and people. But the city is still the region's most valuable asset in attracting economic investment. It should operate prudently and responsibly. In a contemporary metropolitan setting, even a well-run central city will be unable to address effectively the barrage of problems which it continually confronts, but it is too crucial a cog in the metropolitan system to leave these problems unattended.

NOTES

1. The main contemporary works on the general economic history of metropolitan Chicago are Berry et al. (1976), Solomon and Bilbija (1959), Cutler (1982), Mayer and Wade (1969), and McDonald (1984). The interested reader should consult these works. Mayer and Wade (1969) is notable as a remarkable photographic record of the economic history of metropolitan Chicago. In the field of regional economics there are three alternative concepts which are used to define regions: the homogeneous region, the nodal region, and the planning region (see Richardson, 1978). The homogeneous region is thought of as a point in space. The focus of efforts to model a homogeneous region is on its macro-economic features (imports and exports, industrial composition, unemployment rate, investment and rate of economic

growth, etc.). It is assumed that the important characteristics of a regional economy can be captured by the use of macroeconomic analysis applied at the subnational level. Metropolitan Chicago has often been considered a region in this sense; a recent example of a regional econometric model for metropolitan Chicago is provided by Duobinis (1981).

This approach obviously ignores the spatial patterns of economic activity within the metropolitan area. In the concept of the nodal region, the interdependence of the different components within the region are emphasized. Nodal regions are composed of heterogeneous units that are closely interrelated by flows of population, goods and services, communications, and traffic. Further, these flows tend to polarize toward a dominant center, usually a large city or the central business district (CBD) of a large city. Metropolitan Chicago clearly is a good example of a nodal region; its constituent parts (CBD, the rest of the city, and suburban ring) are very different, but they are closely interrelated. Indeed, the nodal region is normally the model used to study the economy of metropolitan Chicago. (See McDonald, 1979, 1984 for extensive discussions of such studies.) Lastly, the concept of the planning region is based on the notion that a region can be defined in terms of coherence and unity of economic decision making. In this essay, all three concepts of region will be used at different points to discuss the economy of metropolitan Chicago.

2. The major sectors of employment are construction; manufacturing; transportation, communications, and utilities; wholesale trade; retail trade; finance, insurance, and real estate; services; and government. This is the U.S. Department of Commerce one-digit Standard Industrial Classification (SIC) system.

3. The conclusions in this paragraph are based on an empirical study conducted by the second author of the three related incubator hypotheses. This study used the Northeastern Illinois Planning Commission (1965) data described in the text. Areas near the central business district had relatively large firm birth rates of relocation into them. Areas near the central business district also had high rates of out-migration of firms relative to in-migration and low rates of firm deaths relative to out-migration. Taken together, these findings are consistent with the incubator hypothesis. The empirical results of this study are available from John McDonald upon request. More studies of the incubator hypothesis are needed. If it is confirmed that the central city is a good incubator for new firms, then policy should seek to expoit that advantage. Other areas in the SMSA that are good incubators should also be identified and made part of a comprehensive economic growth strategy for the metropolitan area.

4. See Solomon (1980) for general studies of post-industrial cities and suburbs.

5. Consider a numerical example in a form similar to the "prisoner's dilemma" game. Suppose the metropolitan area has two counties, Cook and DuPage, and each county can pursue three kinds of economic development

Table 6–9. Local Economic Development Game

		DuPage County		
		Do Nothing	Draw Firms from Cook	Attract New Jobs
	Do nothing	200[a]	300	250
		500	400	500
Cook	Draw firms	100	200	150
County	from DuPage	600	500	600
	Attract new	200	300	250
	jobs	550	450	550

[a] The top number is jobs in DuPage County; the bottom number is jobs in Cook County.

strategies: (1) do nothing, (2) try to draw firms away from the other county (using tax breaks, ets.), and (3) engage in efforts to assist existing firms in the county to grow and attract new business. Table 6–9 shows the outcomes in terms of the number of jobs in each county for the nine possible combinations of strategies. If both counties do nothing, Cook has 500 jobs and DuPage 200 jobs. If the counties only try to draw firms away from each other, their efforts cancel out (and are wasted). If only one county tries to draw firms away from the other, 100 jobs will move. If that county instead engages in efforts to assist existing firms to grow and to attract new business, 50 new jobs will be created. It is harder to have success with these creative efforts than it is to simply draw firms away from the adjacent county. The rest of the elements in Table 6–9 are filled in, using these assumptions. For example, if DuPage County engages in efforts to attract business from Cook County while Cook works to attract new firms, the net result is 300 (200 + 100) jobs in DuPage and 450 jobs (500 − 100 + 50) in Cook. The message from this example is simple; the metropolitan area has more total jobs (250 + 550 = 800) if *both* counties work to attract new firms and assist existing firms to grow. But *each* county has a stronger incentive to go after the jobs in its sister county because that strategy leads to more jobs in that county *regardless* of what strategy is followed by the other county. This is the dilemma of the game of local economic development. What can be done about this inherent problem? We believe that there is an important role for political leadership here. We need leaders who can see the possibilities for the metropolitan area, and we need incentives for local policies to be cooperative rather than competitive.

REFERENCES

Berry, B., et al. 1976. *Chicago: Transformations of an Urban System.* Cambridge, Mass.: Ballinger.

Chicago Area Transportation Study. 1959. *Chicago Area Transportation Study: Final Report,* Vol. 1. Chicago: Chicago Area Transportation Study.

Christian, C., and S. Bennett. 1973. "Industrial Relocation from the Black Community of Chicago." *Growth and Change* 4:14–20.

City of Chicago Department of City Planning. 1961. *Industrial Movements and Expansions, 1947–1957.* Chicago: Department of City Planning.

Cutler, I. 1982. *Chicago: Metropolis of the Mid-Continent,* 3rd ed. Dubuque, Iowa: Kendall/Hunt.

Duobinis, S. 1981. "An Econometric Model of the Chicago Standard Metropolitan Statistical Area." *Journal of Regional Science* 21:293–319.

Hoch, I. 1959. *Economic Activity Forecast for the Chicago Region: Final Report.* Chicago: Chicago Area Transportation Study.

McDonald, J. 1979. *Economic Analysis of an Urban Housing Market.* New York: Academic Press.

———. 1984. *Employment Location and Industrial Land Use in Metropolitan Chicago.* Champaign, Ill.: Stipes.

———. 1989. "Econometric Studies of Urban Population Density: A Survey." *Journal of Urban Economics,* forthcoming.

Mayer, H., and R. Wade. 1969. *Chicago: Growth of a Metropolis.* Chicago: University of Chicago Press.

Mayor's Committee for Economic and Cultural Development of Chicago. 1966. *Mid-Chicago Economic Development Study.* Chicago: City of Chicago.

Mayor's Council of Manpower and Economic Advisors. 1974. *Chicago's Economy.* Chicago: City of Chicago.

Melvin, E. 1965. "Factors Relating to Recent Industrial Movements and Expansions in the Chicago Area." *Bulletin of the Illinois Geographical Society* 8:1–10.

Meyer, J., J. Kain, and M. Wohl. 1965. *The Urban Transportation Problem.* Cambridge: Harvard University Press.

Nealon, M. 1978. *The Movement of Firms in the Chicago Area.* Chicago: First National Bank.

Northeastern Illinois Planning Commission. 1965. *Metropolitan Guidelines, Phase One: Background Documents, Industrial Development.* Chicago: Northeastern Illinois Planning Commission.

Norton, R. 1979. *City Life-Cycles and American Urban Policy.* New York: Academic Press.

Richardson, H. 1978. *Regional Economics.* Urbana: University of Illinois Press.

Solomon, A., ed. 1980. *The Prospective City.* Cambridge: MIT Press.

Solomon, E., and Z. Bilbija. 1959. *Metropolitan Chicago: An Economic Analysis.* Glencoe, Ill.: The Free Press.

State of Illinois, Department of Labor. 1984. *Where Workers Work.* Chicago: State of Illinois, Department of Labor.

U.S. Department of Commerce, Bureau of the Census. 1947, 1954, 1958, 1963, 1968, 1972, 1977, 1982. *Census of Manufactures.* Washington, D.C.: U.S. Government Printing Office.

————. 1947, 1954, 1958, 1963, 1967. *Census of Business.* Washington, D.C.: U.S. Government Printing Office.

————. 1972, 1977, 1982. *Census of Retail Trade.* Washington, D.C.: U.S. Government Printing Office.

————. 1972, 1977, 1982. *Census of Wholesale Trade.* Washington, D.C.: U.S. Government Printing Office.

U.S. Department of Commerce, Bureau of Economic Analysis. 1982. Data requested by authors.

Williamson, H., Jr. 1969. *An Empirical Analysis of the Movement of Manufacturing Firms in the Chicago Metropolitan Area.* Ph.D. dissertation, Yale University.

Political Change in the City: Black Politics in Chicago, 1871–1987

7

Michael B. Preston

One of the most significant developments in the political history of the Chicago metropolitan area, especially during the second half of the twentieth century, has been the emergence of blacks as a potent political force in the city of Chicago. It is a story that will rank in importance with that of the immigrants' rise to political power in the early and middle 1900s. It is too early to say anything definitive about the era of black political domination in Chicago, but one thing is clear: its eventual shape and ultimate impact will depend, in part, upon factors outside the boundaries of the city, as well as within it.

Harold Washington's election in 1983 as the first black mayor of the city of Chicago and his subsequent reelection in 1987 dramatically changed the political landscape in Chicago and is likely to have a significant impact on the politics of the metropolitan region as well as the state. As mayor of the city of Chicago, he had to deal with the various ethnic constituencies within the city, as all other mayors have had to do in the past. However, he also had to confront an imposing force in metropolitan and state politics with which earlier mayors did not have to deal: the suburbs. Further compounding the situation is the fact that the factional splintering of the once formidable Chicago machine meant that the mayor had to confront this imposing new political force under a severe handicap.

To address this dimension of the restructured political configuration in Illinois, we begin with a brief political history of blacks in Chicago. Only by recounting this history can we understand the origins of the racial splintering that paralyzed the city's political machinery in the 1980s and promises to handicap its future relations with other forces in the state and nation. We begin with an overview of black political history in Chicago up to the Daley years. Then we examine the underpinnings of the growing disaffection between the Democratic machine and its black constituents during the Daley and post-Daley era. Finally, we examine the Washington administration, with a particular emphasis on its relations with the remnants of the Daley machine. In conclusion, we talk about what this means for Chicago's relations with other forces in its political environment.

Before we begin our overview, it is useful to make several general observations about black politics in Chicago. Chicago has been called by many people the most political city in the world. In many respects this climate has provided fertile grounds for the development of aspiring black political leaders. Chicago has had black elected officials as far back as 1871, when the first black was elected at large from the city as a county commissioner. In 1928 Chicago also elected the first northern black congressman. Indeed, from the city's Republican era (1871–1930) through the Democratic era (1931–1987), blacks have been elected to city, county, state, and federal offices. In 1987, two of the most prominent black politicians in America resided in Chicago: Harold Washington, the city's first black mayor, and the Reverend Jesse Jackson, the country's first serious black candidate for president of the United States. Black political representation in Chicago has been enhanced because of their strong allegiance and loyalty to the Republican and Democratic parties.

Black political representation, however, has not always been readily translated into political influence. The experience of blacks has differed in important ways from that of the white ethnics who dominated Chicago politics for much of this century. Five patterns have emerged since the late 1800s that set the stage for black political development through 1983:

1. Party identification and loyalty have been consistently given to the party that has more closely aligned itself with civil rights issues important to black voters;
2. The increase in black political representation in both the Republican and Democratic era seldom led to more influence for the black community;
3. Black political leadership, whether based on clientele, interest group, or machine politics, has meant allegiance to a powerful white patron first and the black community second;
4. Black politicians were not allowed during either era to establish black independent power bases; and
5. While many black politicians were successful in fighting for civil

and political rights for blacks, they had to do so within the confines of the political structures of the time. The result has been a defensive, often conservative politics, based on what was possible rather than what was needed (Branham, 1984:370–71).

The following sections develop these points more fully and provide insight into how they contributed to the overt racial strife that has characterized Chicago politics for the past decade.

Black Politics in Chicago, 1871–1955

Today it is difficult to associate politics in Chicago with anything but the Democratic party. It is certainly true that the Democrats have exerted virtually uninterrupted control over city government since the election of Anton Cermack as mayor in 1931 (Wilson, 1960:77). Yet there was a time when the Republican party ruled Chicago. Considering today's general perception of Democrats as embracers of civil rights and Republicans as defenders of the status quo, it is even more surprising to learn that blacks provided a substantial and loyal portion of the Republican vote from Reconstruction through the New Deal. There are several events, elections, and trends during the Republican era (that is, Chicago politics before 1931) which should be noted because they help set the stage for later black developments in politics.

Black identification with the Republican party had its roots in the Civil War. The Republican party was the party of Lincoln, the author of the Emancipation Proclamation. The bond between blacks and the Republican party engendered by a shared philosophy on the subject of slavery solidified when blacks began to attain positions of political power as members of the party.

The first black to be elected at large from the city—or for that matter, to any public office in Cook County—was a Republican. John Jones was elected as a county commissioner in 1871. Other black Republicans were elected to countywide offices also, but only after a lapse of twenty-two years (Gosnell, 1935:82–83). Theodore W. Jones was elected a representative of the county board in 1894, and Edwin H. Wright was elected to the same position two years later. After Wright, who is considered the "father of modern black politics" (Branham, 1983:6), black candidates were unsuccessful until 1904, when Oscar DePriest was elected (Gosnell, 1935:83). Those electoral successes occurred—despite the fact that only 3 percent of the city's population was black—because, before 1908, county commissioners were elected by slate. Slates were nominated at party conventions, so that the vote was party-based and not based on the race of a particular individual. With the passage of the so-called "Primary Law" in 1908, however, county commissioners were nominated in the party primary. After 1910, no blacks were elected to county offices until 1938 (Branham, 1984:373).

Aldermanic elections, however, were an entirely different matter. Oscar DePriest was elected the first black alderman in 1915, and, after many ups and downs in his political fortunes, he eventually served as the nation's first northern black congressman (Gosnell, 1935:180). By 1918, the black electorate was able to put another black candidate into office. When ward lines were redrawn in 1921, two wards (the second and the third) were each able to elect a black alderman (Wilson, 1960:78).

By 1900, half the city's black population lived in three contiguous South Side wards (Branham, 1983:6). James Q. Wilson attributes the ability to elect black aldermanic candidates in the early 1900s as at least partly a result of this demographic happenstance. In his book *Negro Politics: The Search for Leadership,* he states: "Of great importance for the political history of Chicago was the fact that the Negro population was, from the first, concentrated in contiguous, all-Negro tracts which grew by peripheral expansion . . . this meant that as early as 1915, the Negroes constituted a majority of one ward" (1960:77). In addition, more and more blacks were coming to Chicago. The city's black population more than doubled in five years. It grew from 50,000 in 1915 to 109,000 by 1920. In the decade between 1910 and 1920, the black population increased by 148.2 percent (Preston, 1979:26).

Perhaps the most striking thing about the black vote in Chicago was its consistency despite the virtual absence of rewards. Although passed over for the requisite patronage benefits due them in view of their overwhelming support for the Republican party, blacks continued to provide Republicans with unwavering support. The irony of this situation is embodied in the personage of William "Big Bill" Thompson. Although Thompson recognized the political significance of the black vote and brought a fair number of blacks into the patronage system, the gains made by blacks were not commensurate with the level of support they extended to Thompson.

In his first election as mayor, Thompson carried 73 percent of the city's black vote. In 1919, that percentage soared to 91 percent (Preston, 1979:26) and remained high in 1926 and 1931, when Thompson captured around 85 percent of the black vote in Chicago (Gosnell, 1935:27, 44, 58). Black support was not limited to Thompson personally; from 1918 to 1932, with the exception of the 1923 campaign when Thompson was not a candidate, the black electorate supported

Republican candidates with 66 percent or more of their vote. And in 1931—when the rest of the city's support for Thompson dropped off by 14 percent—Thompson won 82 percent of the vote in the black second and third wards (Gosnell, 1935:27, 44, 58). The reasons for his success among black voters were Thompson's flamboyant personality and flair for fiery oratory. These caught the attention of the black electorate. His passionate diatribes against those who ignored the significance of the black community's support were a source of great solace to black voters.

During this period, then, black identification with the Republican party, which was rooted in the Civil War, was nurtured by the election of black Republicans to various public offices. Blacks found a candidate who recognized their potential for political support in William Hale Thompson and supported him in great numbers. But during this period, black-white relations were not as harmonious as might be surmised from the number of blacks elected to office. The 1919 race riot was explosive evidence of the underlying strains partly caused by black politicians operating within a system which was not structured to meet the needs of the black community. In order to gain power, blacks accommodated themselves to rules set out by white bosses. By operating within the political system in Chicago—and thus becoming a part of it—blacks could not challenge that system with any great degree of force. Their electoral power was directed toward maintaining the status quo, toward keeping the same people in office. As a result little changed.

While blacks continued to support Thompson in 1931, wholesale shifts to the Democratic party by other voters were occurring. Anton Cermack, the "father of the modern Democratic machine" (Branham, 1983:6) was elected in 1931. When Cermack was assassinated in 1933, another Democrat, Edward J. Kelly, aggressively courted the black vote. Kelly appointed the first black member of the school board and worked closely with the city's two black aldermen. Despite Kelly's overtures to blacks, however, he never received more than 56 percent of the black vote in his years as mayor from 1933 to 1946. Martin Kennelly, the reform-oriented Democratic mayor from 1947 to 1955, fared no better with black voters; he garnered only 51 percent of the black vote (Grimshaw, 1980:chapter 2).

The next stage in the development of black politics in Chicago might be dubbed the "sub-machine" era, when blacks not only worked with the machine but became part of it in the form of a sub-machine. William L. Dawson was first elected Republican alderman of the second ward in 1935. His rise to the top of the machine-dominated political power structure, however, came about only after he — with the active support of Mayor Edward Kelly — entered the Democratic party as committeeman of the second ward in 1939 (Wilson, 1960:78). Thus, 1939 marks the start of the black Democratic "sub-machine." James Q. Wilson explains the elements necessary to the building of the black sub-machine:

> The existence of a Negro machine, as in Chicago, is dependent upon the existence of a white machine. Machine politics requires a centralization of leadership, a sizable stock of tangible incentives with which to reward contributors, a large group of people in the city who would be attracted by kinds of rewards a political machine can distribute and (usually) a ward district system of selecting party leaders, aldermen and candidates for public office. The machine can flourish in the Negro wards largely because of the status and needs of the Negro. . . . Low paying jobs, political favors, and material assistance are still as important to many Negroes as they once were to foreign born whites [1960:23, 54].

William Dawson used these needs for tangible rewards to his own advantage. After modest early electoral success during the 1940s, Dawson was winning by huge margins during the 1950s. In the 1958 congressional election, he lost only 5 of 350 precincts in his district (Wilson, 1960:66). As Wilson notes, "Dawson, by virtue of his considerable political skill, the patronage placed at his disposal and a favorable public opinion, not only secured his own position but created a network of obligations and loyalties which brought under his control the organization of five or six Negro wards" (1960:50).

This network of influence was aptly demonstrated by Dawson's ability to elect his own candidates. By the mid-1950s, he had his own followers at the head of each of the largest ward committees in the predominantly black areas of the city (Wilson, 1960:50). In 1955, Dawson was one of the leaders who persuaded the County Central Committee to drop Mayor Martin Kennelly and slate Richard J. Daley instead. Daley's majority of about 125,000 votes was produced largely by the black wards (Wilson, 1960:81).

The Roots of Black Independence: The Daley and Post-Daley Era

Just when it seemed Dawson had achieved unprecedented control over the black sub-machine, his political influence within the Daley machine began to wane. This is a significant development in Chicago's political history because it had important implications for the political fortunes of Chicago blacks within the machine and, ultimately, for the future of the machine itself. It is ironic that the rift between blacks and Chicago Democrats began in the Daley era because a major source of Daley's strength was the overwhelming support of the black wards. During his entire career, Daley received an average of over 75 percent of the vote in these wards.

While this figure undoubtedly indicates a high level of black support for the Daley machine, William Grimshaw makes a compelling case for the gradual dissipation of black support during the latter half of Daley's term in office—a decline that reflected growing strains between Daley and his black constituents (1979:8–14). He points out that Daley had a decreasing plurality in every ward of the city—including his own—but the decline was more drastic in the city's predominantly black wards. Grimshaw divides the Daley reign into three distinct phases: (1) 1955–63, when Daley's primary base support was located in the inner city; (2) 1966–69, when the machine began to lose black support as its primary base shifted toward the white outer-city wards; and (3) 1970–75, when there was a radical transformation of the machine's organizational structure.

The impact of those shifts can be seen in changes in the overall ranking of the black wards in terms of their support for Daley. In 1955, all the city's black wards were in the top fifteen (in terms of Daley's plurality); by 1975, only one-half of the inner-city wards remained among the top fifteen (Grimshaw, 1979:7). At the core of these changes in black loyalties were the racist overtones in the policies of the Daley machine, especially in the areas of public safety, public employment, and public housing. Daley's policies kept black voters away from the polls, if not away from Daley himself.

The Racial Shift Thesis

Ralph Whitehead, Jr., (1977) has advanced what he terms a "racial shift" thesis to explain the evolving relationship between the Daley machine and its black supporters. Whitehead contends that the machine's support was never citywide before 1966 and that, after his second election, Daley shifted away from his initial base of support, which was the inner city. Pro-machine voting percentages of 85 percent were not uncommon in those wards and were sufficient to offset losses in the outer ones. Daley's close reelection in 1963, in which the black vote was crucial to the machine's victory, was a critical turning point in the machine's relationship to its black constituency. The narrow margin of Daley's victory, combined with other developments, led Daley to broaden his electoral support to embrace white ethnics in the outer wards, where they had moved to escape the influx of blacks.

To do this, Daley instituted the "politics of property values and potholes." That is, he made sure that garbage was picked up and that streets were clean and repaired. And he held the line on property taxes. As these wards became more white and lower-middle class, Daley put in new organizational personnel and beefed up the benefits. By 1970 the Daley strategy had succeeded. As the vote margins in the black wards were slipping, they were being offset by blue-collar votes in the outer wards.

Once Daley had solidified his base, he no longer needed Dawson, whose independent power base within the machine was viewed uneasily by the Daley cohort. Thus, rather than being able to capitalize on his growing influence within the black community, Dawson was stripped of his power (Whitehead, 1977). Blacks never received the spoils of the victories to which they contributed; the spoils, if they had been forthcoming, would have made it more difficult for the Daley machine to solidify the support of the white ethnic communities it so earnestly sought.

This tension contributed to Daley's evolving strategy of shifting his electoral base. But other factors also contributed to this shift — factors that led Daley to question the continued support of the black community. Most important among these was the civil rights revolution ushered in by Reverend Martin Luther King, Jr. It raised the consciousness of blacks about the indignities they had suffered at the hands of the Daley machine. During this period, blacks began to protest against police brutality, segregated housing, and employment discrimination.

Black dissatisfaction with Mayor Daley was heightened when Daley attempted to punish Congressman Ralph Metcalfe for his criticism of police brutality in Chicago. Without touching bases with representatives of the black community, Daley slated one of his black cabinet members, Edwin France, to run against Metcalfe in the primary. Blacks rejected France for the congressional seat. The issue of police brutality, and the shooting death of Black Panther leader Fred Hampton by police, further incited blacks and led to an increasing number of black anti-machine voters by 1975. Indeed, while only 19.5 percent of blacks voted against the machine in 1955, the number had climbed to 51.8 percent by 1975 (see Table 7–1).

Table 7-1. Anti-Machine Vote in Black Wards

Year	Votes for Machine Candidate	Votes Against Machine Candidate	Percent Against in Black Wards	Percent Against Machine All Wards
1955	73,336	17,775	19.5	51.0
1975	85,668	92,090	51.8	42.2
1977	71,427	74,757	51.1	48.9
1979	74,805	110,683	59.7	51.0

Source: *Chicago Reporter*, 1979.

Post-Daley Developments

The failure of blacks to receive their due from the Daley machine, and the impact of the civil rights movement upon blacks' demands for progress in political, social, and economic matters, combined with the ethnic biases of the Daley machine's hierarchy to produce a shift in the organization's electoral strategy. What would have happened if greater efforts had been made to integrate blacks into the machine cannot be known. What is interesting, however, is that the conflicts between blacks and the machine politicians did not spawn an independent black movement after Daley's death, when the machine began to splinter. Blacks remained within the Democratic party. Despite this, the die was cast during this period for unprecedented tumult within the machine, caused in large part by the black community's increasing independence from the machine.

Nowhere can this be seen more clearly than in the events immediately following Daley's death. In a rebuke to Wilson Frost, a black Democratic loyalist who as vice-mayor was arguably in line to succeed Daley, the city council appointed Michael Bilandic, who later won a special mayoral election in 1977. In 1979, however, Bilandic was challenged and defeated by Jane Byrne, a former loyalist turned reformer. Bilandic's defeat in the 1979 primary election was one of the major political upsets in the nation's history. Black voters gave Byrne almost 60 percent of their votes in the primary, as can be seen in Table 7-2.

Any doubt that a new, more independently minded black voter had emerged in Chicago was dispelled by the black community's role in Byrne's primary upset. At the same time, this election was only the most visible manifestation of increasing black dissatisfaction with the white-dominated Chicago machine. The anti-machine vote in the black wards had been notable throughout the 1970s (see Table 7-1). Since

Table 7–2. Voting in Predominantly Black Wards[a] in 1979 Mayoral Primary Elections

Percent of Turnout Voting Democratic	Bilandic Votes		Byrne Votes	
	Total	Percent	Total	Percent
98.2	106,995	42	146,468	58

[a] Includes all wards with a black majority: wards 2, 3, 4, 5, 6, 7, 8, 9, 10, 15, 16, 17, 20, 21, 24, 27, 28, 29, 34, 37.
Source: Unofficial returns for 1979 Mayoral Election, *Chicago Sun-Times*, April 5, 1979.

1975, black wards have turned in larger anti-machine voting percentages than non-black wards. Black independence was further demonstrated in the 1980 Illinois primary. Jane Byrne's choices for political office were soundly defeated in the black wards. The anti-Byrne sentiment in the black community was due to Byrne's failure to fulfill a variety of campaign promises and her insensitivity to black concerns in a variety of areas, notably some key personnel appointments and practices. She also failed to restructure the extant patronage system in order to provide more and better jobs to the black community. Instead, after her election she began to dominate rather than dismantle the system. Moreover, there was no change in the quality or quantity of patronage jobs available to blacks. Probably the most serious blow to black voters was the realization that Byrne was neither anti-machine nor a reformer. After her election, she embraced the very machine politicians whom she had criticized earlier. The results of the 1980 primary election reflected their degree of dissatisfaction.

The Washington Era

The realization that the interests of the black community were once again thwarted led black leaders to challenge the machine directly. Bolstered by a strong turnout in the 1982 gubernatorial election— one that almost led to a stunning upset by Adlai Stevenson III— black leaders drafted Harold Washington to run in the 1983 primary, registered 200,000 new black voters, and mobilized the black vote to an unprecedented degree. In a three-way primary, Washington won with 37 percent of the vote. In the end, 78 percent of the registered black voters voted and 73 percent voted for Washington (see Table 7–3 for the mayoral primary results). This was particularly notable in that he was opposed by 18 of the 23 black state legislators and 9 of the 15 black aldermen.

Table 7–3. Chicago 1983 Democratic Mayoral Primary Results

	Vote					
	Washington		Byrne		Daley	
Ward Type	Total	Percent	Total	Percent	Total	Percent
Black						
Majority	335,369	78	66,614	16	27,521	6
Black						
Plurality	17,783	32	16,193	30	20,603	38
Hispanic						
Majority	8,569	17	24,454	47	18,582	36
Hispanic						
Plurality	4,206	12	18,473	50	14,110	38
Lakefront	23,717	21	51,984	45	38,879	34
Other	33,045	8	210,387	45	224,215	47
Total City	422,689	37	388,105	33	343,910	30

Source: Data reported in Preston, 1983:486–88.

In one of the most bitter campaigns in Chicago's colorful political history, Harold Washington won the 1983 mayoral election over a previously unknown Republican, with 51.4 percent of the vote. The city had an unprecedented turnout rate of 82 percent. The turnout in the black wards was even higher, 83.68 percent. No black ward had a turnout of less than 73 percent, and blacks gave Washington 96 percent of their vote. Washington also captured over 50 percent of the Hispanic vote.

After the election, Mayor-elect Harold Washington dubbed the Chicago machine "a mortally wounded animal." The results of both the primary and general election would certainly lead one to believe he was correct. Not only did Harold Washington defeat the machine candidate (Jane Bryne) in the primary, but other machine candidates in several wards lost decisively. The tendency to reject machine-endorsed candidates was especially evident in the largely black wards. Given these events, it is easy to understand why most political analysts predicted no insurmountable obstacles for Washington in his dealings with the city council. The prognosis was encouraging. Analysts observed that Washington had a coalition of 16 black aldermen and 4 white independents who campaigned for him after the primary. In addition, they pointed out at least nominal commitment from the Democratic ward organization of 10 or more white aldermen. Hidden among all of these promising reports, however, were two sentences in a *Chicago Tribune* editorial that sounded a cautionary note: "This is Chicago's first post-machine city council. And no one knows how the creature will act."

Its unpredictability soon became obvious. After a prolonged dispute with the remnants of the machine, Washington adjourned his first council meeting and walked out along with 21 aldermen. The remaining 29 aldermen, under the leadership of Edward R. Vrdolyak and Edward Burke, voted on resolutions creating a new system of city council leadership and rules. The 29 voted to expand the number of council committees from 20 to 37 and gave all but 3 council committee chairs to white machine stalwarts opposed to the mayor. With the Vrdolyak-Burke forces in charge of such key committees as zoning, police and fire, and finances, they could thwart the mayor's efforts to make appointments while exerting considerable control over the flow of legislation. Even more important were the rule changes voted in by the so called "Vrdolyak 29." Among the most significant of these was one that required a two-thirds vote to force proposed legislation out of council committees.

Weeks after this debacle, the mayor's forces and the Vrdolyak 29 were still locked in a bitter dispute over the reorganization plan. Circuit Judge James C. Murray ruled that Vrdolyak and his supporters acted legally in approving the chair appointments and rule changes; but he also ruled that the mayor could veto spending resolutions for committees. The inability of both forces to come to some agreement during repeated negotiation attempts, especially over the issue of who would lead the finance committee, kept council business at a standstill. The Illinois Supreme Court refused to rule on the city council dispute, effectively upholding the legislative dominance of the Vrdolyak-Burke coalition.

The result of these developments was that although Washington was elected, he was unable to govern. The Vrdolyak-Burke faction of the machine controlled the city council and held hostage Washington's administrative appointments and legislative initiatives. This stalemate lasted three years and ended only when a federal court ordered a ward redistricting in the city after a successful lawsuit by black and Hispanic voters. The subsequent special election permitted Washington forces to capture 4 additional seats, knotting the city council at 25 on both sides and giving Washington the tie-breaking vote. After one last court battle, initiated by the Vrdolyak faction, Washington was able to reorganize and work with the city council. The infamous "Council Wars" seemed to be over.

The respite was brief, however, as the conclusion of the "Council Wars" was on the eve of the 1987 mayoral election. Within weeks of the machine's legal challenge to Washington's reorganization of the council, machine stalwarts were circulating petitions to hold a referendum on whether the mayoral election should be nonpartisan. This format would have required a runoff between the top two candidates in the primary election—a runoff the white ethnics did not believe Washington could win. The anomalous nature of a nonpartisan mayoral election in Chicago notwithstanding, astute legal maneuvering by Washington kept the referendum off the ballot. But the "Mayoral Wars" had begun.

Chess-like maneuvering before the 1987 mayoral primary led Washington to refrain from announcing whether he would run as an independent or a Democrat until just before the filing date. He ultimately filed to run in the Democratic primary. Two of the white candidates elected to run as Independents, leaving Washington to go one-on-one with former mayor Jane Byrne in the Democratic primary. Washington won the primary with a healthy 53.1 percent of the vote. The vote was largely along racial lines, with Washington getting 98 percent of the vote in the black wards and Byrne getting 87 percent of the vote in the white wards. Washington improved his 1983 showing in the more liberal lakefront wards and among Hispanics.

This victory still left Washington to face the white candidates, Edward Vrdolyak (the Solidarity party candidate), Thomas Hynes (the Chicago First party candidate), and Donald Haider (the Republican party candidate), in the general election. Haider was never a significant factor in the race, and intense pressure was brought to bear on the other candidates to force one to withdraw. Hynes finally withdrew two days before the election but to no avail. Washington prevailed again, with over 53 percent of the vote.

One of the most significant aftermaths of the election was the shift of council control to Mayor Washington. Before the 1987 election, the council split showed pro-Washington forces with 25 votes while the anti-Washington faction had 25 votes. The mayor used his vote to break the tie. On April 17, Mayor Washington and his allies in the city council, backed by desertions from Burke's bloc, rolled to an overwhelming 40–9 victory in their reorganization of the city council. They dumped opponents from most leadership posts. Some former opponents were given new posts or allowed to keep their old ones, but all committees had Washington majorities.

The reelection of Harold Washington in the general election and the election of new pro-Washington aldermen signaled the beginning of a new era within the city. Another factor fostering a more peaceful coexistence within the city and the party was the resignation of Edward

Vrdolyak as Cook County party chairman. He was replaced by George Dunne, who was backed for the job by Mayor Washington. All of this portends well for harmony within the city. At the same time, the history of the Vrdolyak-Burke faction suggests that they will not accept easily their losses within the city. "Council Wars" and their aftermath have already spilled over into state and metropolitan politics, and it may well be that the next theater of the ongoing efforts of old party stalwarts to reassert their power may be played on a larger stage, where the Vrdolyak-Burke faction may hope to find new allies and more favorable terrain.

Chicago and Its Political Environment in the Washington Era

In addition to the tumult just noted, the 1983 election of Harold Washington as mayor of Chicago had political consequences beyond the city itself. One was a split in the Chicago delegation in Springfield that led to a loss of influence for the mayor and the city of Chicago. White Chicago state legislators took their signals from their Cook County Democratic chairman, Edward Vrdolyak, while black legislators took their signals from the mayor. This was in stark contrast to the situation under Mayor Daley, when the high level of cohesiveness within the Chicago bloc enabled the city to exercise disproportionate influence within the state legislature. This cleavage within the Chicago Democratic contingent during an era of population and economic losses only compounded the city's political problems in the state legislature and further contributed to the political refiguration of state forces.

One manifestation of the political rupturing of the city along racial lines has been the efforts by the white ethnic bloc within the city to search for common ground with suburban political leaders. In their battle to save Park Superintendent Edmund Kelly's job, which controls a large number of patronage jobs, the Vrdolyak-Burke faction negotiated an understanding with some suburban Republican leaders that may have long-term implications for the future of political relations between the city and its suburban collar. In exchange for state legislation securing Kelly's job, the white Chicago legislators, mostly in the General Assembly, agreed to support legislation creating a regional airport authority to govern O'Hare airport, which has traditionally been run by the city. The plan only fell through when a number of white Chicago Democrats in the state senate balked at the O'Hare giveaway.

Despite the failure of these initial efforts to broaden the battlefield upon which intracity racial battles are waged, the possibility for a white ethnic-suburban coalition remains, and it can portend only ill for the welfare of the city as a whole if it develops. Airport issues, such as noise control and expansion, remain fertile ground for the nurturing of such a coalition, largely because the airport is controlled by the city while the suburbs absorb many of its undesirable diseconomies. Other areas, however, include the Regional Transportation Authority and major state-subsidized building projects, such as the McCormick Place expansion and the construction of different sports complexes. The defection of the white ethnic bloc can only enhance the power of the governor, as well as the burgeoning suburban delegation, in matters affecting the welfare of the city. This, of course, makes more difficult the job of the mayor of Chicago, whose position in the state has already been eroded by population losses, the loss of patronage power, and continued economic diffusion.

Equally ominous was Vrdolyak's announcement that he was converting to the Republican party. This conversion might have little impact on the political makeup of the city government. However, a traditional source of political strength for Chicago mayors over the past fifty years has been their ability to generate large vote totals in the city and Cook County for Democratic presidential and gubernatorial candidates. Population shifts have already reduced their ability to match vote totals of several decades ago. To the extent that Vrdolyak is able to develop a viable Republican organization in the Southwest Side and Northwest Side white ethnic strongholds, the ability of the mayor to perform as a powerful vote broker in state and national elections will be further eroded—so will the political position of Chicago, the city which long boasted that it put John F. Kennedy "over the top" in the 1960 election.

These possibilities are obviously not inevitable, although Washington's untimely death will make them more difficult to forestall. There are a variety of steps that future mayors of Chicago can take. First, future mayors will have to make racial and ethnic peace. One way to do this is for the mayor to spread the spoils of his/her office more widely, keeping in mind the knowledge that the Daley machine's failure to do this contributed mightily to the loss of its black constituency. Washington moved in this direction in the latest reorganization of the city council. Cooperative white ethnic politicians were left as chairs of some of their old council committees, while others were given new committee chairs or positions on important committees.

Future strategies for working with ethnic communities can take several approaches. First, the mayor should push "linked development" programs in which white ethnics have a great deal of interest. Linked development means asking contractors to contribute money for neighborhood improvements in areas where development is likely to have an adverse impact. Second, if future mayors can hold the line on taxes, they will satisfy both black and white homeowners. Third, they should adopt a policy of support for various ethnic groups in foreign countries. Washington was successful in his support for immigration rights of Soviet Jews, his support for the Solidarity party in Poland, and his policy of not reporting undocumented workers to immigration authorities under current conditions. Finally, working on behalf of federal legislation to help guarantee minimum resale values for people with homes in changing neighborhoods would let these communities know that the mayor is concerned about their interests.

If these efforts are successful, they should help unify the Chicago legislative delegation in Springfield. But the mayor should not be content with merely making peace within the city limits. He/she should take the lead in forging a coalition with suburban political leaders to further a metropolitan agenda. The careful identification of shared interests can form the basis for such cooperative efforts. The goodwill these efforts generate may well spill over into areas where city and suburban interests differ. Such efforts would not only further the interests of the city and the metropolitan region, but would thwart the efforts of those who would seek to exploit the racial cleavages within the city, to its detriment.

Future mayors of Chicago can also seek to protect the interests of the city by maximizing their visibility in the state and nation. As a big-city mayor, he/she can and frequently does speak for other mayors in Illinois and the nation. Washington, for example, visited cities throughout Illinois to push his and their urban agenda in Springfield and Washington. His agenda of more funding for schools and jobs also included a plea to the state and federal governments for a return of a fair share of taxes to the state and region. Such an agenda had much appeal to many downstate mayors. Finally, if the mayor of Chicago can link the plight of Chicago with cities downstate, as well as push the sale of Illinois coal and help for the farmers, the city's interests can be protected. Stated differently, appeals should be based on putting common interest over ideology.

Future mayors can also enhance Chicago's political position by taking great care in backing Democratic gubernatorial and, especially, presidential candidates. If the next president is a Democrat, especially one backed early and supported strongly, the mayor of Chicago will be in a strong position to use his/her influence for the benefit of the city, state, and region. Moreover, it is likely that mayors and other political leaders throughout the state will seek his/her assistance and advice. If the mayor can capitalize on such opportunities, much can be done to shore up Chicago's sagging political fortune as well as stem further losses.

REFERENCES

Branham, Charles. 1983. "A History of Black Politics." *Chicago Journal*, January 19:6.

———. 1984. "Accommodation Politics before the Great Migration." In Melvin G. Holli and Peter d'A. Jones (eds.), *Ethnic Chicago.* Grand Rapids, Mich.: Eerdman.

Gosnell, Harold F. 1935. *Negro Politicians: The Rise of Negro Politics in Chicago.* Chicago: University of Chicago Press.

Grimshaw, William. 1979. *Union Rule: Big City Politics in Transformation.* Lexington, Mass.: Lexington Books.

———. 1980. *Black Politics in Chicago: The Quest for Leadership, 1939–1979.* Chicago: Center for Urban Policy, Loyola University.

Preston, Michael B. 1979. "Black Machine Politics in the Post-Daley Era." In *The Chicago Political Papers.* Urbana, Ill.: Institute of Government and Public Affairs.

———. 1983. "The Election of Harold Washington: Black Voting Patterns in the 1983 Chicago Mayoral Race." *P.S.* (Summer):486–880.

Whitehead, Ralph, Jr. 1977. "The Organizational Man." *The American Scholar* 46(3):351.

Wilson, James Q. 1960. *Negro Politics: The Search for Leadership.* New York: Free Press.

PART IV

Political Manifestations
of Regionalism:
Some Empirical Assessments

Representation, Elections, and Geo-Political Cleavages: The Political Manifestations of Regionalism in Twentieth-Century Illinois

8

Michael W. Frank, Peter F. Nardulli, and Paul M. Green

From earliest history Illinois has seen geography shape its politics. Its geo-political cleavages have not, however, remained constant. The interaction of regional factors with social and economic developments has produced varying political manifestations of regional divisions over time, often with different consequences. The early nineteenth century saw the state's more heavily settled southern section dictating the course of early Illinois politics (see Sutton, chapter 4 herein). Parties were not relevant to governance; rather, the state was run by a group of politicians with southern roots who were committed to the Jeffersonian vision of an agrarian democracy. Before the Civil War, Illinois Democrats—like their national counterparts—split geographically on the slavery issue. Central and northern Illinois Democrats revolted against the southern Illinois, pro-slavery wing of the party. Only the personality and political wizardry of Stephen Douglas held them together. The fledgling Republican party quickly grew into a major political alternative not only because of its anti-slavery stand and the divisiveness of the Democratic party, but also because population migration patterns found northern Illinois growing far more rapidly than southern Illinois (see Atack, chapter 3 herein).

After the Civil War Illinois became a predominantly Republican state. In only a few sections of the state could Democrats produce local victories. Not until immigration patterns made the Democrats dominant in Chicago did the Republicans face any strong opposition in statewide elections. In the New Deal era, both the popularity of Franklin D. Roosevelt and the dense population of Chicago turned Illinois into a highly competitive political state, especially in national elections. State Republican party leaders saw their best hope for political victories resting on a strategy that isolated Chicago, while molding, as best they could, the rest of the state into a cohesive bloc.

The centrality of geo-political cleavages in these various political eras is clear, and the importance of them has been a principal theme in most discussions of Illinois politics. Unfortunately, most of these discussions have been framed in a Chicago-downstate dichotomy. For decades this dichotomy has been used to characterize the political differences in Illinois and to generalize about the attitudinal and cultural diversity of Illinoisans. This dichotomy has been based on a variety of stereotypes concerning life-style, ethnicity, religion, and economic vitality. These stereotypes have some validity, and, for some purposes during periods of Illinois history, it is both useful and meaningful to talk in terms of a Chicago-downstate dichotomy. In other respects, however, this is an overly simplistic depiction of the state's regional mosaic. On the one hand, it overplays the significance of the differences between Chicago and downstate; on the other, it does not do justice to the differences and cultural fissures within these two broad groupings. Moreover, recent decades have seen the emergence of a powerful new regional force in the state's political realm: Chicago's suburban collar.

The subtleties of the state's geo-political structure have shaped the craggy terrain that has characterized Illinois politics for so long. Recent demographic shifts, which have remolded the regional structure, increase the importance of obtaining a refined understanding of this terrain. The newest regional fissure (the suburban collar) has made it more difficult to compromise, satisfy regional needs, and understand the trade-offs necessary to resolve legislative and political impasses. Moreover, these changes come at a time when both political parties have organizational problems and personal and political loyalty is becoming an anachronism. This makes the brokering of regional differences all the more difficult because a strong, broad-based party system is one of the few mechanisms that can effectively bridge regional cleavages.

This chapter outlines and clarifies, in a limited way, the political manifestations of regional cleavages in twentieth-century Illinois. We begin with a discussion of reapportionment and legislative representation. Nowhere is the essence of regional political conflict clearer than in issues involving the allocation of legislative seats and leadership. In these reapportionment battles, the seeds were sown for political conflicts that sprouted long after the reapportionment issue was settled. It was also this long-standing battle which, more than any other political issue, reinforced the Chicago-downstate dichotomy that has dominated discussions of Illinois politics for so long. Next, we turn to an examination of partisan voting patterns in the twentieth century. From presidential voting data aggregated at the county level (with the exception of Chicago and the Cook County suburbs, which we separate), we use similarities in partisan preferences and trends to construct a new picture of regional electoral alignments in the state. We also examine how they have changed over the course of the century. The results challenge the overly simplistic picture of the Chicago-downstate dichotomy that was so strongly etched in people's minds by the decades-long battle over reapportionment—a battle that was a struggle over power as much as policy differences. Next, we use these new regional definitions to examine shifts in the balance of voting power in the state over the course of the century. We conclude with some observations on the implications of our results for Illinois' political map.

Representation, Regionalism, and Reapportionment

The roots of the reapportionment controversy in Illinois lie in the 1870 Illinois constitution. It mandated that legislative districts be based on the principle of equitable statewide representation. For the next thirty years, Illinois legislators reapportioned their district boundaries four times, in 1872, 1882, 1893, and 1901. In the first three instances, census data were used to guide the procedures, and the process was completed with little fuss or furor. In 1901, however, the regional population imbalance in Illinois became so great that reapportionment created a major uproar within the legislature.

Most redistricting conflicts are the result of three conflicting historic themes: territory versus population, geography versus party, and incumbent versus challenger. Although each of these themes was involved in 1901, the controversy boiled down to a statewide reaction to the growth of Chicago. Chicago was becoming a looming giant that most other Illinoisans feared would swallow up the rest of the state.

Both political parties had benefitted from the rapid growth in Chicago's population, but downstate legislators—both Democratic and Republican—were unimpressed with their new big-city allies. Neither longtime southern Illinois Democratic party leaders nor central and northwest Illinois Republican stalwarts were eager to give up their geographic or political power base to newcomers from Chicago. A resolution introduced by state Senator John McKenzie of Jo Daviess

County captured the mood of non-Chicagoans. It proposed a constitutional amendment to limit permanently Cook County's legislative representation to one-third of the members. Bitter debate ensued on McKenzie's resolution. It came within an eyelash of becoming state law, falling short because enough Chicago Republican legislators voted for geographical fairness and personal political interests. Chicago was, after all, solidly Republican during this period.

Nonetheless, from 1901 to 1955 the Illinois legislature refused to reapportion and redistrict its legislative districts in the state, despite the provisions of the 1870 constitution and the growing mismatch between population growth and legislative representation in the General Assembly. The effects of this failure to reapportion can be seen in Table 8–1. The balance between population and legislative representation is fairly good until 1910. The percent imbalance doubled between 1910 and 1930, from a 6 percent deficit to a 14 percent deficit. At its worst point (the 1930s and 1940s), Cook County was shorted eight legislative districts in both the Senate and the House. If the legislature had been correctly apportioned, Cook County would have enjoyed a majority as early as 1930. The legislative imbalances began to be corrected in 1955, several years before the U.S. Supreme Court decision in *Baker v. Carr* (1962). After some of the most grueling negotiations in Illinois' political history, the legislature reached a compromise on reapportionment: the House of Representatives would be apportioned by population, while the Senate would be based on area (see Steiner and Gove, 1962:chapter 4). By 1965, both houses were based on population as a result of the U.S. Supreme Court's decision in the reapportionment cases.

Perhaps no single governmental factor contributed to statewide regional distrust as much as the legislature's blatant disregard of the law and fundamental democratic processes for over half a century. For Chicagoans the state legislature became the chief symptom of a statewide political disease that sought to disfranchise and isolate Illinois' biggest city. The city council became Chicago's critical legislative arena, and the office of alderman was far more coveted than that of state legislator. On the other hand, non-Chicagoans saw the legislature as their political Alamo—a formidable holdout against the onslaught of a continuously growing army of atypical and often strange-speaking Illinoisans living in a small corner of their state.

The ultimate triumph of the "one person, one vote" principle did much to satisfy the legal claims of Chicagoans and their sense of fair play, even if it did nothing to lessen the regional animosities that had raged for over half a century. However, in a bitter twist of irony,

Table 8-1. Trends in the Balance between Population and Legislative Representation in Illinois, 1870–1970

		Illinois Senate					Illinois House of Representatives				
Year	Percent of Illinois in Cook County	Number of Districts in State	Number of Districts in Cook County	Percent of Districts in Cook County	Percentage Imbalance Favoring Areas Outside Cook County	Number of Seats Needed to Adjust Imbalance	Number of Districts in State	Number of Districts in Cook County	Percent of Districts in Cook County	Percentage Imbalance Favoring Areas Outside Cook County	Number of Seats Needed to Adjust Imbalance
1870	14	51	7	14	0	0	51	7	14	0	0
1880	20	51	10	20	0	0	51	10	20	0	0
1890	31	51	15	29	+2	1	51	15	29	+2	1
1900	38	51	19	37	+1	0	51	15	37	+1	0
1910	43	51	19	37	+6	3	51	19	37	+6	3
1920	47	51	19	37	+10	5	51	19	37	+10	5
1930	56	51	19	37	+14	8	51	19	37	+14	8
1940	52	51	19	37	+14	8	51	19	37	+14	8
1950	52	51	19	37	+14	8	51	19	37	+14	8
1955	52	58	24	41	+11	6	59	30	51	+1	0
1960	51	58	24	41	+10	6	59	30	51	0	0
1965	51	58	30	52	−1	0	59	30	51	0	0
1970	49	58	30	52	−3	−1	59	30	51	−2	−1
1971	49	59	30	51	−2	−1	59	30	51	−2	−1

Source: Data reported in Green, 1982:4.

Table 8–2. Chicago's Population, 1870–1980

Census	Chicago's Population	Total Population Cook and Collar Counties	Percent Cook and Collar Counties' Population in Chicago	Total Illinois Population	Percent Illinois' Population in Chicago
1870	298,977	493,513	61	2,539,891	12
1880	503,185	771,445	65	3,077,871	16
1890	1,099,850	1,391,890	79	3,826,352	29
1900	1,698,595	2,084,770	82	4,821,550	35
1910	2,185,283	2,702,465	81	5,638,591	39
1920	2,701,705	3,394,996	80	6,485,280	42
1930	3,376,438	4,449,636	76	7,630,654	44
1940	3,396,808	4,569,643	74	7,897,241	43
1950	3,620,962	5,177,898	70	8,712,176	42
1960	3,550,414	6,220,923	57	10,081,158	35
1970	3,366,957	6,978,947	48	11,113,976	30
1980	3,005,072	7,103,624	42	11,418,461	26

Source: U.S. Census. Data. Decennial Population Figures (1870 through 1980) for Chicago and Illinois.

Chicago's long-sought-after power base in the state legislature began to unravel almost as soon as it was solidified, for both demographic and political reasons. The most obvious of these was the declining population in the city and the corresponding gains in its suburban collar. This can be seen clearly in Table 8–2. In 1950, 42 percent of the entire state lived in Chicago; in 1980, that figure had dropped to 26 percent, and only 42 percent of the population in Cook and the surrounding collar counties lived in Chicago.

These changes in Chicago's population and legislative power base were set in motion during the 1960s and early 1970s. Then, in the late 1970s and early 1980s, several political events occurred that contributed to a further restructuring of regional power bases in the Illinois General Assembly. Perhaps the most important was the death of Mayor Richard J. Daley. His passing liberated Chicago Democrats from one-man rule, but it also created a chaotic situation inside the once cohesive Democratic organization and confusion among those downstaters and suburbanites who had spent a lifetime running against Daley Democrats. Related to these developments were the racial divisions that challenged party loyalty and geographical location as the main determinants of legislative behavior (see Preston, chapter 7 herein). Racial politics hit Democrats the hardest. It complicated their legislative strategy, added uncertainty and divisiveness to an already confusing political situation in the General Assembly, and contributed to the further demise of Chicago's position in the General Assembly.

Patterns in Partisanship

Although the general populace in Illinois apparently felt very strongly about reapportionment, reapportionment was a legislative battle fought largely by political elites over power bases. No legislators want to see their seats eliminated, and most people presumably would prefer to have more rather than fewer representatives from their district. Thus, the controversy over reapportionment was simply a manifestation of the age-old fear of political domination by one group over another. Its primary effect was to reinforce regional animosities, particularly between Chicago and the rest of the state. It is, therefore, an important part of the history of geo-politics in Illinois. But on another level, it tells us very little about differences in and the structure of other types of political preferences across the state. A firm grasp on the distribution of these preferences is crucial to an understanding of geo-political cleavages within Illinois; it can help us determine whether regional animosities that surfaced throughout the reapportionment controversy are rooted in fundamentally different sets of attitudes, values, and cultural norms, and, if so, to what degree. It can also lead us toward a more refined understanding of the contours of geographically based political cleavages in the state.

A fairly refined examination of the regional distribution of attitudes, values, and policy preferences is reported later (Nardulli and Krassa, chapter 10 herein). That analysis, however, speaks to only the most recent phase of Illinois' political history. Here we use voting preferences in presidential elections to address this very important dimension of geo-political cleavages. By examining differences in voting patterns for the entire century, we are able to add an important historical dimension to this aspect of our overall inquiry. The cost, however, is obvious. Data on voting preferences are a poor substitute for refined survey data on attitudes, values, and policy preferences. This notwithstanding, voting data can be useful in generating insights into regional differences because they reflect regional responses to a common stimuli. To the extent that different presidential candidates represent different packages of ideas, values, and policies, we can say something about regional differences across the state. At the very least, we can something about differences in political party allegiances.

Measuring Regional Patterns in Partisanship

The use of county and subcounty voting data to outline the political contours of the state provides us with a number of opportunities and challenges. On the one hand, the availability of these data over a long period of time frees us from the constraints of the regional categorizations laid out earlier (Nardulli, chapter 1 herein). As we did not need to structure our data collection to conform to an a priori set of groupings, we were able to use patterns within the data to define the regions. To do this, however, we had to "denationalize" local voting figures as well as devise a scheme for categorizing individual counties.

Denationalization of the local data was necessary because national influences are often much stronger than regional ones and tend to obscure underlying regional preferences. An example of this can be seen in the voting behavior of Champaign County. The conventional wisdom is that Champaign County is largely Republican, yet the Democratic presidential candidate carried the county in 1912, 1932, 1936, and 1964. Each of these elections, however, was marked by events at the national level causing the nation as a whole to be more Democratic: Teddy Roosevelt's Bull Moose campaign in 1912, the beginning of the New Deal era in 1932, and landslide victories by Franklin Roosevelt in 1936 and Lyndon Johnson in 1964. These Democratic victories in Champaign County may have been more reflective of transient national influences than enduring local preferences, especially if the local margin of victory was smaller than the national margin.

To correct for the effect of these national influences, we measured a county's vote margin in terms of its deviation from the national margin.[1] This allowed us to gauge more accurately the underlying local preferences. Under this procedure, if a county votes less Democratic (Republican) than the nation, it is considered Republican (Democratic). If it votes more Democratic (Republican) than the nation, it is considered Democratic (Republican). On the off-chance the county votes exactly the same as the nation, it is held to be competitive. If we reconsider Champaign County in light of this procedure, we see that in each of the aforementioned elections the county is classified as Republican because the margin by which the Democrats carried the county was less than the national margin.

Figure 8–1 contains plots of vote margins in presidential elections for both Illinois and the nation. It shows in a graphic way the effect of national influences (positive values indicate Democratic victories and negative values Republican ones). It also demonstrates a wide variability in vote margins when national forces are not controlled

Figure 8–1. State and National Vote Margins, 1900–1984

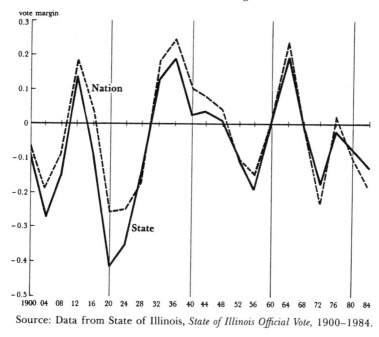

Source: Data from State of Illinois, *State of Illinois Official Vote*, 1900–1984.

Figure 8–2. Denationalized Vote Margin, 1900–1984

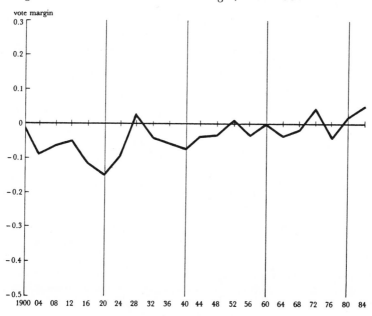

Source: Data from State of Illinois, *State of Illinois Official Vote*, 1900–1984.

for. Notice that the years 1912, 1932, 1936, and 1964 are all strongly Democratic, just as they were in Champaign County. This picture should be contrasted with Figure 8–2, which shows the denationalized state figures. The state votes substantially more Democratic than the nation in only a handful of these elections (1928, 1972, 1980, and 1984). Moreover, the trend is far less volatile, enabling us to make more informed and parsimonious judgments about underlying partisan preferences.

When national forces are taken into account, Illinois appears to be a highly competitive state, especially in the postwar years. However, visual inspections of the vote margins for individual counties indicate this pattern does not hold at the substate level. Indeed, the state as a whole is competitive because certain parts of the state are strongly Republican or strongly Democratic and tend to offset one another at the state level. These inspections also demonstrate that partisan preferences of some counties change markedly over time. Both of these criteria—strength of affiliation and trend in political preferences— were used in an effort to define the political regions of the state. In our scheme, counties comprise a region if they are geographically contiguous and exhibit roughly similar preferences over time. Figure 8–3 is a map of the average partisanship of each county over all twenty-two presidential elections in this century. To construct it, we took the mean of the denationalized vote margins in a county for all presidential elections in the twentieth century and classified it as follows: if the average margin is between −.05 and +.05, the county is competitive; if the average margin ranges from −.05 to −.15, the county is Republican (+.05 and +.15 for Democrats); and if the average margin is more than −.15, the county is strongly Republican (+.15 for strongly Democratic).[2]

Interestingly, the city of Chicago is classified as competitive, a result of its voting Republican until 1928 and Democratic thereafter (also see note 6). A large number of counties, located in the northern and east-central sections of the state, are either strongly Republican or Republican. The remaining regions are generally competitive—Republican and Democratic counties are scattered about—with two exceptions. Three counties at the southern tip (Johnson, Pope, and Massac) are strongly Republican, much more so than the surrounding counties. In the western part of the state, a smattering of Democratic counties appear, most notably Madison and St. Clair in the St. Louis area. In all, the state is divided diagonally by a line running from northwest to southeast. Those areas above the line are generally Republican (except Chicago); those below are more diverse.

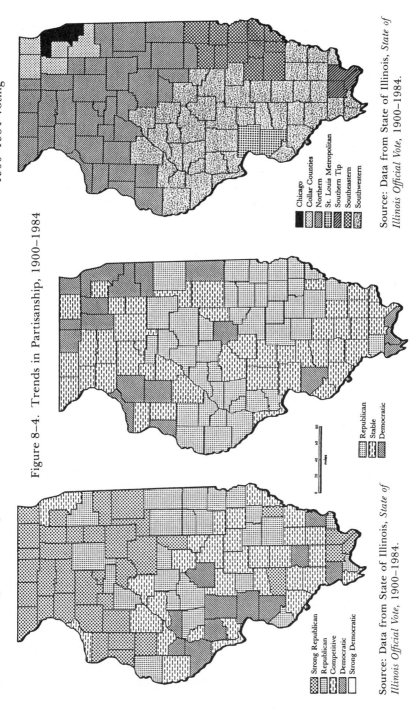

Figure 8–3. Average Partisanship, 1900–1984

Figure 8–4. Trends in Partisanship, 1900–1984

Figure 8–5. Regional Classification Based on 1900–1984 Voting

Strong Republican
Republican
Competitive
Democratic
Strong Democratic

Source: Data from State of Illinois, *State of Illinois Official Vote*, 1900–1984.

0 20 40 60 80
miles

Republican
Stable
Democratic

Source: Data from State of Illinois, *State of Illinois Official Vote*, 1900–1984.

Chicago
Collar Counties
Northern
St. Louis Metropolitan
Southern Tip
Southeastern
Southwestern

Source: Data from State of Illinois, *State of Illinois Official Vote*, 1900–1984.

While the strength of a county's party affiliation gives us some indication of regional boundaries, it does not tell the whole story. Nowhere can this be seen more clearly than in the case of Chicago. Despite the existence of a strong Democratic organization that has turned in lopsided Democratic totals in recent decades, it is classified as competitive. This is, as noted above, due to its voting Republican in the early part of the century. Early Republican victories and recent Democratic ones suggest, of course, a trend toward the Democratic party and underscore the importance of considering both strength and trend in our categorization scheme.

To determine whether political preferences in a county are stable over time, we regressed the denationalized vote margin on year, controlling for autoregression, and used the parameter estimates to determine whether preferences changed over time.[3] If the estimate for a county was not significant,[4] the trend was said to be stable. By stable we mean the county may vote consistently for one party, or it may oscillate between one party and the other. If the parameter estimate was significant, then the trend is toward Republican if negative and Democratic if positive. The results of this procedure are displayed in Figure 8–4.

The figure demonstrates that while much of the state is stable, some clusters of counties exhibit similar trends. There are two pockets of growing Republican affiliation: one in east-central Illinois and the other starting in Livingston County and extending southwest to the border. Each of these areas began the century voting Democratic and has gotten progressively more Republican. Republican strength has become more firmly entrenched in east-central Illinois because these counties were less Democratic at the outset; counties in the west-central pocket were part of the Democratic base of power at the turn of the century. This is why the west-central pocket is competitive and the east-central one Republican in Figure 8–3. As expected, Chicago evidences a significant Democratic trend, but so do some of the strongly Republican counties surrounding it. The latter trend is undoubtedly due to the out-migration of Chicagoans to the suburbs in the post–World War II era. Its impact is minimal, however, and it does little to change the overall composition of the collar counties, which are strongly Republican. In contrast, the partisan shifts in Chicago have moved it from a strongly Republican region to a strongly Democratic one.

Political Regions in Illinois

This analysis led us to define seven political regions in the state, which are depicted in Figure 8–5.[5] The first is Chicago,[6] an obvious choice because its increasing Democratic tendencies over the past sixty years are so different from the tendencies of its neighboring counties. The second region consists of the strong, stable Republican counties surrounding Chicago: suburban Cook, Lake, McHenry, Kane, DuPage, and Will. Third is the northern region, which includes thirty-six counties and is stable and Republican. Another is the St. Louis area, where two counties (Madison and St. Clair) have become more Democratic over time. Next is the southern tip, a handful of counties which are and have been strongly Republican. A sixth region is southeastern Illinois, twelve counties that began the century voting Democratic but are now reliably Republican. The last region is the southwest, which is comprised of forty-three counties and is the most competitive part of the state.

To better portray the differences and similarities among these seven regions, we graphed their partisan preferences over the course of the century. We did this by averaging together the denationalized vote margins of the counties in each region for each election. Before we present these data, however, we should compare the regional map that these deliberations produced with the a priori map used to guide many of the other analyses in this volume (see Nardulli, chapter 1 herein). If we set aside the two "point" regions that our analyses uncovered (the St.Louis area and the southern tip, which together comprise only 5 of the 102 Illinois counties), we see a great similarity between the two regional maps. The basic difference is that a distinctive central region is far less prominent in the voting data. The northern region seems to extend farther to the south and into the eastern edge of the state. What was termed the southern region is really a southwestern swatch that consumes much of the west-central part of the state. What is left is a small group of counties in the southeastern part of the state that, as we shall see, is becoming increasingly similar to the northern tier.

To more clearly illustrate the similarities and differences of the voting trends in the various regions, we separated those that evidenced largely Democratic preferences from those that were more Republican. Figure 8–6 graphs the denationalized vote margins for the more Democratic regions (the city of Chicago and the St. Louis metropolitan area). As is evident, Chicago normally voted Republican until 1928 and Democratic thereafter. The plot displays a clear trend toward a strong affiliation with the Democratic party. The St. Louis area roughly parallels Chicago's pattern, except it was more competitive early in the century and turned Democratic earlier, by about 1920. Although there was a rough correspondence between Chicago and the Illinois counties in the St. Louis metropolitan area between 1928 and 1964, the counties became markedly less Democratic after the Johnson land-slide.

Because their preferences shift over time in a manner that is quite different from either the Democratic or Republican regions, the south-west and southeast are displayed separately in Figure 8–7. In the early part of the century, these regions were the most Democratic in the state, although they were clearly in the southern wing of the party. Just after Chicago and the St. Louis counties began to register strong Democratic tendencies, the southwest and southeast began in 1936 to vote less Democratic than the nation as a whole. For the past forty years, the southwest region has been the most competitive area in the state, while the southeast is more Republican.

The traditionally Republican regions within the state (the suburban collar, northern Illinois, and the southern tip) are displayed in Figure 8–8. The plots show continuous and marked Republican preferences. Although the intensity of their preferences varies at different times, at no point do they come close to voting less Republican than the nation as a whole. In the early part of the series, the southern tip and the collar counties show strong Republican preferences, while northern Illinois is less strong. Note that although all three regions become more Republican during the New Deal era, they became less so after 1944. The variation among these regions has declined since that time, although recent elections show some separation.

Trends in Electoral Power

Partisanship patterns provide information concerning which regions are affiliated with which party and how strongly, as well as how these have changed over time. Most interesting, perhaps, is the rise of Democratic voting in Chicago and its decline in the southwest and southeast regions, along with the solidification of Republican voting in the collar counties and northern Illinois. No less important to an understanding of the geo-political cleavages in the state is an analysis of shifts in electoral power over time. Such an analysis can tell us which regions produce the most votes, and how vote distributions have changed since 1900. It locates the bases of the parties' power and illustrates how regional voting patterns have affected the outcome of statewide elections.

To examine electoral power, minor changes in the regional classi-fications were necessary. Since three of our regions (southeastern, St. Louis, and the southern tip) account for less than 5 percent of the vote in any election, analyzing them separately proved difficult and, ultimately, not very informative. Therefore, the southern tip and St. Louis regions have been included in the southwestern region, and southeastern Illinois in what we will now refer to as the northeastern region. Given the relatively small number of votes involved, this presents no problem for the southwestern region, even though the two regions included behave somewhat differently, especially the southern tip. In the case of southeastern Illinois, its behavior is not dissimilar to that of the northern counties for the past fifty years, and the region has produced Republican margins comparable to those in the northeastern region. Thus, four regions will be used in this analysis: northeastern Illinois, southwestern Illinois, the city of Chicago, and Chicago's suburban collar (including suburban Cook County). Since we are interested in the contribution a region makes to the total votes in the state, the total Democratic votes, and the total Republican votes, we simply added the number of, say, Democratic votes in a region and divided by the number of Democratic votes in the state to arrive at the percentage of Democratic votes provided by the region.

Figure 8–9 contains the percentage of total votes for each region. The plot for Chicago increases until 1948, when it accounts for 46 percent of the state vote, and decreases dramatically thereafter. In 1980 and 1984, only 25 percent of the state's votes come from there. The percentage of total votes from the collar counties shows a moderate increase until 1948, after which it begins to increase more rapidly. The percentage has grown from 7 percent in 1900 to 17 percent in 1948 and 36 percent in 1984. Thus, the collar now produces more votes than does Chicago. The northeastern and southwestern regions display coinciding trends. The northeast declines from 32 percent in 1900 to 20 percent in 1984, while the southwest declines from 28 percent to 18 percent. Moreover, both regions have remained fairly stable since 1944.

The percentage of Democratic votes is displayed in Figure 8–10. Chicago again increases until 1948, when it reached 54 percent. But whereas total votes decreased by 21 percentage points, Democratic votes decreased by 17 points, falling to a level of 37 percent by 1984. The collar counties increased from 5 percent in 1900 to 27 percent in 1984. The northeast exhibits a gradual decline from 28 percent in 1900 to a stable 16 percent to 17 percent since 1944. The plot for the southwestern region shows a dramatic decrease in 1928. Before this time it produced 30 percent to 35 percent of the state's Democratic votes; it subsequently dropped to around 20 percent. This drop is due to the sudden increase in 1928 of Democratic votes in Chicago especially, but also in the collar. The drop is not the result of either

Figure 8-6. Denationalized Vote Margin for Democratic Regions

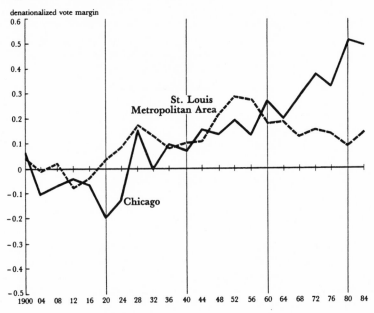

Source: Data from State of Illinois, *State of Illinois Official Vote*, 1900–1984.

Figure 8-7. Denationalized Vote Margin for Southeastern and
Southwestern Regions

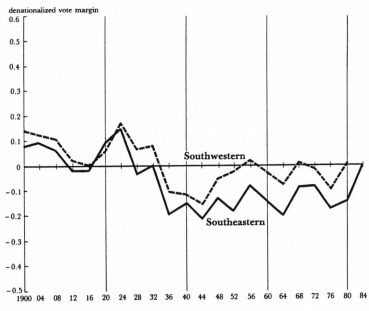

Source: Data from State of Illinois, *State of Illinois Official Vote*, 1900–1984.

Figure 8–8. Denationalized Vote Margin for Republican Regions

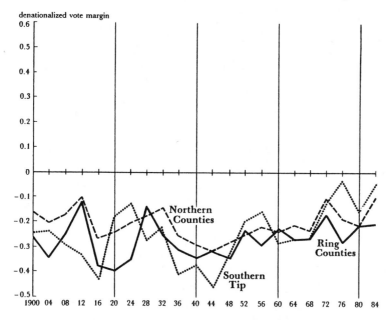

Source: Data from State of Illinois, *State of Illinois Official Vote*, 1900–1984.

Figure 8–9. Percent of Total State Vote by Region

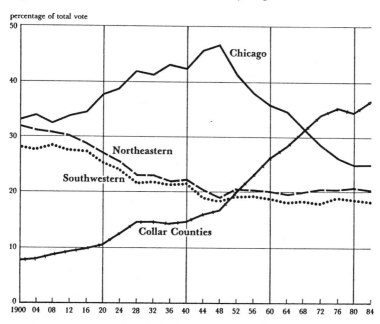

Source: Data from State of Illinois, *State of Illinois Official Vote*, 1900–1984.

Figure 8–10. Percent of Democratic State Vote by Region

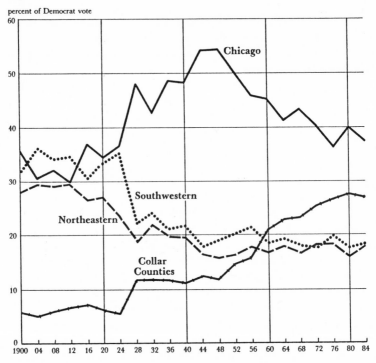

percent of Democrat vote

Source: Data from State of Illinois, *State of Illinois Official Vote*, 1900–1984.

Figure 8–11. Percent of Republican State Vote by Region

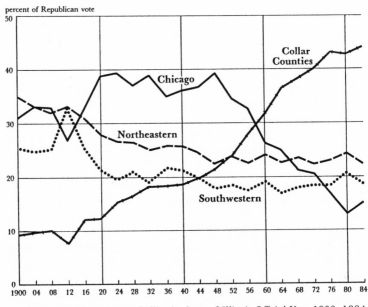

percent of Republican vote

Source: Data from State of Illinois, *State of Illinois Official Vote*, 1900–1984.

a switch of allegiance to the Republican party (discussed below) or widespread apathy, as can be seen in Figure 8–9. The sudden shift in the Democratic base of power is one of the interesting puzzles uncovered by this analysis.

That there was not a corresponding increase in the percentage of Republican votes coming from the southwest can be seen in Figure 8–11. Except for an upward spike in 1912, the plot indicates a slight decrease, from 25 percent in 1900 to 19 percent in 1984. Again, the plot for Chicago shows a dramatic decrease beginning in 1948, from 39 percent to 15 percent. A second puzzle, then, is the across-the-board decrease in Chicago's contribution since 1948. Republican votes from the collar counties increase dramatically over the century, from 9 percent to 44 percent. The northeastern plot indicates a steady decrease from 35 percent to 22 percent.

The three figures together demonstrate a decline in the importance of the northeast and the southwest. Chicago and the collar counties, on the other hand, exhibit contrasting trends. Chicago held unprecedented power until 1948, when that power began to decline. Meanwhile, the collar's power has increased dramatically; it has provided more of the total votes in the state than any other region since 1972 and more Republican votes since 1960. More significant and less obvious, the suburban Democratic vote will be more important to presidential candidates than the city vote, if present trends continue.

We now turn to what is, in a very real sense, the ultimate question. To what extent have the differences in partisan preferences and the distribution of total votes affected the outcome of presidential elections in the state? In other words, to what extent have elections represented regional victories? What regions have held the balance of power, and how has this balance changed over time, if at all? To examine these important questions, we examine the raw vote margins (total Democratic votes minus total Republican votes) for each of the four regions just analyzed for every presidential election in the twentieth century. These vote margins are reported in Figure 8–12. Bars above the line indicate a net Democratic victory in a region, those below the line a net Republican victory; the longer the bar, the greater the victory.

What we would expect to see, based upon conventional wisdom concerning Illinois politics, is Chicago on one side of the line and the other regions of the state on the other, with the size of the margins in the various regions determining the electoral outcome in the state. But reality is a far different matter. The Chicago-downstate dichotomy characterizes Illinois elections in only seven of the twenty-two elections

Figure 8–12. Vote Margins in Presidential Elections by Region

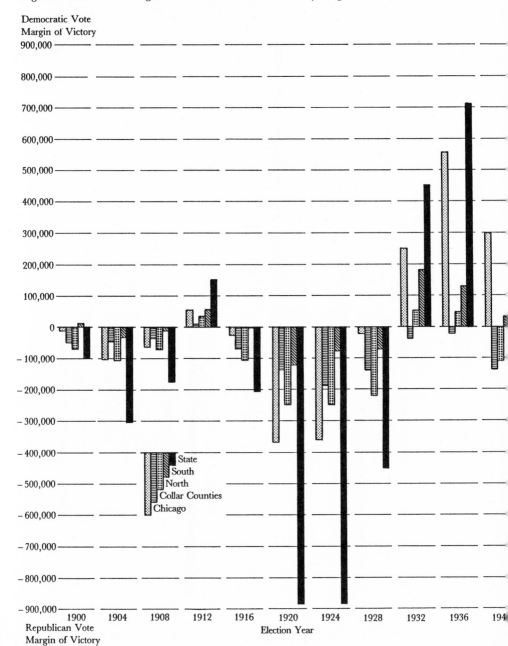

Democratic Vote
Margin of Victory

900,000

800,000

700,000

600,000

500,000

400,000

300,000

200,000

100,000

0

−100,000

−200,000

−300,000

−400,000

−500,000

−600,000

−700,000

−800,000

−900,000

State
South
North
Collar Counties
Chicago

1900 1904 1908 1912 1916 1920 1924 1928 1932 1936 1940
Republican Vote
Margin of Victory

Election Year

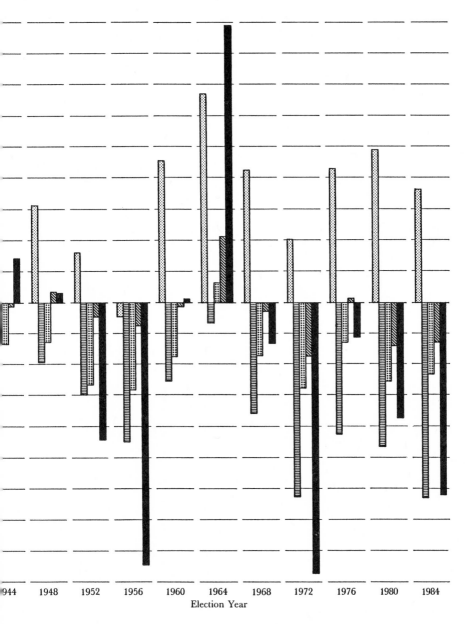

Source: Data from State of Illinois, *State of Illinois Official Vote*, 1900–1984.

in this century and in no election before 1944. In only two of those elections (1944 and 1960) did Chicago's preferences (Democratic) prevail over those of the other regions of the state. The remaining five elections, all won by Republicans, were in 1956, 1968, 1972, 1980, and 1984. Thus, the stereotypic pattern characterizes recent Illinois elections, but only decades after the dichotomy was well etched in Illinois' political lore. Interestingly, these elections occur only after the balance of power between Chicago and the collar began to converge.

In addition to the Chicago-downstate pattern, three others were observed: consensus, a Chicago-southwest coalition, and a Chicago-southwest-northeast coalition. Consensus across all regions was the typical pattern of Illinois elections early in the century. In eight of the twenty-two elections, all regions favored the same candidate, but seven of them came before 1932 (1904–28).[7] The other consensus election was 1956. Chicago and the southwest — backing the Democratic candidate — were pitted against the collar and the northeast in three elections (1940, 1948, 1976), and this coalition prevailed in the first two of them. In three elections (1932, 1936, 1964), the collar counties voted out of step with the other regions in the state, but they never prevailed.

From these findings, it is possible to discern three broad periods in the electoral history of Illinois. From 1900 to 1928, there was consensus among the regions (except in 1900, but see note 7). The Republican candidate won every election save 1912, when Teddy Roosevelt attracted a large number of would-be Republican voters. The second period extends from 1932 to 1964, i.e., from the beginning of the New Deal to the beginning of the Great Society. The Democrats won most of the elections, the exceptions being 1952 and 1956. Moreover, each of the four voting patterns was observed in this period (one consensus, three Chicago-northeast-southwest, two Chicago-southwest, and three Chicago versus downstate). The third period runs from 1968 to the present. Again, only Republican candidates have won. Four of the five elections saw Chicago lose to the other regions, and in 1976, the collar counties and the northeast bested the Chicago-southwest coalition for the first time.

Conclusions

If any firm conclusion can be drawn from this fairly narrow examination of electoral politics in Illinois, it is that the state's regional mosaic is much different from, and more complex than, the simple

Chicago-downstate dichotomy. While the origins of this dichotomy can clearly be traced to the emergence of Chicago as a major urban center and the long battle over reapportionment, partisan preferences were never quite so distinct or simple. These preferences differed across various parts of the state, but our analyses suggest that as many as seven regions existed, not just two. Moreover, regional preferences in some parts of the state have changed markedly over time, as have partisan alignments within it. Only in the latter part of the century have the implications of the Chicago-downstate rivalry been borne out, long after the reapportionment battles on which it is based were fought. Not since 1960, and only once before then, was the margin in Chicago enough to overcome the margins in the other parts of the state. Given the trends in voting strength, it is unlikely that a repeat of 1960 will occur ever again.

Particularly interesting is the discovery of three periods in the electoral history of Illinois, which correspond to the changing trends in electoral power. The state was consensually Republican from 1900 to 1928. A second, Democratic period is comprised of the elections from 1932 to 1964, during which time Chicago was the major base of Democratic power and the most powerful region in the state. A third period began in 1968, just after the collar began contributing more votes to the state's total than Chicago did. Illinois has since been Republican. If the trends in electoral power continue, Illinois seems destined to be a state capable of producing Republican victories on a reliable basis. Furthermore, should Chicago's suburban collar continue to grow relative to the other regions, it will soon be able to deliver Republican victories alone, no longer failing in its attempt to do so. This time, however, reapportionment will not be a viable strategy for the weaker regions.

As a whole, the trends and patterns we have uncovered display a great deal of change over the course of the century. Nothing suggests that this ongoing evolution of the structure of electoral politics in the state will stop. Indeed, the mushrooming strength of the collar in both Democratic and Republican domains, and the possibility of a Republican defection on the part of white ethnics in Chicago, suggests that we may be on the brink of a major reshuffling of electoral alignments and power within the state.

NOTES

1. Our measure is

$$y = (a - b) - (c - d)$$

where a is the Democratic proportion of total votes in the county, b is the Republican proportion of total votes in the county, c is the Democratic proportion of total votes in the nation, d is the Republican proportion of total votes in the nation, and y is the denationalized vote margin. Y can theoretically range between -2.0 (the Republican candidate captured every vote in the county and none in the nation) to $+2.0$. In fact, however, the minimum value is -0.950 and the maximum is 0.554. The mean of Y is -0.105 and the standard deviation is 0.181.

2. There is no simple translation of these values into the percent of the vote captured by the two parties because of the presence of third party candidates. Assuming, however, no third party activity, a value of -0.05 translates into a 52.5 percent to 47.5 percent Republican victory, and a $+0.15$ value into a 57.5 percent to 42.5 percent victory for the Democrats.

3. When autocorrelation is present, the ordinary least squares (OLS) parameter estimates are not efficient and the standard error estimates are biased, affecting significance tests. Therefore, we used the first order autoregressive model

$$y_t = x_t B + v_t$$

where y_t is the denationalized vote margin, x_t is the election year, and the error component $v_t = e_t - a_1 v_{t-1}$. The error occurring at the present time point is e_t, and the error from the previous time point is $a_1 v_{t-1}$.

4. At the .05 level of significance.

5. While we strove for objectivity, it was necessary to use our judgment in letting the data decide the regional boundaries. As noted above, in some cases the trend in partisanship was more important than its strength, and in other cases just the opposite. We allowed our knowledge of the area to influence this choice.

6. Cook County encompasses two distinct components: the city of Chicago and the suburbs. Through the mapping stage, the two were combined because of a limitation in the mapping software. In subsequent analyses, specifically the plots of the vote margin over time and electoral power, the Cook County suburbs are included in the collar counties and Chicago stands by itself.

7. In 1900, Chicago, the collar counties, and the northeast voted Republican while the southwest voted Democratic. The margin of victory in the southwest, however, was only 8,840 votes. With no knowledge of the voting patterns prior to 1900, it does no damage to include this along with the consensus votes. Thus, the consensus period ran from 1900 to 1928.

REFERENCES

Green, Paul M. 1982. "Legislative Redistricting in Illinois, 1871–1982: A Study of Geo-political Survival." In Anna J. Merritt (ed.), *Redistricting: An Exercise in Prophecy.* Urbana: Institute of Government and Public Affairs.

State of Illinois. 1900–1984. *State of Illinois Official Vote.* Springfield: State of Illinois.

Steiner, Gilbert, and Samuel K. Gove. 1962. *Legislative Politics in Illinois.* Urbana: University of Illinois Press.

U.S. Census. Data. Decennial Population Figures (1870 through 1980) for Chicago and Illinois.

Money, Politics, and Regionalism: 9
Allocating State Funds in Illinois

James W. Fossett and J. Fred Giertz

Few issues in Illinois politics incite the level of rancor that attends discussions of the regional distribution of state spending. Debates over spending proposals in the state legislature and other public forums are marked by vociferous complaints from all participants that they are not receiving their fair share of state support. Representatives of the Chicago suburbs contend that since they pay a large share of state taxes, they are entitled to a fair return in the form of state services instead of being required to subsidize what they view as overly generous and wasteful welfare programs in Chicago or other state activities from which they derive no benefit. Chicago representatives counter that there is a mismatch between social problems and local resources, which the suburbs have helped to create and from which they benefit unfairly, making it only fair that the suburbs be required to support programs which benefit the city. Variations on these themes have been pressed during debates on school-aid reform, the Build Illinois public works program, reform of the Rapid Transit Authority, the Chicago World's Fair, and practically every other major spending proposal advanced during the last several years.

This chapter tests the relative merits of these claims by examining the geographic distribution of state funds in Illinois and the underlying demographic and political causes of this distribution. It first examines the broad outlines of how state spending is distributed across Illinois regions without adjusting for any need factors. Then an attempt is made to judge how fair this distribution is according to criteria which have been developed for different types of programs. Differences in per capita expenditures among regions are not necessarily a sign of inequities since there are great disparities in the regional distribution of problems and needs in the state. In addition, a variety of competing

Table 9–1. State per Capita Spending, Major Budget Categories and Total, by Region, 1984

	Elementary/ Secondary Education	State Payroll and Operations	Highways	Public Aid	Total[a]
Cook	$167.86	$151.72	$15.32	$184.98	$606.53
Collar counties	144.20	145.15	19.89	40.51	433.57
North	157.15	250.12	58.48	50.85	631.69
Central	149.46	437.81	98.09	63.27	853.81
South	224.56	360.96	56.42	83.72	912.46

[a] Includes programs not listed separately.

Source: Compiled from data reported in Illinois Legislative Council, 1984.

but legitimate objectives drive state policies that affect the distribution of expenditures. After adjustments for these factors are made, it is suggested that the regional inequities are much less severe than is often believed.

The conclusions are mixed but suggest that many state programs which should focus or target spending on the harder-pressed areas of the state are in fact spread broadly across the state, with limited attention to program need. This tendency to spread state funds is explained in terms of political changes within the state legislature that have made it increasingly difficult to assemble and sustain coalitions in support of spending funds in the state's most distressed areas.

I. The Distribution of State Resources: A Regional View

Most of the debate over the distribution of state funds centers on figures like those in Table 9–1, which displays per capita state spending for major budget categories and overall expenditures in the various regions of the state. While these figures are, almost inevitably, incomplete and subject to a number of qualifications, they provide a broadly accurate picture of where state funds are spent.

These numbers indicate that state spending is unevenly distributed across the five regions. Spending is highest in the downstate regions, particularly the central and southern regions, and lowest in the collar counties. The southernmost downstate regions receive particularly large shares of state spending for payroll and operations, largely because of the spending associated with such major state institutions as universities, prisons, and the state capital complex in Springfield. The southern region and Cook County also receive large amounts of public aid—largely AFDC (Aid to Families with Dependent Children) and Medicaid payments—per capita relative to the other three regions. The collar counties, by comparison, receive the lowest amount of state funds per capita of any of the five regions in three of the four major budget categories and less total state spending per person.

Earlier analyses of the geographic location of state spending suggest that this broad spending pattern of major regional disparity and heavy spending in downstate areas has existed for at least the last twenty years (Kane, 1973). State institutions have historically been located downstate, and recently constructed facilities, particularly prisons, have been built in this same pattern. Most state programs aimed at redressing the problems of lower-income groups have spent the bulk of their funds in Chicago and depressed downstate areas. Quite clearly, if disparities in spending mean unfairness, then the state spends its funds unfairly and has done so for some time.

It is far from clear, however, that the simple existence of disparities in spending provides any evidence, much less conclusive proof, that the distribution of state expenditures is inequitable. First, there is no necessary connection between where the funds are spent and who benefits from this spending. College students from DuPage County who attend the University of Illinois receive benefits from spending in Champaign County; residents of Cook County experience reduced crime rates when Cook County felons are incarcerated in state prisons in Will or Menard counties. Second, some state programs are explicitly intended to provide services to lower-income or other groups and *should* be spent where these groups are located, rather than being equally spread across all areas of the state. It would obviously be a waste of money to spend the same amount of money to educate handicapped children in counties where there are few such children as in counties where there are large numbers of these children. Quite clearly, inequality in spending does not mean unfairness.

The four sections that follow analyze the equity and efficiency of the regional distribution of state expenditures in Illinois. Section II presents alternative theoretical views of what constitutes equity in regional distributional decisions. Section III discusses the goals of various state programs, along with their regional implications. Section IV addresses the distribution of problems and needs in the state's regions. Section V analyzes the actual distribution of state resources and compares it with the distribution of problems.

II. Fairness and Efficiency in Distributional Decisions

All government programs involve either the explicit or implicit redistribution of resources. Sometimes the redistribution is intended as the primary goal of government policy, such as social security and welfare programs. Other times, the redistribution is the unintended by-product of activities undertaken for other purposes, such as road construction and the siting of schools, prisons, and hospitals. The concern for the geographic distribution of the benefits of government programs (and of the costs in the form of taxes) affects all levels of government and is almost always a controversial and divisive issue. For example, the distribution of state aid to local schools has generated interregional conflicts in Illinois for decades. The distribution of federal expenditures is of great concern to many states such as Illinois, which receive a disproportionately small share of federal activities.

As with all government programs, activities involving redistribution should be judged according to the general guidelines of efficiency and equity. Unfortunately, these are often competing goals. For example, building public facilities in prosperous and rapidly growing areas of the state may be among the most efficient programs for promoting economic growth, yet these programs may divert resources from other areas that are deserving on equity grounds. Channelling resources to impoverished areas may reduce state activities that have a greater development potential in other parts of the state.

Even the equity goal alone is ambiguous. Few if any people would disagree with the statement that government policies should distribute resources among various regions in a fair or equitable manner. Equity, like beauty, is often in the eye of the beholder, however.

What factors should influence the distribution of state expenditures? One approach suggests distributing state expenditures on the basis of need or productivity alone, without regard to the contribution that various regions make to financing the cost of government programs. A competing approach that is increasingly advocated suggests that regions are entitled to a fair return of government expenditures based on the taxes collected in the region. Not surprisingly, almost every region believes it is not receiving a fair return on its tax dollars. The suburbs of Chicago are among the most vocal groups in this regard. These high-income areas bear a large share of the state's tax burden, yet they receive relatively little in various kinds of state aid, such as that distributed under the school-aid formula.

One response to allegations of inequity would be to deny the legitimacy of regions as an entity for calculating expenditures and tax payments. Under this approach, different state activities would be targeted to meet the needs of citizens in different circumstances. There would be no explicit state policy regarding the regional distribution of state activities. The overall regional distribution of state expenditures would simply be the sum of the effects of the various individual programs operated by the state. A region's share would be determined by the economic and demographic characteristics of its residents. If the underlying distribution rules for distributing expenditures among citizens are accepted, the existence of regional disparities would not indicate unfairness to a region.

If regions do matter, the question of what constitutes a fair distribution among regions must be addressed. A fundamental element of this question deals with what is actually being distributed among regions. Is it expenditures or government services or both? The distribution of expenditures among regions involves the place where government dollars are actually spent. The distribution of services involves the place where the benefits of government activities are realized. Sometimes it makes little difference which concept is used. For example, the distribution of the benefits and the distribution of expenditures for state aid to local schools or for welfare aid to the poor is basically the same.

For state activities such as mental health, higher education, and the prison system, the geographic distribution of expenditures may be quite different from the distribution of the benefits of the services provided by these programs. For these activities, expenditures are concentrated in a relatively few places where the state facilities are located. The benefits, however, are spread more evenly over the state, depending on the regional origin of the individuals receiving the service.

It is clear that equity in the distribution of state expenditures or services is a subjective concept. Reasonable individuals can differ over what constitutes a fair distribution. However, an understanding of these alternative views of equity can help to focus the discussion on the key aspects of distributional issues.

It would be naive to suggest that actual decisions about the regional distribution of state activities are determined solely by the equity and efficiency considerations discussed here. Ultimately, decisions about these matters are made by elected officials, which means that they are intrinsically political in nature. Elected officials, in general, desire to remain in office. This means that they must be concerned about their standing with their constituents and with other groups to whom they are obligated. Politicians are interested in directing both expenditures and services to the districts they represent and to the groups to whom they owe debts. These interests will always be weighed against the broader statewide goals of interregional equity or efficiency.

III. Programmatic Criteria for Evaluating Distribution Patterns

There are a variety of different goals that state programs are designed to achieve. Some of these activities have an explicit regional dimension while others do not.

Programs Targeted on Individuals

Many redistributional programs are entitlement programs distributing state aid to persons in particular categories. Programs such as Aid to Families with Dependent Children, unemployment compensation, and aid to the medically indigent have a regional distribution that is determined by the distribution of the individuals qualifying for such aid. If the programs distribute aid among persons in an appropriate way, the regional distribution of expenditures (whether it results in great disparities or virtual equality) should be of little concern. Individuals, not regions, make a difference in these types of programs.

Recently, the state has become increasingly active in providing direct aid to individuals and corporations to encourage economic development. The goal of such aid is to promote economic growth in the state and not necessarily to respond to problems of poverty (although the use of enterprise zones combines the goals of economic development and poverty).

Programs Targeted on Local Governments

Many state programs provide aid not to individuals but to local governments. Some types of intergovernmental aid are not meant to be redistributive in nature. For example, the state uses its superior position in levying an income tax to collect and distribute one-twelfth of its income-tax receipts to municipalities and counties on the basis of population. The state also distributes a portion of the motor-fuels tax to local governments. Such programs make no effort to target aid according to any standard of need.

Other state intergovernmental aid, however, is targeted to assist governments in dealing with special problems. Infrastructure-development funds are often awarded to local governments for road, sewer, and water systems. Need in this case is not synonymous with the lack of local resources, but rather with the lack of such facilities or their obsolescence. The bulk of this type of spending should be directed to growing areas where infrastructure development is needed.

Other types of aid to local governments are designed to compensate for differences in economic capacity among various jurisdictions. State aid is targeted to reduce or eliminate these disparities. Without such aid, poorer districts would have to tax themselves much more heavily than more prosperous areas to provide the same service levels. State aid to local school districts is the best example of this type of program.

Statewide Programs

Many programs provide services on a statewide basis. Programs such as higher education, mental health, and the criminal justice system do not have an explicit regional focus, although the location of state facilities providing these services determines the distribution of expenditures (as opposed to services). The location of such facilities should be based on such factors as cost and availability to the clientele served. The regional distribution of services depends upon the origin of those receiving the services, as opposed to the location of the state facilities.

From the discussion presented thus far, it is clear that the analysis of the actual pattern of regional distribution of state activities must be undertaken with great care. There are difficult issues that must be resolved (often in rather arbitrary ways) to apportion expenditures or services among regions. Because state activities are designed to meet a variety of different goals, no single measure will allow conclusions to be drawn concerning either the equity or efficiency of existing distribution patterns. Since differences among regions do not necessarily imply inequities among various areas, the equity question is much more complex than simply comparing per capita expenditure or service patterns among regions.

IV. The Distribution of Problems and Needs in the State

The distribution of problems or needs in the state must be examined before any meaningful conclusion can be drawn concerning the equity or efficiency of the distribution of state activities. Table 9–2 displays a variety of measures of social and economic characteristics for the five regions in the state. The values in the table are averages for the counties in each region which have been assembled from a variety of state and federal data sources. While these figures conceal variations between rich and poor counties within regions (particularly in the three downstate regions that contain large numbers of counties), they provide a useful summary of the important attributes of the major areas of the state.

These figures confirm that the Chicago suburbs are the wealthiest and most rapidly growing area in the state. The five collar counties

Table 9–2. Economic and Demographic Characteristics of Regions

	North	Central	South	Collar	Cook
Population change, 1970–84 (percentage)	9.2	7.5	13.9	35.0	−11.2
Poverty population, 1980 (percentage)	7.5	10.2	13.4	4.9	13.9
Per capita income, 1984	12,623	11,809	10,565	15,452	14,199
Per capita income Growth, 1975–84 (percentage)	106.8	87.3	102.3	121.6	100.0
Earnings growth, 1975–84 (percentage)	53.6	39.7	48.5	61.1	46.8
Unemployment rate, 1984 (percentage)	10.1	10.9	14.6	7.2	8.6
Population, 1984	1,129,100	1,944,400	1,221,600	1,945,500	5,270,400
Number of counties	17	45	34	5	1

Source: Compiled from data reported in U.S. Bureau of Census, "County Statistics File," 1985.

have the highest per capita income, the highest rates of growth in population, income, and earnings, and the lowest levels of poverty and unemployment in the state. There has been a major decentralization of employment in the Chicago area over the last twenty years. Almost two-thirds of the manufacturing, retail, and wholesale jobs in the metropolitan area are now located in the suburbs, compared with less than half in the late 1960s. This movement of jobs, wealth, and people has led to an increasing disparity between Chicago and its suburbs in terms of both problems and resources.

These numbers also suggest that the southern Illinois region has a high concentration of social and economic problems. Recent declines in agriculture and particularly coal mining in this area have produced relatively high rates of poverty and unemployment and a low growth rate of earnings. The region has always had a lower than average level of income. The northern region appears to be somewhat more prosperous than the central; it has lower levels of poverty and unemployment and higher levels of income and earnings growth.

The figures for Cook County are harder to interpret. Because little of the socio-economic data and none of the state expenditure data are available below the county level, we are unable consistently to separate the city of Chicago from suburban Cook County and hence cannot observe the distinction between Chicago and the suburbs used elsewhere in this volume.

The available data suggest, however, that most of Cook County's social problems are concentrated in Chicago. Eighty-five percent of Cook County's poor live in Chicago, compared to about 60 percent of the total population, and unemployment in the city is well above that in the remainder of the county. Chicago has lost large numbers of entry-level manufacturing and retail jobs to the suburbs over the last fifteen years while experiencing growth in high-skill service industries. Because of housing costs and discrimination in the suburbs, lower skilled city workers have been unable to gain access to suburban jobs, leading to increased poverty and unemployment rates (Fossett and Orfield, 1987).

By contrast, much of suburban Cook County is relatively prosperous. A number of inner-ring suburban communities, particularly on the city's South Side, are beginning to experience problems of concentrated poverty and unemployment; but the city's northern and western suburbs inside Cook County closely resemble the balance of the suburban area.

In summary, the problems in the state are not evenly distributed geographically. Instead, they are concentrated in a small number of places—such as Chicago and a few downstate cities (in addition to certain areas in the south)—that suffer from high unemployment, poverty, slow income growth, and loss of manufacturing jobs.

V. The Distribution of State Resources

In this section, we examine the way in which the state distributes its resources relative to the governmental and social problems discussed in the previous section. It will be remembered from earlier discussion that the state spends much larger amounts of money downstate than in the Chicago area, particularly for the support of such public institutions as prisons, universities, and mental hospitals. Chicago area residents, however, use these facilities more intensely than downstate residents. Here we examine the extent to which this spending pattern targets or focuses state resources on areas of need and to what extent it appears to be influenced by regional or political factors.

We used quantitative analyses to investigate both the distribution of expenditures and the distribution of services. The quantitative analysis is supplemented with related observations about various state programs. Multiple regression analysis was used to investigate these relationships between various measures of state spending for different services and program need. Data on state spending and need were collected at the county level. The spending data came from a report on 1984 state spending prepared by the Illinois Legislative Council (1984), and program-need information came from various federal sources.

Since this study reports spending only at the county level, we are unable to systematically distinguish spending in Chicago from that in the balance of Cook County. The high concentration of low-income groups inside the city, however, suggests that public aid, which is largely composed of Aid to Families with Dependent Children (AFDC) and Medicaid, should be spent largely inside the city—as should aid to primary and secondary education, which is allocated in part on the basis of the number of lower-income children. Similarly, state spending for services such as mental health or services to families and children which aid lower-income groups should mainly benefit city residents. In contrast, spending for state payroll and operations and for such programs as highways should be more broadly dispersed across the county.

Regional factors were measured by a series of regional dummy variables defined relative to Cook County, so that the coefficients on these variables measure how much more or less per capita each downstate region received relative to Cook County once need factors are taken into account. Separate regressions were estimated for each of the major classes of state expenditures defined in earlier sections.

The results of this analysis, which are reported in Table 9–3, suggest that the state's record of spending money in areas that have problems is distinctly mixed. In some functional areas, the state appears to have done well in spending money where there are problems; in others, the relationship between spending and need is much weaker. Public aid and assistance to primary and secondary education both appear to focus fairly directly on the problems they are supposed to address. State education assistance is higher in counties with higher poverty rates, lower incomes, and a higher proportion of school-age children. It does not appear to be distributed with any particular regional bias and may be judged, at least at the county level, to be relatively well targeted on the proper areas.

More detailed examinations of how funds are distributed to individual school districts, however, have indicated that this finding may

Table 9-3. Regional Distribution of per Capita Expenditures, Regression
Analysis

Explanatory Variables	Dependent Variables			
	Primary and Secondary Education	Payroll and Operations	Highways	Public Aid
North	8.665	411.639	−8.845	80.699
	(0.19)	(0.50)	(−1.00)	(−3.90)**
Central	−15.322	409.652	22.537	−73.189
	(−0.34)	(0.94)	(0.26)	(−3.52)**
South	25.794	416.613	−20.099	−64.496
	(0.56)	(0.64)	(−0.22)	(−3.11)**
Suburban	52.452	431.065	−18.448	−87.120
	(1.08)	(0.26)	(−0.20)	(−4.06)**
Children, age 5–7 per 1,000 population	1.173 (4.61)**			
Poverty rate	993.031 (5.98)**			
Per capita income	−.974 (−2.56)*	−.026 (−1.79)*	.003 (0.46)	
Poverty rate of children				842.018 (4.49)**
Proportion of population black				119.865 (2.44)*
Proportion of population urban		176.122 (2.03)*	−111.675 (−2.95)**	
R²	.82	.10	.15	.66
F	27.58**	1.79	2.84	31.03**

t statistics in parentheses.
* Significant at the .1 level.
** Significant at the .01 level.

need to be qualified because the formulas used to distribute state aid
do not sufficiently recognize variations among districts in revenue-
raising ability. Other students of state school finance have argued that
the manner in which state funds are distributed is insufficiently responsive to the variations in costs facing individual districts and needs
to be modified to reflect these differences.

Public-aid spending is closely related to the poverty population and to the black population, which is generally more economically disadvantaged than other groups. In contrast to education aid, however, there is evidence that Cook County receives more public-aid funds than other regions, even after adjustments for need have been made. Closer examination, however, suggests that this may be the result of differences in program need not recognized in the regression equation rather than politically induced regional bias.

One of these differences is in the age of the poverty population. A larger share of the poor are elderly in rural areas than in Cook County, where the bulk of the poor are younger families composed largely of single mothers and their children. Income support for the lower-income elderly is provided by the Supplemental Security Income program (SSI), which is totally funded by the federal government and hence does not appear in these figures, while assistance to poor families with children is provided by AFDC, which is jointly funded by the state and federal governments and is fully counted in these data. Higher than expected rates of spending in Cook County may simply reflect the fact that larger numbers of its poor are eligible for state-supported programs, while many poor families elsewhere in the state receive funds from other sources.

Second, the high level of public-aid spending in Cook County appears to reflect high levels of spending for Medicaid, which funds medical care to lower-income groups. It is possible to be eligible for Medicaid without having an income below the poverty level, and more Medicaid enrollees are concentrated in Cook County than are poor people. Cook County contains almost 67 percent of the state's Medicaid enrollees, compared to about 57 percent of the state's poverty population.

Other types of state spending, particularly for the construction and operation of state facilities, are less closely related to program need and show no particular regional bias. Spending for state payroll and operations has a weak negative relationship to per capita income, which may reflect the location of state prisons in downstate rural areas. It is related positively to urbanization, which may reflect the concentration of state administrative offices in Chicago and Springfield and the location of universities in smaller urban areas, such as Champaign-Urbana and Bloomington.

State-supported capital spending for highways shows no strong regional pattern nor any particular association with measures of need, including measures of regional economic growth not shown in these equations. (The same is true for other capital funds allocated through the Capital Development Board, although the results are not reported here.) As noted earlier, however, there is no particular policy reason for the distribution of these types of expenditures to be closely related to the measures of need used here, so the absence of any relationship between state spending and local problems cannot be cited as evidence of inequitable spending patterns.

For other state programs, the lack of any relationship between spending and program need is a matter of greater concern. The distribution of the local government share of state income tax revenue is made on the basis of population, which provides more funds to growing areas and relatively less to declining areas that are likely to be under greater financial stress. Similarly, the state's program of assistance to public transit systems provides less assistance to Chicago systems, and more to several smaller downstate systems, than the comparative scale and economic importance of these systems would suggest. Many downstate systems, which serve small and thinly settled cities that provide limited numbers of riders, recover a much smaller share of their expenses from fare-box revenues than do the state's larger systems and are hence financially dependent on state subsidies for their continued existence.

State spending in other program areas, which cannot be distinguished in the data used in this study, may also be less well targeted on problem areas than is desirable. One set of such programs which have been studied in some detail is a series of block-grant programs in community development, job training, and community services, created in 1981 by the Omnibus Budget and Reconciliation Act. This legislation consolidated a number of small categorical programs into the block grants and provided state governments considerable control over how these funds were to be allocated and spent. Several studies have found that this shift from federal to state control in Illinois produced a spreading of program funds away from Chicago and other harder pressed localities to more prosperous areas.[1]

The state's several economic development programs are also potentially fruitful for further research. While there has been little attention—either journalistic or scholarly—to the distribution of state economic development funds of various types, there is at least informal evidence that the state has subsidized considerable development in its more prosperous areas. The state has granted enterprise-zone status to such well-off cities as Springfield and Urbana and has spent considerable funds to attract the Diamond-Star plant to Bloomington-Normal, which has one of the lowest unemployment rates in the state, and to stimulate high-tech development along the corridor

Table 9-4. Regional Distribution of State Services, 1984

	North	Central	South	Collar	Cook
State university freshmen	1,585 (10%)	3,692 (16%)	2,365 (11%)	4,144 (17%)	10,720 (46%)
Community college freshmen	2,920 (13%)	4,209 (19%)	3,304 (15%)	3,074 (14%)	8,894 (40%)
Mental health admissions	1,371 (6%)	1,709 (8%)	1,254 (6%)	1,461 (7%)	15,318 (73%)
Corrections admissions	769 (6%)	1,500 (12%)	1,080 (9%)	925 (8%)	7,857 (65%)
Population	1,129,100 (10%)	1,944,400 (17%)	1,221,600 (11%)	1,945,500 (17%)	5,270,400 (46%)

Note: Totals may not add to 100% due to rounding.

Sources: *Data Book on Illinois Higher Education, 1984; Mental Health Statistics FY84; 1984 Annual Report to the Supreme Court of Illinois.*

in Dupage County, which is among the most rapidly growing areas in the country.[2] While these investments may well be defensible on other grounds, they do indicate that large amounts of state economic development funds have been used to encourage growth in expanding areas rather than in depressed areas.

In terms of the distribution of services as distinct from expenditures, Table 9-4 shows the regional distribution of several important state activities. The table suggests that, taking its population into consideration, Cook County receives a disproportional share of state services in the area of mental health and the criminal justice system. The county has an approximately proportional share of university and community college freshmen. A regression analysis similar to that for the distribution of expenditures in Table 9-3 was conducted in an attempt to explain the service distribution by county for state universities, community colleges, state mental hospitals, and prisons. The results are presented in Table 9-5.

Surprisingly, the collar counties are not disproportionately represented in terms of freshmen college enrollment. The distribution of students roughly corresponds to the distribution of population, and the regional variables have no statistical significance. Only per capita income is important in explaining enrollments in state universities. There also appears to be no distinct regional pattern to community college enrollment. Here, however, income is negatively related to enrollment.

Table 9-5. Regional Distribution of State Services, Regression Analysis

Explanatory Variable	Dependent Variables (per 1,000 of population)			
	State University Freshmen	Community College Freshmen	Mental Health Admissions	Correction Admissions
North	.403	2.649	−1.244	−.550
	(−.57)	(1.04)	(−2.39)*	(−1.34)
Central	.332	−.381	−1.562	−.508
	(.05)	(−0.15)	(−2.49)*	(−1.26)
South	.399	1.638	−1.265	−.487
	(−.56)	(0.64)	(−2.49)*	(−1.20)
Suburban	−.225	1.819	−1.366	−.690
	(−.30)	(0.67)	(−2.51)*	(−1.57)
Persons aged 17 per 1,000	18.813	−130.002		29.034
	(−0.56)	(−1.09)		(1.49)
Per capita income	.0001	−.0003		
	(2.52)*	(−2.94)*		
Crime rate				.00007
				(2.99)**
Proportion of population black			3.423	
			(4.07)**	
R²	.19	.25	.36	.28
F	3.72*	5.27*	10.69**	5.15*

t statistics in parentheses.
* Significant at the .1 level.
** Significant at the .01 level.

All of the non–Cook County regions have less than proportional representation in prison and mental health admissions because of Cook County's domination in this area. The regional pattern is especially important in mental health admissions; all downstate regions have a significantly lower rate, even after adjustments have been made for race. Admissions to corrections facilities are, not surprisingly, related to crime rates. Regional factors are marginally significant; all downstate regions have lower admission rates than Cook County, even after adjusting for crime rate differences.

Accounting for this apparent overconsumption of mental health and prison services in Cook County is difficult, since it seems unlikely that Chicago legislators spend an undue amount of time lobbying to get constituents into prison or psychiatric facilities. This pattern more likely reflects, as in the case of public aid, demand variables not included in these equations or institutional or procedural factors that lead to more intensive use of state facilities. The lower-income mentally ill or retarded, which one might expect to be concentrated in Cook County, for example, are unlikely to have access to private psychiatric facilities or out-patient programs and may be institutionalized largely because of a lack of viable alternatives.

Similarly, the "overuse" of prison facilities by Cook County may simply reflect a concentration of more serious crimes, whose perpetrators are more likely to receive prison sentences. The conventional FBI "index crime" rate figures used here include a number of offenses—such as burglary and larceny—which are relatively common and rarely rate a prison sentence, even for repeat offenders. By contrast, so called "Class X" offenses—such as murder or forcible rape—which have mandatory prison sentences under current Illinois law, may be more concentrated in Cook County than are the less serious crimes included in conventional crime rates. Requiring prison sentences for these crimes may have disproportionately increased the number of prisoners in Cook County relative to other parts of the state and may account for its apparent overconsumption of prison facilities.

This analysis does not support the widely held and frequently articulated conviction of many downstate legislators that Chicago is unduly benefitting from state services at the expense of the rest of the state. Cook County does receive larger than expected shares of state spending for public aid, prison, and mental health commitments, but closer examination suggests that this "bias" would largely disappear with the inclusion of better need measures or a closer accounting of how services are allocated. While the extent of state spending in Chicago as distinct from the rest of Cook County is difficult to assess with any degree of precision, the analysis here suggests that most of this spending is likely the result of the concentration of lower-income groups, which this spending benefits inside the city, rather than any particular political bias. Considering the severity of their problems, Chicago and other hard-pressed areas are receiving relatively less state funds from a number of program areas, while the prosperous areas are receiving relatively more. The state appears to be spreading funds more broadly than the distribution of social and governmental problems would suggest is desirable. The next section of this paper addresses some of the possible causes of this spending pattern.

VI. Politics and Prospects

It should first be noted that much of this spreading of funds is both desirable and proper. As argued earlier, much state spending is intended to provide services to the state as a whole rather than to redistribute resources among areas or groups. Further, some state programs are intended to provide support for members of particular groups, whether they live in rich areas or poor ones. The large absolute number of poor who live in the otherwise prosperous collar counties, for example, means that these counties will (and should) receive larger dollar allocations from income-support programs than do downstate counties, which have larger proportions of their populations below the poverty level but smaller absolute numbers of poor. Quite clearly, much state spending *ought* to be widely dispersed.

The analysis presented above, however, suggests that much state spending which should be redistributive in nature—support for local school systems and general governments, much economic-development support, and federally financed but state-administered programs for social services, job training, and community development—is also spread across areas that have limited program need. Prosperous areas receive large allocations relative to the severity of their problems, and hard-pressed areas—particularly Chicago—receive relatively less. Close examination suggests that the major reason for this pattern of spending may be political rather than demographic. Political leaders in Chicago and other hard-pressed areas are experiencing increasing difficulty in developing and maintaining coalitions in Springfield to support state spending on programs which address their problems.

The reasons for these increasing political problems are complex, but in general they relate to shifts in influence within the state legislature, the deterioration of traditional links between Chicago mayors and Illinois governors, and changes in the career orientation of state legislators. More precisely, the increased spreading of state spending appears to be a function of a decline in the size, cohesiveness, and influence of the Chicago delegation, a corresponding increase in the influence of the suburban bloc, and legislators' increased attentiveness to distributive questions.

The Decline of Chicago

Perhaps the major reason for the increasing difficulty of Chicago and other hard-pressed areas in securing state funding has been the erosion of the city's influence in Springfield. Traditionally, the city's position was secured by dealings between Mayor Richard Daley and a succes-

Table 9-6. Geographic Division of Illinois Legislature, 1967-68 and 1985-86 (percent share of seats)

	House of Representatives		Senate	
	1967-68	1985-86	1967-68	1985-86
Cook County	50.8	35.6	51.7	35.6
Collar counties	13.6	27.1	15.5	27.1
Downstate	35.6	37.3	32.8	37.3
Total	100.0	100.0	100.0	100.0

Sources: Compiled from data in Van Der Slik and Redfield, 1986, and State of Illinois, *Blue Book, 1967-68.*

sion of Illinois governors from both parties.[3] Besides controlling the Chicago and Cook County Democratic delegations by dominating the candidate slating process, the mayor also exercised considerable influence over downstate Democratic delegations by virtue of his prominence on the state central committee and his ability to deliver votes for statewide Democratic candidates. This influence put him in a strong political position in dealing with governors of either party. Perhaps ironically, Daley's most successful collaborations were with Republican rather than Democratic governors, who were rivals for influence in the state party.

Succeeding mayors have been unable to maintain this collaboration successfully. Mayor Jane Byrne attempted to strike several Daley-style deals with Governor James Thompson, but she had only limited success. Harold Washington had even less success in securing gubernatorial support for the city's legislative initiatives. Mayor Washington and Governor Thompson in fact clashed publicly—a historic rarity—over administrative appointments to the McCormick Place convention center and the new White Sox stadium authority, the mayor's alleged failure to adequately support the governor's proposals for state tax increases, and the responsibility for providing funds to settle a Chicago teachers' strike. Chicago's influence in Springfield has clearly declined.

The reasons for this decline are complex, but three factors appear to have been particularly important. First, the city delegation in the state legislature is considerably smaller than it once was. Over the last twenty years, the city and, to a lesser extent, Cook County have lost considerable population and legislative seats, in spite of aggressive manipulation of the redistricting process. Table 9-6 displays the geographic division of seats in both houses of the state legislature for selected sessions over this period. In the 1967 session, slightly over half of the members of both houses were from Cook County; by the 1985–86 session, this share had fallen to just over one-third. The city's representation has fallen even more sharply. In the 1967–68 session, about one-third of the legislature was elected from Chicago districts; by 1985, less than one-fifth came from districts completely contained in the city. While several other districts which extend from the city into suburban Cook County have been carefully drawn to maintain city (and Democratic) majorities, the representatives from these districts are likely to come under increasing pressure from suburban constituents to take their interests into account and to be less oriented toward city concerns. The size of the city's bloc in Springfield, and hence its influence, has slipped sharply.

It should also be noted that the state's other hard-pressed areas have been losing population and representation as well. Such downstate cities as Peoria and Kankakee—whose problems of unemployment, poverty, and job loss are as severe as Chicago's—have also experienced losses of population and a dilution of their legislative influence through the redistricting process.

This decline in the size of Chicago's delegation has been exacerbated by the increasing contentiousness within its ranks. The well-publicized "Council Wars" between Mayor Washington and Alderman Edward Vrdolyak have spilled over into the legislative delegation as well, so that Vrdolyak supporters in Springfield have increasingly made common cause with suburban Republicans to support anti-city legislation. The most prominent recent example of this collaboration came in the 1986 legislative session, when suburban Republicans backed a Vrdolyak measure to prevent the mayor from replacing Chicago Park District Director Ed Kelly in exchange for support on an attempt to create a suburban-dominated regional airport authority, which would take much of the control of O'Hare Airport away from the city (McClory, 1986). While both measures eventually failed, the split in Chicago's delegation seems likely to persist, if not intensify. Not only does Chicago have less representation in the state legislature, but what representation it has is increasingly divided, leading to a further decline in its influence.

A third factor reducing the city's influence is that Chicago politicians historically have not placed a high priority on developing and maintaining stable, ongoing coalitions with other parts of the state (Gove, 1982:207). During Daley's tenure as mayor, the state legislature was generally viewed as the "minor leagues" to which promising organization politicians were sent to acquire experience before being "promoted" to vacancies on the City Council or the Cook County Board.

Under these conditions, members of Chicago's delegation remained largely oriented toward maintaining and enhancing their positions within the city's political hierarchy rather than attempting to develop an independent political base in Springfield. More recently, the city's incentives to develop stable political ties with other parts of the state have been weakened by the city's status as a home-rule municipality under the 1970 state constitution. This change, which provided the city with more control over its own affairs, reduced its need for state legislation and hence lessened the need for city representatives to do business on a regular basis with the rest of the legislature. Since the establishment of home rule, most of the city's efforts in the legislature have been directed toward defensive attempts to prevent encroachment on the city's power—as in the O'Hare Airport–Park District case—or large expensive projects—such as the Chicago World's Fair and subsidies for the Regional Transit Authority—which benefit only the city. Downstate legislators are unlikely to see themselves as having much stake in alliances with the city on either type of issue. In fact, they may have more to gain politically by opposing Chicago initiatives.

These changes have substantially weakened the city's position in dealing with both the state legislature and the governor. The city's own legislative delegation is smaller and more fragmented than in the past, and recent mayors have been unable to develop ties with downstate delegations to replace Daley's prominence in the state Democratic party. Given these conditions, it is perhaps not surprising that the city's ability to secure state funding has declined.

The Rise of the Suburbs

A second major factor which has altered the politics of state funding in Illinois has been the increasing political prominence of the Chicago suburbs. As earlier argument suggests, population and legislative representation have moved out of Chicago and into the collar counties and suburban Cook County. As the data in Table 9–6 indicate, the size of the suburban delegation in the state legislature has increased from less than 15 percent of the seats in 1967–68 to almost 30 percent in 1985–86.

This increasing size has been accompanied by increasing cohesiveness and activism within the suburban delegation.[4] As a result of the cutback amendment to the 1970 constitution, which replaced multi-member house districts in which minority party representation was guaranteed with single-member districts, the suburban delegation has become overwhelmingly Republican. Democrats occupied the constitutionally prescribed one-third of suburban house seats in 1967–68;

but only three of the thirty-two suburban seats in 1985–86. This shift in partisan composition has increased suburban influence among legislative Republicans and led to the selection of suburbanites as minority leaders in both houses in 1983.

Both minority leaders have been active in establishing control over their delegations and in pressing for a larger share of state funding for the suburbs, largely at Chicago's expense. Capitalizing on anti-Chicago sentiment has proven effective — both as a campaign issue in suburban districts and as a device for maintaining cohesion inside the delegation (McClory, 1986:19). The increased size and cohesion of the suburban delegation, at a time when the city's delegation is divided and widely seen as politically vulnerable, have significantly altered the balance of power in the legislature and made the spreading of funds to more prosperous areas politically necessary.

Legislative Careerism

A third factor that has made it politically difficult to target state funds on areas with the most severe problems has been the increasing careerist orientation of many state legislators. Unlike their predecessors, current legislators are more likely to see their legislative duties as a full-time job with many of the characteristics of a career. Almost half of the members of the 1983 General Assembly, for example, listed their occupation as full-time legislator, compared to less than 5 percent twenty years earlier (Van der Slik and Redfield, 1986:72). This orientation stems from the legislature's expanded work load, which has increased both the amount of time the legislature spends in session and the level of demands for constituent-service activities. This expanded work load has reduced the time legislators have available to spend on law practices and other career interests, which has increased the cost of losing their seat — a cost which has been further raised by increases in legislative pay and pensions. As a result of these changes, more legislators may place a higher premium on holding onto their seats than was previously the case.

Another factor which has likely enhanced legislative careerism is the so-called "cutback amendment" to the state constitution, which reduced the size of the House of Representatives by one-third and replaced a cumulative voting system (in which each district chose three members and each party was guaranteed at least one member in every district) with a single-member-district system. The reduction in the size of the House has increased the work load and the public visibility of individual representatives, likely making them more concerned about potential electoral challenges. This concern may have been enhanced by the elimination of the cumulative voting system, which was described by one scholar as a method of "institutional[izing] noncompetition" (Fenton, 1966:209). The shift to a single-member system may have also made representatives more concerned about potential electoral challenges and hence more attentive to the electoral consequences of particular votes.

This careerist perspective may have led many legislators to focus solely on potential local gains when voting on distributive issues. Local government units and other institutional claimants for funds—such as school boards, the employees of state facilities, and local economic development groups, which are among the more visible and vocal constituents—are likely to press for the largest possible share of funds from most programs and to gauge the performance of individual legislators by how well they do in securing support. A desire to be well thought of by these groups, which control a disproportionate share of campaign resources, may have made legislators less willing to support measures that do not provide a politically acceptable level of funding for their districts.

This increased local orientation may have complicated the task of legislative leaders in assembling coalitions, particularly among Democrats and downstate representatives. Because they perceive their performance is being watched by politically important groups in their district, these representatives may be less willing to go along with party leaders on one vote in exchange for support on another. Downstate Democrats, who were once willing to take their cues from Mayor Daley on Chicago-related issues, for example, may be more insistent on getting commitments for their fair share of funds from party leaders as the price for their support.

This career-based localism may partially account for the tendencies toward "four parties (one centered around each of the four major legislative leaders) rather than two" and *ad hoc* interest-brokering as the major method of legislative bargaining, which have been noted by close observers of the Illinois legislature, including members of the legislative leadership (Ross, 1984:31; 1985a:8–10; 1985b:11). Because of the increased unwillingness of legislators to support a particular measure unless they get something from it, there is less basis for stable coalitions within which legislators can trade support across issues. Support for each issue increasingly has to be assembled from scratch by each legislative leader, with the result that versions of bills differ as do the supporting coalitions assembled by each leader. These competing versions of legislation must be reconciled, which is most frequently done by spreading enough benefits to secure a majority.

One example of this method of brokered distribution occurred in successful attempts to increase the state subsidy for the Chicago Rapid Transit Authority in the 1985 legislative session. Support for this measure was assembled by increasing the comparable state subsidy for several downstate transit districts, most of which are small, financially marginal, and heavily dependent on state support.

Conclusions and Solutions

The political reasons for the spreading of funds across the state with limited attention to program need are straightforward. The poorer areas of the state, particularly Chicago, have been losing representation and have been unable either to keep their own delegations in line or to develop coalitions among themselves, while the more prosperous suburban areas have been gaining both representation and political cohesion. When coupled with an increased tendency for legislators to demand tangible benefits for their districts as the price for support for particular programs, this shift in political power has led to a shift of funds away from poorer areas to wealthier ones. Distributive decisions that were made in the past by party leaders— primarily Mayor Daley of Chicago and the governor—are now largely bargained on an *ad hoc* basis between legislative leaders and the governor.

The significance of these political changes for the geographic distribution of state spending should not be overstated, particularly given the findings cited earlier on the historical stability of state expenditures. Much, if not most, state spending still goes where it always did, in spite of these shifts in the political center of gravity in the state legislature. This spending is driven by factors that are responsive to political forces only in the long run. The location of state facilities (such as universities, prisons, and office complexes), which is the main determinant of state spending for operations and payrolls, can be altered only slightly from one legislative session to the next. AFDC and Medicaid expenditures are heavily constrained by federal regulations that severely limit state discretion. These results do suggest, however, that Chicago and other depressed areas are doing much less well at influencing the flow of state funds than they once did. The Washington administration, for example, advanced several unsuccessful proposals to replace the loss of federal general revenue-sharing funds.

There is no reason to expect these political changes, or the demographic trends which underlie them, will abate or reverse themselves in the near future. Most population projections envision a static population in Chicago, continued decline in other hard-pressed areas, and continued growth, although at a lower rate, in the suburbs. If borne out, these projections suggest a further redistribution of legislative seats away from poorer areas toward richer ones after the 1990 census. Further, the tendency for brokered coalition-building to be the dominant method of assembling coalitions around bills which allocate money seems likely to continue. The spreading of funds, therefore, might continue or intensify.

The major conceivable exception to this trend lies in the possibility of a more stable coalition between Chicago and the more depressed downstate areas. As noted earlier, the city has made relatively little effort to develop any stable political ties with these areas, particularly the harder-pressed downstate cities. While there was some limited cooperation between Chicago and other cities over the Build Illinois program, and Mayor Washington made several widely publicized swings through downstate to rally support for the general revenue-sharing program, there is still little ongoing contact of the type necessary for a stable alliance to develop.

NOTES

1. The Job Training Partnership Act (JTPA), which replaced the Comprehensive Employment and Training Act (CETA), is examined in Orfield and Slessarev (1986) and Oldakowski, Marczak, and Geraci (1985); other programs are evaluated in Hull House Association (1985).

2. For a detailed account of the state's role in attracting the Diamond-Star plant, see Lind and Elder (1986:19–23).

3. This section draws heavily from Gove (1982).

4. See McClory (1986:18–19). For evidence on the increasing political importance of the Chicago-suburban cleavage, see Ross (1983:8).

REFERENCES

Data Book on Illinois Higher Education, 1984. 1984. Springfield: State of Illinois Board of Higher Education.

Fenton, John. 1966. Midwest Politics. New York: Holt, Rinehart, and Winston.

Fossett, James, and Gary Orfield. 1987. "Market Failure and Federal Policy: Low Income Housing in Chicago, 1970–1983." In Gary Tobin (ed.), Divided Neighborhoods. Beverly Hills: Sage.

Gove, Samuel K. 1982. "State Impact: The Daley Legacy." In Samuel K. Gove and Louis Masotti (eds.), After Daley. Urbana: University of Illinois Press.

Hull House Association, Research and Advocacy Department. 1985. *Tracking Federal Dollars: Categorical Grants, Block Grants and the Issue of a Fair Share for the Poor of Illinois.* Chicago: Hull House Association, Research and Advocacy Department.

Illinois Legislative Council. 1984. *1984 State Tax Collections and Expenditures by County,* File 9-477. Springfield: Illinois Legislative Council.

Kane, Douglas N. 1973. *Regional Distribution of Taxes and Expenditures in Illinois.* Ph.D. dissertation, Department of Economics, University of Illinois.

Lind, Nancy, and Ann Elder. 1986. "Who Pays? Who Benefits?: The Case of the Incentive Package Offered to the Diamond-Star Automotive Plant." *Government Finance Review* 2 (December):19–23.

McClory, Robert J. 1986. "O'Hare: First Battle in a Long War?" *Illinois Issues* 12 (August-September):16–19.

Mental Health Statistics FY84. 1984. Springfield: Illinois Department of Mental Health and Developmental Disabilities.

1984 Annual Report to the Supreme Court of Illinois. 1984. Springfield: Administrative Office of the Illinois Courts.

Oldakowski, Raymond, Lauri Marczak, and Ann Geraci. 1985. "Job Training Partnership Act Funds: An Evaluation of Their Allocation in Illinois." *Illinois Business Review* 42 (1):7–10.

Orfield, Gary, and Helen Slessarev. 1986. *Job Training under the New Federalism: JTPA in the Industrial Heartland.* Chicago: Illinois Unemployment and Job Training Research Project.

Ross, Diane. 1983. "The Ascension of Michael Madigan." *Illinois Issues* 9 (May):6–12.

———. 1984. "Pate Philip: The Unambiguous Leader of the Senate GOP." *Illinois Issues* 10 (March):30–32.

———. 1985a. "A Few Words from the Governor." *Illinois Issues* 11 (January):6–19.

———. 1985b. "Phil Rock: Holding Together a Raucous Caucus." *Illinois Issues* 11 (April):8–14.

State of Illinois. 1969. *Blue Book, 1967–68.* Springfield: State of Illinois.

U.S. Bureau of Census. 1985. "County Statistics File."

Van der Slik, Jack, and Kent Redfield. 1986. *Lawmaking in Illinois.* Springfield: Sangamon State University Press.

Regional Animosities in Illinois: Perceptual Dimensions

10

Peter F. Nardulli and Michael Krassa

Conventional wisdom, based on folklore handed down by generations of Illinoisans, holds that Illinois is a deeply divided, heterogeneous state. As some of the other essays demonstrate (Wirt, chapter 2 herein), it was settled at different times by people with very different backgrounds and orientations. Many believe that these regionally based subcultures persist today, producing individuals who approach life and the world in distinctive and sometimes conflictual ways. These cultural differences have been exacerbated by differences in regional economic systems. Different sectors have developed at different rates and at different times, giving rise to regionally based differences in economic interests and needs (Atack, chapter 3 herein). Bitter political battles over slavery, the structure of education, prohibition, redistricting, and a host of other issues have divided the state in the past (Sutton, chapter 4 herein) and continue to do so, to a degree, today (Frank, Nardulli, and Green, chapter 8 herein).

This chapter seeks to examine, directly and empirically, the structure of regional divisions that have been part of the state's folklore for so long. This examination is important for several reasons. First, it has never been done before. Much of the conventional wisdom about the beliefs, perspectives, desires, and attitudes of Illinois residents is based on the views of political and civic leaders as well as the media. While there may be observable differences across the state, accents and dress codes tell us little about one's belief system. The only truly empirical bases for much of the conventional wisdom about regional differences in Illinois are voting and census data. However, they are not always precise, informative, or to the point.

A second reason for this examination is that much has changed in post–World War II society, and many of these changes may have mitigated whatever regionally based cultural differences existed in the past. The revolution in transportation and communications has made both the state and the world a smaller place in which to live. A package can be received overnight anywhere in the state, in some cases in a matter of hours. Friends, family, and business associates are as close as a telephone. Illinois is tied together by a network of superhighways inconceivable just thirty years ago; in addition, more people have more cars with which to traverse those highways. Regional airports across the state have made various cities even more accessible to businesses and political leaders. Indeed, a state "fly around" is almost mandatory today for those announcing for statewide office in Illinois. Unlike fifty years ago, Illinois residents throughout the state have daily access to major newspapers as well as radio and television stations.

These changes mean that even those who remain in one locale for most of their lives are being exposed a broader array of stimuli and ideas than would have been the case in an earlier era. A related societal change is the increased mobility of the American people. The social pluralism that Wirt (chapter 2 herein) describes as characterizing Illinois in the post–Civil War era was diffused throughout the state at an increasingly rapid rate over the past forty years. Fewer people are living most of their lives in one locale, and the migration patterns are leading to less distinctive regional populations. Major urban areas, while still very diverse, are no longer dominated by impoverished enclaves of immigrants speaking foreign languages, practicing different religions, and observing strange customs. The reapportionment issue has been largely defused by the Supreme Court. In Chicago, the sons and daughters of these immigrants have migrated to suburban areas, as well as other parts of the state, and are no longer manipulated by urban pols in ways that made the nativists in rural areas suspicious and hostile. They have adapted their views, wants, and life-styles to their new environment; they have also had an impact on the local cultures with which they have come into contact. The technological revolution in farming has decreased the demand for farm laborers and has led to an out-migration from rural areas, a trend only briefly interrupted in the 1970s. For decades would-be farmers have been in search of other jobs, leading to even more diversified regional populations.

A final factor that may be relevant here is the increasing uniformity in public elementary and secondary education that exists within the state of Illinois. Despite the great disparities in spending, district size, and the quality of physical structures that still exist, the differences are certainly not as great as they were fifty years ago. Curricular mandates, statewide teacher certification, and a funding formula that makes some effort to equalize per pupil expenditures have all contributed to a greater degree of uniformity. There are no longer uncertified teachers using outdated textbooks and teaching in "one room" school houses. Throughout the state we now find modern, well-equipped schools that are able to take advantage of the latest educational innovations.

Understanding Regionalism: A Statewide Survey

To obtain a better understanding of the regionalism in Illinois, we undertook a statewide telephone survey. The state was divided into five regions—northern Illinois, central Illinois, southern Illinois, the city of Chicago, and the suburban collar around Chicago. The latter sample included the Cook County suburbs (see Nardulli, chapter 1 herein: Figure 1–1). A random sample of respondents was selected in each of these regions, using an exhaustive list of telephone exchanges and random digit dialing. In all, 2,751 male and female heads of households responded to the rather lengthy questionnaire (448 in the northern subsample; 471 in the central; 452 in the southern; 682 in Chicago; 698 in the suburban region). Using a weighting scheme, we are able to talk about views of Illinois residents as a whole as well as those in the different regions.[1]

The survey was designed to achieve a number of objectives. First, we wanted to see how Illinoisans viewed the state. To do this, we asked them open-ended questions about how they described "their part of the state," as well as if and how they saw the state being divided. Second, we wanted to capture how the respondents viewed people who lived in other parts of the state. Were they similar to themselves? Did others think highly of them? Were those in other parts of the state concerned with their welfare? How about legislators from other regions of the state? Were they concerned with the welfare of the state or with narrow, localistic concerns? To what degree did people in different parts of the state adhere to stereotypes of others?

The third part of the survey examined the bases for whatever regionally based animosities existed. Were these animosities based on real differences in how residents viewed life or in what they wanted out of life or out of their government? Or were these animosities reflections of a past not yet caught up with the present? A final section of the survey dealt with the demographic characteristics of the respondents (age, race, sex, religion, ethnicity, income, and education). If regionally based differences in attitudes, wants, demands, and the like emerged, we wanted to be able to determine whether they were based on different subcultures or were simply due to differences in education levels, family structures, racial compositions, and so forth, across the different parts of the state.

A review of these survey data will help us obtain a better sense of the depth and structure of the regional cleavages within Illinois; it may also help us understand their foundation. We begin with a review of how people view the state; then we turn to how they view others. Finally we examine, by region, differences in respondents' attitudes, wants, and demands.

Perceptions of Regional Divisions within Illinois

We start our analysis of regionalism by examining how respondents viewed Illinois. We used a series of questions to probe these perceptions, beginning with one on how they described *their* part of the state. The vast majority of respondents used geographic or regional descriptors, as seen in Table 10–1. About 5 percent could not provide any description, and another 8 percent used a non-regional term. Of those using regional terms to describe their locale, only a small portion used a term different from those used to organize this study (i.e., eastern Illinois or western Illinois). Over 86 percent of those interviewed (over 90 percent of those who could provide some sort of description) used a term that corresponded to one of our subsamples.[2] Most of those who did not use a geographical identifier described themselves as being from an urban area, a rural area, or named a specific town.[3]

We can get a telling assessment of how people viewed the state by examining a second set of questions. One asked respondents whether the state was "pretty much alike" or whether it was composed of "several different regions or parts." If they thought of the state as being composed of several different parts, they were asked to name those parts. Only 21 percent of the respondents who responded to this question thought of Illinois as being pretty much alike; almost three-quarters (73 percent) thought it was composed of distinct regions or parts. Less than 6 percent had no opinion. As Table 10–2 indicates, respondents' views on this question varied somewhat across our five samples. Inhabitants of Chicago's suburban collar were the most likely to see contrasts, while central Illinois residents were somewhat less likely to see regional divisions.

Table 10–1. Part of State in Which Respondent Lives,
Self-Described

Descriptor	Percent of Sample[a] (N)
Northern Illinois	35.3
	(1,577)
Southern Illinois	9.5
	(423)
Eastern Illinois	.4
	(18)
Western Illinois	1.3
	(60)
Central Illinois	18.0
	(806)
Chicago	15.3
	(682)
Chicago suburbs	8.2
	(368)
Other term	7.5
	(337)
No description	4.5
	(199)
[a] Weighted.	(4,470)

Identifying the divisions that people saw within the state was no simple matter. We recorded verbatim, for each respondent, up to seven different terms used to describe these divisions. Over three hundred descriptions were offered. They ranged from topological terms (valleys, flatlands, swamps, etc.), highly specific terms (city and county names), and sociological terms (rural, small town, urban), to the more familiar regional (north, south, central, Chicago suburbs) and subregional terms (east-central, northwest suburbs, etc.).

A comprehensive review of all the descriptors given by respondents would be both cumbersome and counterproductive as our primary concern is with the saliency of regional cleavages. More informative is a simple listing of basic regional terms that were offered by respondents. Table 10–3 lists these for the state as a whole as well as by subsample. Also included in Table 10–3 are data on the percentage of people who offered no within-state divisions as well as those who offered only non-regional divisions. If we begin with these latter two categories, we see that even though over three-quarters of the respondents thought the state was divided, almost 30 percent could not

Table 10–2. Views on Illinois' Homogeneity

	All Respondents[a] % (N)	Northern Illinois Respondents % (N)	Central Illinois Respondents % (N)	Southern Illinois Respondents % (N)	All Downstate Respondents[a] % (N)	Suburban Collar Respondents % (N)	City of Chicago Respondents % (N)
Illinois is:							
Pretty much alike	20.9 (933)	25.2 (106)	29.1 (130)	24.5 (103)	26.8 (420)	16.8 (110)	23.4 (151)
Composed of different parts	73.3 (3,276)	74.8 (314)	70.9 (316)	75.5 (318)	73.2 (1,144)	83.2 (545)	76.6 (495)
Total number of respondents	(4,472)[b]	(420)	(446)	(421)	(1,564)	(655)	(646)

[a] Weighted.
[b] 263 or 5.8 percent of the respondents had no opinion on this question; these respondents were excluded from the statistics in the remaining columns.

Table 10–3. Percent of Cases Listing Various Regional Divisions

	All Respondents[a]	Northern Illinois Respondents	Central Illinois Respondents	Southern Illinois Respondents	All Downstate Respondents[a]	Suburban Collar Respondents	City of Chicago Respondents
North	28.3	39.7	28.9	35.6	33.6	25.4	24.8
South	37.0	46.0	41.2	46.5	43.9	34.5	30.1
East	2.4	1.8	3.0	1.8	2.3	2.0	3.1
West	4.8	4.0	4.0	2.2	3.5	5.3	5.9
Central	18.9	21.4	29.5	22.8	25.5	14.8	15.0
Suburban collar	10.8	4.2	4.5	3.5	4.2	17.2	11.1
Chicago	26.1	24.6	25.9	25.2	25.4	29.4	22.1
No divisions offered	29.2	29.7	34.2	28.2	31.4	24.1	33.6
Only non-regional divisions offered	12.9	11.2	10.6	10.4	10.7	15.0	13.1
Number of cases	4,472	448	471	452	1,672	698	682

[a] Weighted.

say how and another 13 percent did not mention even a single regional division. Indeed, almost half (46 percent) of Chicago respondents offered no regional divisions at all.

If we look at the data on the incidence of respondents' mentioning one of the various regional terms (which will not sum to 100 percent because people could mention more than one), several points are evident. First, those that perceived regional divisions were most likely to see northern, southern, and central Illinois, plus Chicago, as distinct areas within the state. Southern Illinois was the most frequently mentioned as being distinct, followed by northern Illinois and then Chicago. Chicago's suburban collar, the fastest growing, most affluent, and perhaps politically the most pivotal part of the state, was barely perceived as a distinct region. It is also clear that most did not see east-west divisions within the state. These perceptions did not vary much by region of the state, although it is interesting to note that Chicagoans were less likely to see Chicago as a distinct part of the state than those elsewhere. In each of the other regions, the respondents were more likely to see *their* part of the state as a distinct region.

Illinoisans Perceptions of One Another

The set of data just reviewed indicated that Illinoisans viewed the state as being divided, largely along the regional lines that we used to organize this survey. But these data tells us little about how respondents viewed those who lived in other parts of the state. To gauge these perceptions we had to use a rather involved strategy. First, we divided the state into three different sectors (Chicago, the suburban collar around Chicago, and the areas of Illinois outside the Chicago metropolitan area, i.e., downstate Illinois). We then asked how people from one sector perceived those from the other two sectors on several key dimensions. Are *they* similar to us? Do *they* care about us? Are *their* legislators concerned about the *whole* state? The questions used are reported in Table 10–4. A second tact was to obtain reactions from the respondents to a set of social stereotypes of rural dwellers, urbanites, and suburbanites. These questions, unlike those in Table 10–4, were asked of all respondents, enabling us to compare self-perceptions with those of outsiders. These questions are provided in Table 10–5. A third set of questions dealt with people's perceptions of whether one or another of the three regions constituted a financial burden on the state. One last set of questions dealt with whether Chicago should become a separate state and the consequences of such a development.

Table 10–4. Questions Pertaining to How Residents Viewed One Another

General Perception Questions:

G-1   People who live in _____ are pretty much the same as those who live around here (for clarification read: in terms of how they were raised, how they live, and what they think is important).

G-2   Most people in _____ don't think very highly of the people around here.

Questions of Perceptions of Others' Demands on State Government:

D-1   People in _____ want the state government to do a lot more than we do around here.

D-2   _____ want the state government to do a lot less than we do around here.

Questions on Concern for Welfare:

W-1   Most _____ care about the welfare of people around here.

W-2   _____ would support a government program that only benefitted people around here.

Questions on Perceptions of Other's Legislators:

L-1   State legislators from _____ sometimes oppose laws that only favor other parts of the state.

L-2   Legislators from _____ are generally not concerned with the welfare of the *whole* state.

L-3   _____ legislators are too willing to interfere with the legislature's work if they don't get their way.

Table 10–5. Social Stereotype Questions

Chicagoan, "Callous" Stereotype:

C-1   Most Chicagoans are rude to strangers.

C-2   Most people in Chicago are not very neighborly.

Downstaters, "Rube" Stereotype:

R-1   Most downstaters are only concerned with what goes on in their own town.

R-2   Most downstaters are too set in their ways (don't like change).

Suburbanites, "Social Climber" Stereotype:

S-1   People in the suburbs of Chicago are too concerned with getting ahead.

S-2   People in the suburbs are overly concerned with outward appearances (things like fancy cars, big houses, or expensive clothes).

Perceptions of Individuals

Figure 10–1 displays the data on the first general perceptual question (G–1), which asked whether people thought those in other parts of the state were similar to those in their region. A few points are clear. Beginning with the traditional Chicago-downstate dichotomy, it is

Chicagoans' Views of Others

People who live in (the suburbs around Chicago) (in downstate Illinois) are pretty much the same as those who live around here [in terms of the way they were raised, how they live, and what they think is important].

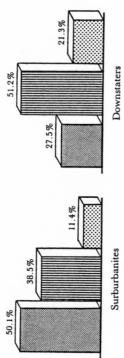

Downstate Residents' Views of Others

People who live in (Chicago) (the suburbs around Chicago) are pretty much the same as those who live around here [in terms of how they were raised, how they live, and what they think is important].

Suburban Residents' Views of Others

People (who live in the city of Chicago) (in downstate Illinois) are pretty much the same as those who live around here [in terms of the way they were raised, how they live, and what they think is important].

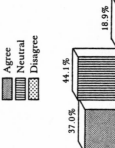
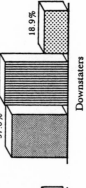
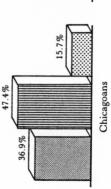
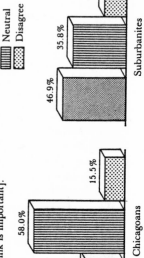

Figure 10–1. Views on Similarity to One Another

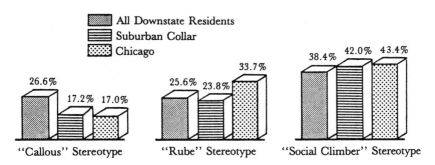

Figure 10-2. Social Stereotypes

apparent that few residents in these two parts of the state believed they were very similar in terms of how they were raised, how they live, and what they think is important. Barely a quarter of Chicagoans agreed with that question when the reference group was "downstate"; about the same proportion of the downstate sample thought they were similar to Chicagoans. About 58 percent of the downstate respondents explicitly disagreed with it. Both Chicagoans and downstaters were more likely to see themselves as more similar to suburbanites—50 and 47 percent, respectively. Suburbanites, however, rejected the comparisons between themselves and downstaters and Chicagoans. Only about 37 percent agreed that they were similar to either group.

We should be cautious in over-interpreting these response patterns. "Different" does not necessarily mean "bad," and we should resist the temptation to place a negative connotation on the findings reported in Figure 10-1. Some light can be shed on this matter by examining the responses to the social stereotype questions reported in Table 10-5. To enhance stability of the perceptions these questions were meant to tap and to simplify the presentation of the results, we combined the data on the three pairs of social stereotype questions (C-1, C-2; R-1, R-2; S-1, S-2) reported in Table 10-5. For each set of questions, respondents who agreed with the views in both were said to adhere to one of three stereotypes: a "callous" stereotype for Chicagoans, a "rube" stereotype for those outside the metropolitan area, and a "social climber" stereotype for suburbanites. The results, depicted in Figure 10-2, lead us to view the findings reported in Figure 10-1 somewhat differently. The lowest overall support for these rather negative stereotypes was for Chicagoans, about 20 percent overall; the highest was for suburbanites, with 40 percent of the weighted statewide sample agreeing with the "social climber" stereotype. About 27 percent agreed with the "rube" stereotype.

Even if we look at the support for these stereotypes by region, this general pattern holds up. Only about a quarter of downstaters agreed with the "callous" stereotype of Chicagoans. About 17 percent of suburbanites agreed with it, which was actually lower than the number of Chicagoans. About a third of the Chicago respondents agreed with the "rube" stereotypes, while less than a quarter of suburbanites agreed with it. Overall about a quarter of downstaters agreed with the "rube" stereotype, but less than 20 percent of those in northern Illinois adhered to it. In contrast, almost 32 percent of those in southern Illinois agreed—about the same number as in Chicago. There was not much regional variation in the "social climber" stereotype, but suburbanites registered the highest overall level of agreement.

The data portrayed in Figures 10–1 and 10–2 provide some revealing insights into the nature of regional cleavages in the state. The existence of regional cleavages in the minds of our respondents was confirmed by the fact that over 77 percent of Illinoisans thought Illinois was composed of "several different regions or parts." Despite the fact that a fairly large number of respondents (almost a third) could not name even a single division, a good number of downstaters rejected any commonalities between themselves and Chicagoans, and Chicagoans did the same. Both saw themselves as more similar to suburbanites, but suburbanites were less likely to see the similarities. At the same time, only between a quarter to a third of downstaters and Chicagoans adhered to negative stereotypes; about two in five had negative stereotypes of suburbanites. Thus, while most contended there were differences, these differences did not appear to extend to a personal level or result in personal animosities.

It should be pointed out that this was not at all clear to many people across the state, as can be seen in Figure 10–3. It reports the distribution of responses to the question that asked people to respond to the statement, "Most people in ——— think very highly of people from around here" (Table 10–4: G-2). Over 46 percent of Chicagoans agreed that downstaters did not think highly of them; approximately the same percent of downstaters agreed that Chicagoans did not think highly of them. Fewer people in both groups thought that suburbanites did not think highly of them (42 percent of Chicagoans; 39 percent of downstaters). Only about 28 percent of suburbanites thought Chicagoans did not think highly of them, but 39 percent felt downstaters did not hold them in high regard—a somewhat surprising finding.

Chicagoans' Views of Others

Most people (in the Chicago suburbs) (downstate) don't think very highly of people around here.

Agree
Disagree
Neutral

41.6% 37.6% 20.8%
Suburbanites

46.9% 26.3% 26.8%
Downstaters

Suburban Residents' Views of Others

Most people (in Chicago) (downstate) don't think very highly of people around here.

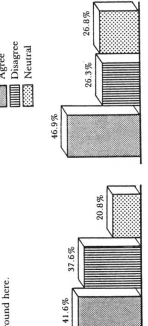

Agree
Disagree
Neutral

27.6% 45.4% 27.0%
Chicagoans

39.1% 32.7% 28.2%
Downstaters

Downstate Residents' Views of Others

Most people who live in (Chicago) (the Chicago suburbs) don't think very highly of the people around here.

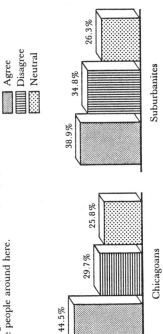

Agree
Disagree
Neutral

44.5% 29.7% 25.8%
Chicagoans

38.9% 34.8% 26.3%
Suburbanites

Figure 10–3. Views on Others' Respect

Perceptions of Political Wants and Political Support

Another source of possible friction among people — one that would lead them to see broad differences among them — is in the political arena. Residents in one part of the state may perceive others as wanting a higher level of services from state government. They may also see others as unresponsive to their wants and needs. We asked several questions to gauge Illinoisans' feelings about these matters (Table 10–4: D-1, D-2). The first dealt with people's perceptions about the relative level of others' wants from state government. The data are reported in Figure 10–4. What is evident from them is that many people outside Chicago thought Chicagoans wanted more from state government than they themselves did. While 35–39 percent of down-staters and suburbanites believed that Chicagoans wanted about the same level of government services as they did, even more thought Chicagoans wanted state government to do more than they wanted it to do. There were even more marked differences in the regional downstate samples. Almost half of northern Illinois residents, for example, thought Chicagoans wanted a higher level of government services. In contrast, only about one-third of downstaters and about one-quarter of Chicagoans thought the suburbanites wanted more than they did from the state. Most of the respondents in these areas thought suburbanites wanted about the same level of services. Essentially, the same pattern prevailed for Chicago and suburban perceptions of downstate desires.

Even more informative than the question on perceptions of what others wanted from the state were the questions on whether respondents thought others were concerned with the welfare of people in "their part of the state" and whether others would support a program that benefitted "their part of the state" (see Table 10–4: W-1, W-2). To simplify the presentation of these data and to garner more insights from them, these two questions were merged into one for purposes of analysis. We produced four relevant categories. One included respondents who believed others did not care about their welfare and would not support a program that benefitted them. A second included respondents who thought others *might* care about their welfare but would still not support a program that benefitted them. A third category included respondents who said others cared but would not support a program for them. The fourth included respondents who thought others cared and would support a program that benefitted them. Most respondents fit into one of these categories, but others expressed contradictory feelings and were placed in a miscellaneous, "mixed feelings" category.

Percent believing Chicagoans want state government to do less, about the same, or more than the people in their part of the state.

All Downstate Residents
Suburban Collar

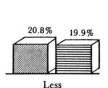
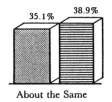
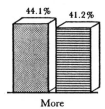

20.8%   19.9%

35.1%   38.9%

44.1%   41.2%

Less

About the Same

More

Percent believing people outside the Chicago area want state government to do less, about the same, or more than the people in their part of the state.

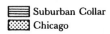
Suburban Collar
Chicago

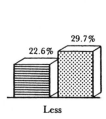
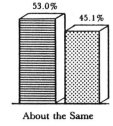
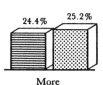

22.6%   29.7%

53.0%   45.1%

24.4%   25.2%

Less

About the Same

More

Percent believing people in the Chicago suburbs want state government to do less, about the same, or more than the people in their part of the state.

All Downstate Residents
Chicago

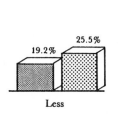
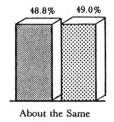
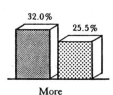

19.2%   25.5%

48.8%   49.0%

32.0%   25.5%

Less

About the Same

More

Figure 10-4. Views on Levels of State Services

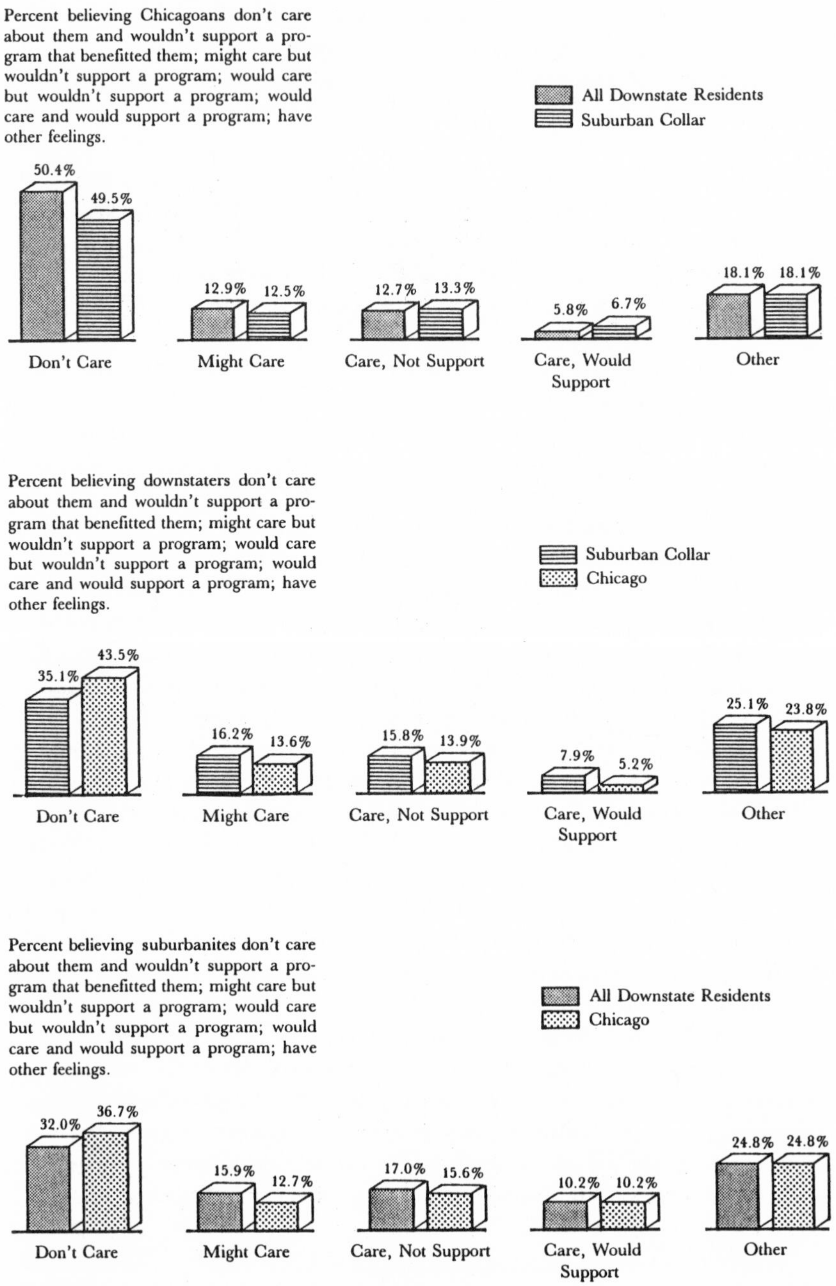
Percent believing Chicagoans don't care about them and wouldn't support a program that benefitted them; might care but wouldn't support a program; would care but wouldn't support a program; would care and would support a program; have other feelings.
All Downstate Residents
Suburban Collar
50.4%
49.5%
12.9%
12.5%
12.7%
13.3%
5.8%
6.7%
18.1%
18.1%
Don't Care
Might Care
Care, Not Support
Care, Would Support
Other
Percent believing downstaters don't care about them and wouldn't support a program that benefitted them; might care but wouldn't support a program; would care but wouldn't support a program; would care and would support a program; have other feelings.
Suburban Collar
Chicago
35.1%
43.5%
16.2%
13.6%
15.8%
13.9%
7.9%
5.2%
25.1%
23.8%
Don't Care
Might Care
Care, Not Support
Care, Would Support
Other
Percent believing suburbanites don't care about them and wouldn't support a program that benefitted them; might care but wouldn't support a program; would care but wouldn't support a program; would care and would support a program; have other feelings.
All Downstate Residents
Chicago
32.0%
36.7%
15.9%
12.7%
17.0%
15.6%
10.2%
10.2%
24.8%
24.8%
Don't Care
Might Care
Care, Not Support
Care, Would Support
Other

Figure 10–5. Views on Others' Degree of Support

Figure 10–5 contains the data for these various categories, by region. If we look at the perceptions of Chicagoans, the results are startling: half of the residents outside the city of Chicago believed that Chicagoans neither cared about their welfare nor would support a program that would benefit them. Overall more than 75 percent thought Chicagoans would not support a program that benefitted them, regardless of whether they believed Chicagoans cared about their welfare. Only 6–7 percent thought Chicagoans both cared and would support a program that benefitted their part of the state. The results did not vary much by regions, although southern Illinois respondents appeared slightly more charitable to Chicagoans than others. Chicagoans viewed others somewhat more favorably, but not much, and the results differed by reference group (downstaters, suburbanites). Only about 44 percent of Chicagoans thought downstaters did not care about their welfare *and* would not support a program that benefitted them. About 71 percent thought they would *not* support a program that benefitted Chicago, regardless of whether they were concerned with the welfare of Chicagoans. Only about 5 percent of Chicagoans thought downstaters cared about their welfare and would support a program that benefitted them. The comparable numbers for Chicagoans' perceptions of suburbanites were 37 percent, 65 percent, and 10 percent. Interestingly, almost a quarter of Chicagoans had mixed feelings on these matters, indicating a good deal of uncertainty over others' feelings about them. These results did not vary much, whether the referent was downstate or the suburbs.

Suburbanites' perceptions of individuals outside the Chicago metropolitan area were more generous than those of Chicagoans. Only about 35 percent thought downstaters did not care about their welfare and would not support a program that benefitted them; 67 percent thought they would not support a program that benefitted the suburbs. About a quarter expressed mixed feelings. Less than one in ten suburbanites (8 percent) thought downstaters cared and would support a program for their benefit. Downstaters' views of suburbanites were similar. About one-third thought they were not concerned with their welfare *and* would not support a program that helped them; almost two-thirds thought suburbanites would not support a program for downstate. Only 10 percent thought suburbanites were concerned with their welfare and would support a program. About a quarter expressed mixed feelings.

A parallel set of questions queried respondents on their perceptions of legislators from other regions (see Table 10–4: L-1, L-2, L-3). The responses to these questions are reported in Figures 10–6 through

Chicago Residents' Views of Others' Legislators

(Legislators from downstate) (Suburban state legislators) sometimes oppose laws that only favor other parts of the state.

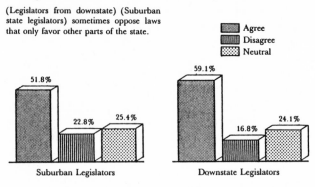

Downstate Residents' Views of Others' Legislators

(Suburban state legislators) (State legislators from Chicago) sometimes oppose laws that only favor other parts of the state.

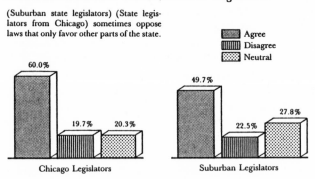

Suburban Residents' Views of Others' Legislators

(Legislators from downstate) (State legislators from Chicago) sometimes oppose laws that only favor other parts of the state.

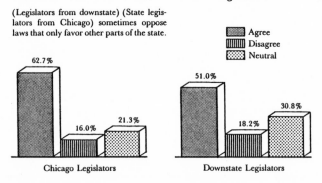

Figure 10–6. Views on Others' Legislators concerning Preferential Laws

10–8. Figure 10–6 deals with the question on whether legislators from one part of the state sometimes oppose laws that benefit other parts of the state (L-1). As is evident, Chicago legislators got the worst marks of all. Over 62 percent of suburbanites agreed with the statement when applied to Chicago legislators, as did 60 percent of downstaters. Downstate legislators did not fare much better, especially in the view of Chicagoans. About 59 percent of Chicagoans thought downstate legislators sometimes opposed laws that only favored other parts of the state; about half of the suburbanites agreed with them. About half of the respondents in the Chicago sample and half in the downstate area agreed with this statement when applied to suburban legislators.

Data on the next question, reported in Figure 10–7, dealt with whether legislators were concerned with the welfare of the entire state (L-2). Here again Chicago legislators got the most negative assessments. About 60 percent of the respondents in the suburban and downstate samples thought Chicago legislators were unconcerned with the welfare of the entire sample; about one in five explicitly disagreed. Only about two in five Chicagoans thought non-Chicago legislators were *not* concerned with the welfare of the entire state, and the percentage did not vary much across regions (downstate, suburban). Almost a full third of the Chicago respondents explicitly disagreed with the assertion that non-Chicago legislators were disinterested in the welfare of the entire state. The highest marks were received by downstate legislators, as perceived by suburban respondents. Only about a third of the suburbanites thought downstate legislators were not concerned with the welfare of the entire state; well over a third of the suburbanites explicitly disagreed with the proposition. Suburban legislators got far worse evaluations from downstate respondents—almost half thought these legislators were disinterested in the welfare of the entire state. Only about a quarter explicitly rejected that proposition.

Perceptions of Fiscal Equity

Besides perceived differences in personal characteristics and political wants and support, another factor that can both create and worsen regional animosities is the perception that one region is a financial drain on the state (i.e., their consumption of state resources exceeds their contribution in state taxes). To determine how people perceived various regions of the state on this key point, we asked respondents their views on whether Chicago, downstate Illinois, or the suburbs were a financial burden on the state. The results are reported in

Chicago Residents' Views of Others' Legislators

(Downstate) (Suburban) legislators are
generally not concerned with the welfare of
the whole state.

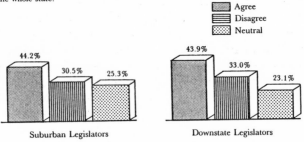

Suburban Legislators   Downstate Legislators

Downstate Residents' Views of Others' Legislators

(Chicago) (Suburban) legislators are
generally not concerned with the welfare of
the whole state.

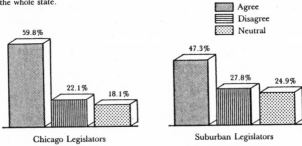

Chicago Legislators   Suburban Legislators

Suburban Residents' Views of Others' Legislators

(Downstate legislators) (Legislators from
Chicago) are generally not concerned with
the welfare of the whole state.

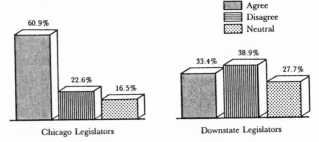

Chicago Legislators   Downstate Legislators

Figure 10–7. Views of Others' Legislators concerning
Welfare of State

Chicago is a financial burden on the rest of the state.

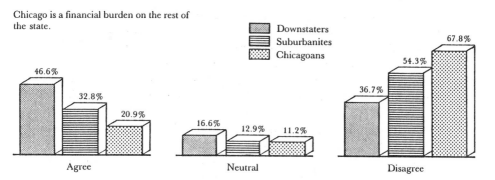

Downstate is a financial burden on the rest of the state.

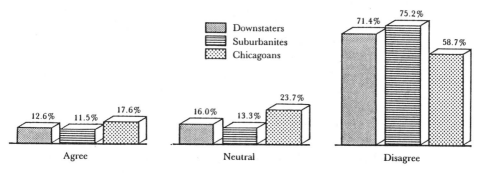

The suburbs around Chicago are a financial burden on the rest of the state.

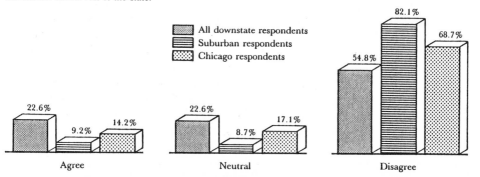

Figure 10–8. Perceptions of Fiscal Equity

Figure 10–8. Interestingly, most people did not view *any* region as a financial burden. But, by a margin of more than two to one, more people thought Chicago was a financial burden than either of the other two regions about which we inquired. Indeed, while Chicagoans were least likely to view Chicago as a financial burden, more Chicagoans thought Chicago was a burden than thought downstate Illinois or the suburbs were a burden. Over 46 percent of downstaters thought Chicago was a burden, while only about 37 percent explicitly disagreed. More than half of those from northern Illinois adhered to the view that Chicago was a financial burden, while only about one-third of suburbanites agreed with that view.

Hardly anyone viewed the downstate and suburban areas as a financial burden, and more than two-thirds of the people in the state as a whole explicitly rejected the proposition. Chicagoans were more uncertain as to whether downstate was a financial burden, but less than one in five agreed with this view. Downstaters were more likely to view the suburbs as a burden than anyone else in the state. The percent of downstaters viewing the suburbs as a financial burden (22.6 percent) was almost twice as high as the percent of suburbanites believing downstate was a financial burden (11.5 percent).

Perceptions of Chicago Statehood

As a means of assessing the depth of the animosities between Chicago and the rest of the state, we asked respondents their opinion of whether Chicago should become a separate state as well as what effect such a change would have on their part of the state. The results, reported in Table 10–6, are informative. Only about 11 percent of the respondents in the state as a whole supported the idea of Chicago becoming a separate state. This ranged from a high of almost 19 percent in southern Illinois (16.9 percent in the downstate area as a whole supported the idea) to a low of about 6 percent in the suburbs. Even more surprising in light of some of the views expressed earlier, only about one in five downstate respondents thought that such a separation would help their part of the state. Only 8 percent of the suburbanites and about 11 percent of Chicago respondents thought that it would help them. Most people, over 60 percent overall, thought such a move would hurt their part of the state, while about a quarter thought it would have no effect upon their part of the state. Even among downstate respondents, almost half thought a Chicago separation would hurt them, more than twice as many as thought it would benefit them.

Table 10–6. Views on Chicago Statehood

	All Respondents[a] % (N)	Northern Illinois Respondents % (N)	Central Illinois Respondents % (N)	Southern Illinois Respondents % (N)	All Downstate Respondents[a] % (N)	Suburban Collar Respondents % (N)	City of Chicago Respondents % (N)
Support idea of Chicago statehood	11.0 (4,240)	17.6 (427)	15.3 (443)	18.8 (420)	16.9 (1,575)	6.2 (695)	9.8 (680)
Believe Chicago Statehood would:							
Help their part of the state	14.0	23.8	22.2	19.5	21.8	8.2	11.1
Hurt their part of the state	60.9	49.9	51.8	44.3	49.3	67.2	68.4
Have no effect upon their part of the state	25.1 (4,023)	26.3 (391)	26.0 (434)	36.2 (406)	28.9 (1,510)	24.6 (638)	20.5 (644)

[a] Weighted.

Summary

What does our review of the survey data tell us about the structure of regionalism in Illinois? First, over 90 percent of Illinoisans had views on regional divisions in the state, and almost 75 percent thought it was composed of "several different regions or parts." However, when asked to identify those parts, *almost 30 percent could not offer even a single division*. Another 12.9 percent did not offer geo-political divisions. Rather, they talked about topological features, city and county names (other than Chicago or Cook), and urban-rural divisions. Another interesting point here is that of the different parts of the state named, Chicago was named by only about a quarter of the respondents. More people named southern Illinois and northern Illinois than Chicago. This is startling in a state that has been talked about by academicians and political and media elites in terms of "Chicago and downstate" for the better part of a century. It suggests that the diffusion of Chicagoans throughout other parts of the state and the explosion of the metropolitan area are beginning to have an impact on people's perception of the state. The contrast between Chicago and the more industrialized urban-northern sector of the state is becoming less clear in the minds of Illinoisans, including Chicagoans themselves. Only 22 percent of Chicagoans identified Chicago as a distinct part of the state (see Table 10–3), and less than half of those in the Chicago sample identified "their part of the state" as Chicago; almost a third identified "northern Illinois" as their "part of the state" (see Table 10–19). It is unlikely that these perceptions would have held twenty to thirty years ago.

These data suggest that regionalism in Illinois is not as clear to many Illinoisans as we would have thought. It is apparent that the prominence of Chicago as a distinctive part of the state is diminishing in the minds of Illinoisans. Moreover, the data on perceptions about those in other parts of that state suggest that more ambiguity exists than one would have thought in a deeply divided state. It is true that most downstaters (58 percent) explicitly rejected the notion that they were similar to Chicagoans, and that almost as many Chicagoans (51 percent) felt the same way about those in downstate Illinois (see Figure 10–1). Only about 27 percent and 28 percent of downstate and Chicago, respectively, were willing to admit to similarities between them, but a good portion (16 percent in the downstate region and 21 percent in Chicago) were not willing to commit themselves (see Figure 10–1). Moreover, both of these groups were more willing to admit to similarities between themselves and suburbanites.

Contributing to the ambiguity over mutual perceptions are the data on social stereotypes (see Figure 10–2). Relatively small proportions of the respondents in any region agreed with these stereotypes, with the exception of the stereotype of suburbanites. Moreover, the proportion of those adhering to the different stereotypes were not regionally skewed; rather, they were fairly evenly distributed across regions, even in the case of the suburban stereotypes. Also relevant here are the perceptual data on financial burdens (see Figure 10–8). Less than a majority of the respondents in any part of the state thought Chicago was a financial burden, and hardly anyone thought any of the other regions were a burden. In light of these various findings, the small proportion of the population favoring the separation of Chicago from the state is entirely understandable, as is the fairly widespread perception that such a separation would hurt "their part of the state" (see Table 10–6).

In contrast to these findings are the data on people's perceptions about others' concern for their welfare. These data seem to get at the heart of the regionally based animosities that seem to characterize the state. Many people (especially Chicagoans and downstaters) did not feel that others thought highly of them (see Figure 10–3), and even more felt that others were not concerned with their welfare (see Figure 10–5). Moreover, the vast majority in a region (up to 76 percent in some cases) did not feel that others would support a program that would primarily benefit their region (see Figure 10–5). There was also a good deal of disaffection for the legislators from other areas (see Figures 10–6 and 10–7). They were viewed as obstructionists who were not concerned with the welfare of the entire state. Downstaters were most likely to feel that others and their legislators were unconcerned and/or ignored their interests.

The Foundations of Regional Animosities in Illinois: An Empirical Examination

Despite the ambiguities that emerge from a careful review of the data presented thus far, it is quite clear that regionally based cleavages and animosities exist in the minds of many Illinoisans, at least on a political level. There is less empirical support for the notion that deeply personal animosities exist. Many people felt that others were "different," but most did not adhere to negative stereotypes of those from other parts of the state. This is an important distinction because of the pervasive and deeply rooted folklore concerning personal tensions between "city slickers" and "country rubes." It also helps us clarify the nature of within-state regional animosities. But we cannot stop here in our attempts to enhance our understanding of these animosities; the survey data permit us to examine, in a limited way, their underpinnings.

Any attempt to clarify the source of regionally based political animosities in a state as large and heterogeneous as Illinois is problematic, at best. However, two broad, generic explanations have a good deal of intuitive plausibility; one is subcultural, the other distributional. The subcultural explanation is based on the historically diverse pattern of settlement and economic development that have characterized the state since its inception (Wirt, chapter 2 herein; Atack, chapter 3 herein). This asserts that people from different parts of the state have different values, priorities, and belief systems which lead to different norms, wants, and political demands. When input into the political system, these differences form the foundation for conflicts and resulting animosities.

The implication of this subcultural perspective can be depicted graphically to clarify what we might expect to find if it had a strong impact upon the values, attitudes, and beliefs of people across the state. The distribution of views toward some very basic referent— say importance of education—in a culturally segmented state would look something like that in Figure 10–9. Regionally distinctive means would exist and, in an extreme situation (one in which cultural influences were very strong), these means would be surrounded by relatively narrow bands of responses, with minimal overlap across regions.

A distributional explanation for regionally based political animosities is quite different from the subcultural explanation, but Figure 10–9 can be useful in differentiating between the two. A distributional explanation is not based on the existence of regionally distinctive values, views, or beliefs, such as those posited in Figure 10–9. Rather, animosities are generated by conflicts over the distribution of public goods and the structuring of the distributional consequences of state policies and programs. Within a distributional explanation, there may be little disagreement over the value of a public education or the importance of a well-developed system of highways. The real conflicts emerge over methods for funding schools, the structure of a school-aid formula, and the determination of which highways get built and maintained. Perceptions that certain parts of the state use "clout" or "illegitimate techniques" (failure to fairly apportion legislative seats) to obtain a disproportionate share of state resources produce regional animosities which persist long after specific conflicts have passed. But these conflicts, according to a distributional explanation, result not

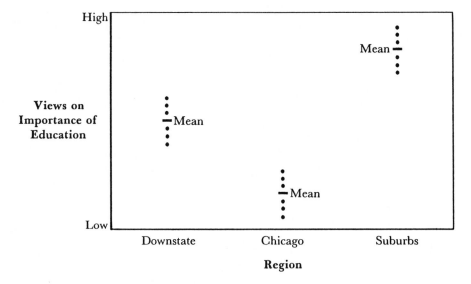

Figure 10–9. Hypothetical Distribution on Views toward Education

from conflicts over *what* to do but rather *how* to do what most agree should be done.

A few points should be noted about these competing explanations. First, they are simply ideal types of explanations that are, in some ways, not mutually exclusive. This means that reality may fall somewhere between the two different sets of explanations. There may be some areas in which marked disparities in attitudes, beliefs, and wants exist across the state; in other areas, there may be much more agreement, with the consensus breaking down over specifics of implementation. In still other areas, disagreement may exist over both ends and means.

A second important point is that our ability to assess the sources of these political animosities is highly limited. We have the means to determine, in a wide variety of areas, whether regionally distinctive patterns exist. However, if marked disparities do not exist, we do not have the ability to determine whether regional animosities are based on perceptions of marked and illegitimate inequalities across regions. Nor can we assume that a high level of homogeneity in values, attitudes, and wants means that the political animosities are the results of perceived distributional inequities. Too many other rival explanations exist to justify such an assumption. In a variant of the subculture explanation, one could just as well contend that while regional differences no longer exist, they once did. The prevailing animosities, it could be argued, are based on these past differences. They persist because they are exploited by self-serving politicians and are constantly in the media. These problems prevent us from making more than a small beginning in trying to understand the underpinnings of political animosities in Illinois.

Regional Diversity

To assess whether there are regionally based subcultures in Illinois, we examine three main areas. We begin with respondents' views on a set of fundamental social issues. Next we look at how they evaluated a variety of factors related to the quality of life in their community. Finally, we examine their preference for state government spending priorities. These sets of inquiries obviously do not exhaust the possible areas of examination. Nonetheless, these analyses should yield some sound insights into whether regionally based subcultures actually exist within the state.

To insure that our quantitative analyses of these data were really measuring geographically based differences, we needed to control for a host of demographic variables. If these variables were not controlled, the analyses might simply have picked up effects resulting from differences in the social composition of the population (age structure, wealth, racial makeup, educational achievement, occupation, etc.) in different regions of the state. People of a different race or in different income brackets might view things differently; but people with similar social characteristics might view these things similarly, regardless of *where* they live in the state. To the extent that the social composition of the population varied by region, these demographic differences could have confounded our efforts to detect the existence of regionally based subcultures. Thus, using analysis of covariance with multiple regression,[4] we tested for the impact of region[5] while controlling for the effects of age, race, sex, income, educational achievement, occupational prestige, religious affiliation, and household structure (marital status, number of income earners, existence of children, own or rent residence).[6]

Social Attitudes

We asked respondents twenty-one questions that tapped their views on matters ranging from the role of God in life and family values to civil rights for homosexuals. We also inquired about views toward women and racial minorities, as well as attitudes toward abortion, the death penalty, and care for the terminally ill.[7] In many instances more than one question on a particular subject was included. This permitted us to attain a higher level of reliability and stability in responses by using factor analysis to reduce the larger sets of variables into a smaller set of composite variables. In some cases this approach was successful; the appropriate variables "hung together" in a sufficiently tight manner to permit the formation of a composite variable. But in other cases this did not occur.

We were able to form sound composites for attitudes concerning the role of God in society, sexual freedom for individuals, and tolerance for homosexuals; a marginal composite emerged from an analysis of the questions on the importance of family.[8] The sets of questions on views toward women and blacks did not permit us to form composite measures and, for a variety of reasons, we do not examine these variables in the following analyses.[9] We only asked one question in the areas of abortion, the death penalty, and the treatment of the terminally ill. They were straightforward questions that were interpretable standing alone (not embodied in a composite variable), and we did subject them to further analysis.

Table 10–7 reports the variables used in the social issues analysis, along with an interpretation of each. As is evident, they tapped a broad range of some of the most controversial issues of contemporary life. The results of the analysis of covariance are reported in Table 10–8. In a fairly sophisticated and comprehensive way, these analyses tested for the existence of regionally distinctive mean scores on the various dependent variables. We first report the gross impact of the dummy regional variables on the dependent social attitude variables (i.e., before the effects of the control variables are partialled out). Next, we report the impact of the dummy regional variables after the control variables have been entered into the analysis. Finally, we report the net impact of the regional variables only for cases where the respondent's family had lived in the same part of the state for at least three generations. The reason for this analysis is that, if deeply rooted cultural differences in fact exist within the state, their presence may be obscured by recent migrants. About half the respondents in the state as a whole had family ties to their part of the state that went back at least three generations. By examining just these respondents, we may obtain a better understanding of whatever regionally based subcultures exist.

The results reported in Table 10–8 provide us with a number of

Table 10–7. Attitudinal Variables Used in Analysis of Covariance

Variable	Interpretation
GODROLE	Those scoring high in this measure believe that a belief in God contributes to a better world and personal happiness.
SEXLFREE	Those scoring high on this measure believe that the informed judgment of individuals should be the primary determinant of their personal sexual practices.
GAYTOL	Those scoring high on this measure believe that homosexuals should not be discriminated against.
FAMLYVAL	Those scoring high on this measure believe that men and women should be ready to sacrifice their career for the happiness of their family.
ABORTION	Those scoring high on this measure believe that a woman should have the right to choose an abortion.
DEATH	Those scoring high on this measure believe that judges should be able to sentence people to death.
PROLONG	Those scoring high on this measure believe that doctors should do everything to prolong the life of a terminally ill patient.

insights. First, the differences in mean scores across regions of the state are not, by and large, very significant. In most instances there are no statistically significant differences, especially when we control for demographic differences. Where statistically significant differences emerge, they are not very large, barely accounting for as much as 1 percent of the variance in the dependent variables.

If we examine the statistically significant differences, we see the basic dichotomy between the downstate area and the Chicago metropolitan area (city and suburbs). Downstate respondents scored significantly higher than those in Chicago and its suburbs on the GODROLE variable and lower on the GAYTOL and ABORTION variables. Downstate respondents were initially lower than Chicago area respondents on the SEXLFREE variable, but the difference was eliminated by the control variables. In no instance did respondents from the northern region of the downstate area differ from those in the central region. However, southern Illinoisans scored significantly higher than other downstaters (as well as those in the Chicago area) on the GODROLE variable; they also scored significantly lower than other downstaters on the SEXLFREE and ABORTION variables. Moreover, in the one instance that breaks with the fairly general pattern noted here, southern Illinoisans and Chicagoans scored significantly higher on the PROLONG variable than did respondents elsewhere in the state. This is the only instance in which a significant difference emerged between Chicago and its suburbs, after demographic differences were controlled. Significant differences between Chicago and the suburbs initially emerged on the GODROLE, SEXLFREE, FAMLYVAL, and DEATH variables, but they were eliminated when the demographic variables were entered into the analysis.

The rather meager pattern of results reported here cannot be attributed to the diluting effect of recent migrants. The analysis of longtime residents revealed only two findings that did not emerge from the analysis of all respondents (DOWNSTATE and SEXLFREE; COLLAR and PROLONG).

A better feel for the magnitude of the differences across regions can be obtained by examining the distribution of raw scores by region. Unfortunately, these scores are not easily interpretable as it is difficult to know what a big difference is on the various scales. To facilitate an assessment of raw differences, we divided the scores on each of the social attitude variables into three categories—high, medium, and low—for the weighted statewide sample. We attempted to create three equal categories, but the distribution did not always permit such a division. In any event, this technique permits us to compare the proportion of respondents ranked low, medium, or high in the state by region. The percentages in the low and high categories are reported in Table 10–9.

If we carefully examine Table 10–9, we see very few instances where the proportion of respondents ranked low or high in a region varies by more than 5–10 percent from the percent ranked low or high for the state as a whole. The few instances in which this did occur involved southern Illinoisans—on the GODROLE, SEXLFREE, and ABORTION variables. A disproportionate number of Chicagoans (43.3 percent) ranked in the high category on the PROLONG variable. Some dramatic differences between selected regions of the state can be found (southern Illinoisans and suburbanites on the GODROLE variable; Chicagoans, northern Illinoisans, and suburbanites on the PROLONG variable), but few of the interregional differences are much more than 10 percentage points. It also should be kept in mind that the data reported in Table 10–9 reflect gross differences in views; demographic effects are *not* removed.

Views on Quality of Life

The next segment of the analysis deals with views on the quality of life. Respondents' preferences on a variety of items were elicited by

Table 10–8. Results of Social Attitudes Analysis

Regional Variables	GODROLE	SEXLFREE	GAYTOL	FAMLYVAL	ABORTION	DEATH	PROLONG
Northern Illinois							
Impact before control variable entered	0	0	0	0	0	0	0
Net impact (after control variables entered; partial correlation coefficient)	0	0	0	0	0	0	0
Net impact for longtime residents only (partial correlation coefficient)	0	0	0	0	0	0	0
Central Illinois							
Impact before control variable entered	0	0	0	0	0	0	0
Net impact (after control variables entered; partial correlation coefficient)	0	0	0	0	0	0	0
Net impact for longtime residents only (partial correlation coefficient)	0	0	0	0	0	0	0
Southern Illinois							
Impact before control variable entered	+++ (.14)	--- (−.10)	0	0	--- (−.10)	0	0
Net impact (after control variables entered; partial correlation coefficient)	+++ (.07)	--- (−.06)	0	0	--- (−.08)	0	+++ (.05)
Net impact for longtime residents only (partial correlation coefficient)	+++ (.09)	--- (−.12)	0 0	0 0	--- (−.12)	0 0	++ (.05)

Downstate Illinois						
Impact before control variable entered	+++ (.16)	--- (-.12)	--- (-.18)	0	--- (-.10)	0
Net impact (after control variables entered; partial correlation coefficient)	+++ (.11)	0	--- (-.10)	0	--- (-.05)	0
Net impact for longtime residents only (partial correlation coefficient)	+++ (.16)	--- (-.05)	--- (-.14)	0	-- (-.05)	0
City of Chicago						
Impact before control variable entered	0	++ (.08)	0	0	--- (-.09)	+++ (.18)
Net impact (after control variables entered; partial correlation coefficient)	0	0	0	0	0	+++ (.09)
Net impact for longtime residents only (partial correlation coefficient)	0	0	0	0	0	++ (.06)
Suburban Collar Counties						
Impact before control variable entered	--- (-.14)	0	0	-- (-.05)	0	0
Net impact (after control variables entered; partial correlation coefficient)	0	0	0	0	0	0
Net impact for longtime residents only (partial correlation coefficient)	0	0	0	0	0	--- (-.09)
Total variance explained by control variables	23	.19	.09	.05	.05	.09
Number of cases	3,937	3,876	3,871	3,944	3,943	3,937

Note: Because of the large sample sizes, we only report findings that are significant at the .01 level or beyond. Positive significant findings at the .01 level are indicated by a ++, negative ones by --; findings significant at or beyond the .001 level are indicated by three symbols (+++ or ---). Partial correlation coefficients are reported in parentheses below these symbols.

Table 10–9. Distribution of Respondents across Trichotomized Social Attitude Variables

	All Respondents[a] (percent)	Northern Illinois Respondents (percent)	Central Illinois Respondents (percent)	Southern Illinois Respondents (percent)	All Downstate Respondents[a] (percent)	Suburban Collar Respondents (percent)	City of Chicago Respondents (percent)
GODROLE							
Lower segment	35.2	30.4	29.5	21.2	27.5	41.6	37.2
Upper segment	33.8	35.0	43.9	48.5	42.8	24.7	34.0
SEXLFREE							
Lower segment	30.6	35.3	36.1	42.9	37.7	27.2	25.1
Upper segment	36.9	29.9	32.9	25.7	30.1	39.7	42.8
GAYTOL							
Lower segment	31.2	37.1	40.1	40.5	39.4	28.5	23.0
Upper segment	35.9	28.3	27.6	28.5	28.1	39.9	41.5
FAMLYVAL							
Lower segment	33.5	37.7	31.2	31.2	33.0	34.1	33.6
Upper segment	32.7	29.2	35.2	35.0	33.6	28.7	37.6
ABORTION							
Lower segment	24.6	29.2	27.4	35.4	30.0	22.0	20.4
Upper segment	42.5	38.8	38.2	31.2	36.5	43.8	49.4
DEATH							
Lower segment	26.1	26.8	20.6	23.9	23.1	25.6	31.1
Upper segment	33.7	34.2	34.4	37.2	35.1	34.9	29.9
PROLONG							
Lower segment	31.9	37.1	35.9	30.8	34.8	35.3	22.7
Upper segment	29.9	23.4	25.7	32.1	26.8	23.9	43.3

[a] Weighted.

Table 10–10. Quality of Life Measures Used in Analysis of Covariance

URBAN AMENITIES	Those scoring high on this composite variable placed a high degree of importance on shopping districts, professional sports, a vibrant nightlife, a fast pace to living, and many different restaurants.
COMMUNITY LIFE	Those scoring high on this composite variable placed a high degree of importance on open spaces, family-oriented activities, good neighbors, and privacy.
INFRASTRUCTURE	Those scoring high on this composite variable placed a high degree of importance upon street lights, well-maintained streets, and good hospitals.

asking them to rate each on a scale from 0 to 10.[10] A rating of 10 means that the item being assessed is very important to the respondent, while a rating of 0 indicates that it is not at all important. The various items that individuals were asked to evaluate all described aspects of an environment in which a person could reside. These items included shopping districts, different restaurants, a religious environment, family-oriented activities, good neighbors, privacy, similarly minded neighbors, a vibrant nightlife, professional sports teams, ethnic diversity, museums, plays and other cultural activities, open spaces, street lights, well-maintained streets, and good hospitals. To simplify the analysis and enhance the stability of the results, we again employed factor analysis to attempt to reduce the large number of variables into a smaller number of independent dimensions.

We were more successful here in that the factor analyses yielded three fairly strong composite variables.[11] These are listed in Table 10–10. One independent dimension dealt with those amenities that only an urban area can provide—large shopping districts, different restaurants, professional sports, etc. It is labeled URBAN AMENITIES. A second dimension that emerged concerned more home- and neighborhood-centered facets of life, such as accessibility to open spaces, privacy, family-oriented activities, and good neighbors. It is labeled COMMUNITY LIFE. The third dimension tapped the importance of a town's infrastructure—street lights, well-maintained streets, and good hospitals. It is labeled INFRASTRUCTURE.

The results of the analysis of covariance are reported in Table 10–11. The patterns that emerge are fairly straightforward but differ somewhat from those in the social attitudes analysis. With respect to

Table 10–11. Results of Quality of Life Analyses

Regional Variables	URBAN AMENITIES	COMMUNITY LIFE	INFRA-STRUCTURE
Northern Illinois			
Impact before control variable entered	0	0	− − − (−.06)
Net impact (after control variables entered; partial correlation coefficient)	0	0	− − − (−.06)
Net impact for longtime residents only (partial correlation coefficient)	0	0	0
Central Illinois			
Impact before control variable entered	0	0	0
Net impact (after control variables entered; partial correlation coefficient)	0	0	0
Net impact for longtime residents only (partial correlation coefficient)	0	0	0
Southern Illinois			
Impact before control variable entered	++ (.04)	0	0
Net impact (after control variables entered; partial correlation coefficient)	+++ (.05)	0	0
Net impact for longtime residents only (partial correlation coefficient)	0	0	0
Downstate Illinois			
Impact before control variable entered	0	+++ (.08)	0
Net impact (after control variables entered; partial correlation coefficient)	0	0	0
Net impact for longtime residents only (partial correlation coefficient)	0	0	0

Table 10–11 (continued). Results of Quality of Life Analyses

Regional Variables	URBAN AMENITIES	COMMUNITY LIFE	INFRA-STRUCTURE
City of Chicago			
Impact before control variable entered	+++ (.22)	--- (−.09)	+++ (.08)
Net impact (after control variables entered; partial correlation coefficient)	+++ (.12)	--- (−.05)	0 0
Net impact for longtime residents only (partial correlation coefficient)	+++ (.11)	0	+++ (.10)
Suburban Collar Counties			
Impact before control variable entered	0	0	0
Net impact (after control variables entered; partial correlation coefficient)	0	0	0
Net impact for longtime residents only (partial correlation coefficient)	0	0	0
Total variance explained by control variables	.13	.07	.06
Number of cases	3,965	3,980	3,982

Note: Because of the large sample sizes, we only report findings that are significant at the .01 level or beyond. Positive significant findings at the .01 level are indicated by a ++, negative ones by −−; findings significant at or beyond the .001 level are indicated by three symbols (+++ or −−−). Partial correlation coefficients are reported in parentheses below these symbols.

the URBAN AMENITIES variable, Chicagoans, unsurprisingly, stood out from the rest of the state. More surprising is the fact that suburbanites' views on these features of life were similar to those of downstaters, with the exception of southern Illinoisans. Southern Illinoisans, quite unexpectedly, were more similar to Chicagoans than those elsewhere in the state. With respect to the COMMUNITY LIFE variable, downstaters scored significantly higher than Chicagoans and suburbanites, and Chicagoans scored significantly lower than suburbanites. Chicagoans scored significantly higher on the INFRA-STRUCTURE variable than respondents in other parts of the state. The only difference among respondents outside the city of Chicago on this variable occurred with respect to those in northern Illinois, who scored significantly lower than those in the other parts of the state. Here again the analyses of longtime residents did not result in any markedly different pattern of results.

Table 10–12 presents the distribution of the trichotomized quality of life variables by region in order to obtain a more concrete sense of the gross differences across regions. The percent of Chicagoans scoring in the high category of the URBAN AMENITIES variable was about 20 points higher than in the downstate and suburban regions. On the COMMUNITY LIFE variable, however, the differences were much smaller. In the high category the differences between Chicago and downstate were only about 3 points; the difference in the low category was about 10 points. The Chicago-downstate differences in the INFRASTRUCTURE variable were in the 8 point range, while the Chicago-suburban differences were slightly greater (9–13 points).

State Fiscal Priorities

The final segment of this analysis deals with views on state government fiscal matters: where ought state spending priorities be focused? We approached this by reading respondents a list of state-supported activities and asking them whether they wanted state taxes and spending to increase, decrease, or remain the same with respect to them. Respondents were also given the option of rejecting a particular activity as a legitimate governmental enterprise.[12] Altogether, we evaluated fourteen activities, ranging from elementary and higher education to economic development, environmental protection, and state highways. Not all activities evaluated were significant components of the state budget, and the results were somewhat repetitive. Therefore, for the sake of simplicity we report results for seven activities: elementary education, higher education, economic development, aid to needy farmers, aid to the poor, public safety, and state highways.

While the absolute levels varied from activity to activity, most respondents across the state favored increased taxes and spending. Thus, for purposes of analysis, we dichotomized the dependent variable: a "1" reflected a desire for increased taxes and spending; a "0" reflected a desire for the status quo or a reduction.

The results of these analyses are reported in Table 10–13. We should focus our attention on the entries in the middle row for each region, for two reasons. First, the introduction of the demographic variables did not generally lead to the elimination of significant findings for the dummy regional variables. Indeed, of the fifteen instances

Table 10–12. Distribution of Respondents across Trichotomized Quality of Life Variables

	All Respondents[a] (percent)	Northern Illinois Respondents (percent)	Central Illinois Respondents (percent)	Southern Illinois Respondents (percent)	All Downstate Respondents[a] (percent)	Suburban Collar Respondents (percent)	City of Chicago Respondents (percent)
URBAN AMENITIES							
Lower segment	32.8	39.7	40.8	33.8	38.6	36.1	19.5
Upper segment	33.5	29.9	26.3	32.5	29.0	27.9	48.7
COMMUNITY LIFE							
Lower segment	33.8	31.3	28.2	27.9	28.9	35.3	38.9
Upper segment	33.2	33.7	36.1	38.3	36.0	30.1	33.4
INFRASTRUCTURE							
Lower segment	32.8	41.1	32.5	30.5	34.3	35.7	26.5
Upper segment	37.7	31.7	35.9	44.2	37.0	33.0	45.7

[a] Weighted.

Table 10–13. Results of State Spending-Priorities Analysis

Regional Variables	Elementary Education	Higher Education	Economic Development	Aid to Farmers	Aid to Poor	Public Safety	State Highways
Northern Illinois							
Impact before control variable entered	0	0	0	0	0	0	0
Net impact (after control variables entered; partial correlation coefficient)	0	0	++ (.04)	– – (–.05)	0	0	0
Net impact for longtime residents only (partial correlation coefficient)	0	0	0	– – (–.06)	0	0	0
Central Illinois							
Impact before control variable entered	0	0	0	0	– – – (–.09)	– – – (–.10)	0
Net impact (after control variables entered; partial correlation coefficient)	0	– – (–.05)	0	– – – (–.08)	– – – (–.06)	– – – (–.08)	0
Net impact for longtime residents only (partial correlation coefficient)	0	– – – (–.08)	0	– – – (–.08)	0	– – – (–.07)	0

Table 10–13 (continued). Results of State Spending-Priorities Analysis

Regional Variables	Elementary Education	Higher Education	Economic Development	Aid to Farmers	Aid to Poor	Public Safety	State Highways
Southern Illinois							
Impact before control variable entered	0	0	0	+++ (.06)	0	0	0
Net impact (after control variables entered; partial correlation coefficient)	0	0	+++ (.06)	0	0	0	0
Net impact for longtime residents only (partial correlation coefficient)	0	0	++ (.07)	0	0	0	0
Downstate Illinois							
Impact before control variable entered	0	0	0	--- (-.09)	0	0	0
Net impact (after control variables entered; partial correlation coefficient)	0	--- (-.06)	+++ (.07)	--- (-.09)	--- (-.05)	--- (-.09)	0
Net impact for longtime residents only (partial correlation coefficient)	0	--- (-.09)	++ (+.07)	--- (-.09)	0	--- (-.09)	0

Table 10–13 (continued). Results of State Spending-Priorities Analysis

Regional Variables	Elementary Education	Higher Education	Economic Development	Aid to Farmers	Aid to Poor	Public Safety	State Highways
City of Chicago							
Impact before control variable entered	+++ (.11)	+++ (.10)	0	0	+++ (.18)	+++ (.14)	0
Net impact (after control variables entered; partial correlation coefficient)	+++ (.10)	+++ (.06)	0	+++ (.07)	+++ (.09)	+++ (.08)	0
Net impact for longtime residents only (partial correlation coefficient)	+++ (.17)	+++ (.09)	0	+++ (.09)	++ (.06)	+++ (.10)	0
Suburban Collar Counties							
Impact before control variable entered	0	0	––– (–.08)	0	0	0	––– (–.14)
Net impact (after control variables entered; partial correlation coefficient)	––– (–.06)	0	––– (–.06)	0	0	0	––– (–.09)
Net impact for longtime residents only (partial correlation coefficient)	––– (–.13)	0	––– (–.07)	0	0	0	––– (–.13)
Total variance explained by control variables	.06	.02	.03	.05	.09	.04	.05
Number of cases	4,000	4,000	4,000	4,000	4,000	4,000	4,000

Note: Because of the large sample sizes, we only report findings that are significant at the .01 level or beyond. Positive significant findings at the .01 level are indicated by a ++, negative ones by ––; findings significant at or beyond the .001 level are indicated by three symbols (+++ or –––). Partial correlation coefficients are reported in parentheses below these symbols.

in which a change in the significance of a regional variable occurred, the regional variable became *significant* in fourteen. Thus, rather than wiping out initially significant regional effects, the control variables actually enhanced their significance. Secondly, the analysis of only longtime residents led to markedly different sets of results.

If we examine the results of the multivariate analyses after the effect of the demographic variables is removed, we see a number of patterns. First, while the overall impact of the regional variables is minuscule, we do find *statistically* significant differences across the three major parts of the state—Chicago, its suburbs, and downstate. In six of the seven areas (all but economic development and state highways), more Chicagoans preferred increased spending and taxes than did people in other parts of the state. The results for the suburbs revealed that suburbanites' preferences were between Chicagoans and downstaters in four areas (higher education, aid to farmers, aid to the poor, and public safety); suburbanites registered the least support in the state for spending increases in elementary education, economic development, and state highways. Downstaters' preferences were similar to Chicagoans with respect to highways; downstaters actually preferred higher levels of spending and taxes with respect to economic development. Downstaters' preferences for increases in every other area— including aid for farmers in financial trouble—were the lowest in the state. This is most revealing, given the earlier finding that downstaters did not believe those in other parts of the state would support programs that benefitted them.

If we examine the three components of the downstate region (northern, central, and southern Illinois), we can see some sporadic differences. The most important of these is the general tendency of central Illinoisans to be the most fiscally conservative.

Table 10–14 reports raw data on the percent supporting spending and tax increases in each category across the region. In only two instances does a regional mean exceed the statewide mean by more than 10 percentage points, and all instances involved Chicagoans (public safety, aid to the poor). About one in five regional means differed by more than 10 points, with most of the larger differences being between Chicagoans and central Illinoisans. The most divisive issue appears to be aid to the poor, where the difference between central Illinoisans and Chicagoans reaches almost 25 percentage points.

Regional Differences in Illinois: A More Refined Examination

It is clear from the above analyses that residents of the various regions analyzed here are not as distinct as Illinois folklore would suggest—

Table 10–14. Distribution of Respondents Supporting Tax and Spending Increases for Various Programs

	All Respondents[a] (percent)	Northern Illinois Respondents (percent)	Central Illinois Respondents (percent)	Southern Illinois Respondents (percent)	All Downstate Respondents[a] (percent)	Suburban Collar Respondents (percent)	City of Chicago Respondents (percent)
Elementary education	65.6	63.2	63.5	62.6	63.2	62.3	73.9
Higher education	57.3	52.7	49.9	55.1	52.0	56.6	66.3
Economic development	62.0	65.2	60.7	69.0	64.2	57.0	66.1
State highways	53.6	57.8	57.7	61.5	58.8	44.6	59.4
Public safety	67.1	60.9	57.1	64.2	60.0	66.9	78.0
Aid to poor	61.7	57.4	51.8	59.5	55.4	58.0	76.4
Aid to farmers	62.8	54.7	54.1	64.8	57.2	65.0	67.9

[a] Weighted.

Table 10–15. Refined Regional Variables

Region	Number of Respondents	Region	Number of Respondents
Downstate		Suburban Collar	
Medium-sized cities (25,000+)	289	North Shore	72
St. Louis metropolitan area	169	Northwest	105
Little Egypt	145	Near West	84
Rural and small towns	789	South	134
Chicago		DuPage	144
South Side	243	Outlying suburbs	143
West Side	96		
North Side	188		
White ethnic	150		

at least with respect to the measures used here. Statistically significant differences emerged across the basic regions of the state, to be sure, and the direction of the differences that emerged was, by and large, predictable. What was surprising was the magnitude of the differences that emerged. In no instance did the variance explained by the regional variables exceed 5 percent of the total variance; after partialling out the variance attributable to demographic differences across the state, the sum of the variance explained by the regional variables never exceeded 2 percent of the total. Nor did restricting the analyses to longtime residents significantly enhance the explanatory power of the regional variables. It should also be stressed that the dummy variable technique employed here maximized the power of region as an exploratory variable.

It could be argued, of course, that the results reported here are misleading because we examined areas not likely to be divisive or to generate regional differences. Yet it would be difficult to think of areas more likely to generate differences across rural, urban, suburban, and small-town dwellers than views on God and religion, sexual mores, abortion, and the death penalty. Our question on the quality of life tapped views on two very basic, age-old dimensions—the importance of urban amenities and the value of communal commodities that cannot be purchased at a shopping mall—plus the attraction of a well-maintained infrastructure. Our questions on state fiscal priorities covered the basic components of the state budget.

A more plausible criticism would relate to the crudity of the regional variables used. Despite the fact that much of Illinois' political history has been discussed in terms of the Chicago-downstate dichotomy and, more recently, the suburbs, reality is far more complex (see, for example, Frank, Nardulli, and Green, chapter 8 herein). While the statistical analysis reported here is faithful to the traditional divisions in the state, the meager results it yielded suggest that a more refined regional breakdown would be a logical next step in the analyses of regional differences within the state. Who familiar with Chicago, for example, would be blind to potential attitudinal and perceptual differences between the largely black South Side, the white ethnic neighborhoods, and the lakefront areas? Moreover, not all suburbs around Chicago are havens of white, affluent professionals; many are dominated by residents who have more in common with various areas of Chicago than with one another. Residents in the rural areas of the outlying ring counties (Lake, Will, McHenry, and Kane) may have more in common with people categorized here as downstaters than with suburbanites. Finally, a glance at what we term "downstate" reveals that we combined cities such as Rockford, Peoria, and Moline with what has traditionally been known as "Little Egypt" (the southern tip of the state). We also lumped that part of the St. Louis metropolitan area in Illinois together with the small-town and rural dwellers across the state.

To refine the analysis of regional differences somewhat, within the constraints of the sampling design, we divided the various subsamples into the subdivisions reported in Table 10–15. The three downstate samples were broken into four categories: medium-sized cities (all cities over 25,000 not in the St. Louis area), the three counties in the St. Louis metropolitan area (Madison, St. Clair, and Monroe), little Egypt (all counties in the southern tip of the state below a line extending from Randolph County to White County), and the rest of downstate (predominantly rural and small-town residents). Little Egypt was separated from the rest of rural Illinois because of its unique settlement patterns and reputation for distinctiveness. We used telephone exchange rates to divide Chicagoans into four groups, which roughly correspond to the basic cleavages within the city: the relatively affluent, largely white North Shore; the largely black South Side; the racially mixed, largely poor West Side; and a "white ethnic" sector composed of the Northwest and Southwest sides. There were not enough respondents to justify creating separate Northwest Side and Southwest Side variables; the demographic similarities between them led us to merge them into a "white ethnic" sector.

The suburbs posed a more difficult challenge because of the number of cities involved in the categorization process and the fact that their development led to more heterogeneity within the suburbs than the casual observer would suspect. Nonetheless, general reputations, reinforced by a very recent, sophisticated analysis of Chicago suburbs by a social geographer (Getis, 1985), make it possible to make some well-grounded distinctions. The most obvious is between the very affluent, prestigious North Shore suburbs (Wilmette, Winnetka, Glencoe, Highland Park, etc.) and the working-class southern suburbs (Stickney, Summit, Robbins, Calumet Park, etc.). Ranking just below the North Shore suburbs in affluence and prestige are the northwestern suburbs (Park Ridge, Arlington Heights, Palatine, Mt. Prospect, etc.) and the somewhat more diverse far western suburbs in DuPage County (Elmhurst, Glen Ellyn, Wheaton, Oak Brook, Bensenville, Addison, West Chicago, etc.). Even more diverse than the DuPage suburbs are those in the near west, which includes River Forest, Oak Park, and Elmwood Park, as well as Melrose Park, Franklin Park, and River Grove. Re-

Table 10-16. Comparison of Refined Regional Analyses
and Earlier Results

Variable	Gross Impact of Regional Variables (change in R^2)	Net Impact of Regional Variables	Gross Impact of Refined Regional Variables
Attitudinal			
GODROLE	.030	.014	.060
SEXLFREE	.020	.005	.030
GAYTOL	.030	.010	.040
FAMLYVAL	.002	.001	.005
ABORTION	.020	.009	.020
DEATH	.010	.000	.020
PROLONG	.040	.009	.060
Quality of Life			
URBAN AMENITIES	.040	.015	.060
COMMUNITY LIFE	.010	.003	.020
INFRASTRUCTURE	.010	.004	.020
Spending Priorities			
Elementary education	.010	.008	.010
Higher education	.010	.002	.020
Economic development	.010	.004	.010
Aid to farmers	.010	.009	.020
Aid to poor	.030	.006	.050
Public safety	.020	.009	.030
State highways	.020	.007	.030

spondents living in one of the four outlying ring counties (Will, Kane, McHenry, and Lake) were assigned to an "outlying suburb" category.[13]

Dummy variables were created for each of the subdivisions listed in Table 10-15. We examined the impact of these dummy variables on the set of dependent variables analyzed earlier, without controlling for the set of demographic variables used in the previous analyses. We did not control for these demographic differences because some of the more refined regional variables were so demographically distinct (North Shore suburbs and median income; Chicago South Side and race; Little Egypt and religion, etc.) that we did not want to obscure whatever raw differences existed across regions. This analysis, then, should give us "high side" estimates of the impact of fairly refined regional variables within the state on our basic dependent variables.

The results of the more refined regional analyses are reported in Table 10-16, along with parallel results for the earlier analyses. All that is reported here are the contributions to the explained variance by the set of regional variables. The number of dummy regional and dependent variables employed was too large to justify reporting more detailed results. Moreover, the relatively marginal impact of these regional variables did not warrant more detailed results; they simply would have obscured the "big picture." The gross impact of the more refined regional variables was, in all but three instances, larger (in R^2 terms) than the cruder regional variables, but by only 1–3 points. In no instance did these variables explain more than 6 percent of the variance in any of the dependent variables, and that figure was not the net influence of the demographic differences. Controlling for them undoubtedly would have considerably reduced the figures reported in column 3 of Table 10–15.

A cursory review of some of the more basic attitudinal variables (GODROLE, GAYTOL, SEXLFREE, FAMLYVAL) reveals that the affluent residents along the northern part of the Lake Michigan shoreline (either suburban or city) tended to be most consistently and distinctively different from residents in Little Egypt and rural Illinois. Chicago blacks on the West Side and South Side differed most from the North Shore residents in their strong desires to do whatever is necessary to prolong the life of the terminally ill. Those living in any section of the city of Chicago and those in the St. Louis metro area were distinctively different from those elsewhere in the state in their high regard for urban amenities; Chicago northsiders again scored the highest on this scale. The only other dependent variable in which at least 4 percent of the variance was explained was the support for spending to aid the poor. The highest levels of support here were found in the largely poor South and West sides in Chicago; the lowest level of support was in the DuPage County suburbs.

We recite these results only to suggest that, to the extent regional differences exist within the state, they do not necessarily conform to long and deeply held beliefs about its makeup. Modern Illinois is not composed of a set of narrow-minded, traditionally oriented, rural downstaters, whose viewpoints are constricted by a rigid social conformism, counterposed against a set of normless, hedonistic urban dwellers, whose values, attitudes, and interests are diametrically opposed to those of downstaters, therefore fueling interminable political conflict.

The meaning of the results of the extensive regression analyses conducted thus far is that the distinctive means portrayed in Figure 10–9 do not exist in Illinois, at least not for the questions examined here. But this is only part of the meaning of the data embodied in the survey. A less obvious point is that the *diversity* of views (as opposed to their central tendency) is fairly similar in separate regions of the state. This is a particularly important point with respect to the downstate and suburban regions, which conventional wisdom holds to be more homogeneous than the Chicago area. This can be illustrated by examining the standard deviation for the different regional groups on the various measures. The standard deviation is a measure of dispersion that reflects the spread of the data in a sample around the mean (Blalock, 1960:67).[14] While it is instinctively difficult to know whether the spread around the mean is "loose" or "tight," all that is necessary for our purposes is to relate the size of the standard deviation in the different regions to the size in the state as a whole. The closer the spread for the regional groupings is to the spread for the state as a whole, the more diverse the region.

Table 10–17 reports the standard deviation for the weighted statewide sample for each dependent variable examined here and expresses the standard deviation for the downstate, Chicago, and suburban regions as a percent of the state standard deviation. In only 6 of the 51 instances was the standard deviation for a region less than 95 percent of that for the state as a whole. In only 2 instances was the regional figure less than 90 percent of the statewide figure—and both were for Chicago, presumably the most heterogeneous regional grouping! Table 10–18 includes similar data for the more refined regional groupings, using only the dependent variable for which the regional variables had the highest impact (R^2 above .05). Here we find more instances of tighter clusters, 8 of 70 had standard deviations that were less than 90 percent of the statewide figures. Some of these were quite small (69 percent, 72 percent), as we might expect as the regional group and sample size become smaller. However, upon closer examination, it can be seen that no pattern exists in the incidence of low figures. We cannot point to any region that was consistently more homogeneous; rather, a region might have had a tight spread with respect to one question and a loose spread with respect to the others.

Summary and Conclusions

In asking people how they viewed others in the state—whether they were similar to themselves, whether others thought much of them, whether others cared about their welfare—it was evident that regional animosities existed within Illinois, at least in the minds of many. Most viewed the state as divided, but far fewer were able to articulate the regional divisions. Chicago was not as prominent in the minds of

Table 10-17. Diversity within Regions of Illinois

Variable	Statewide Standard Deviation	Downstate Standard Deviation (as a % of state S.D.)	Chicago Standard Deviation (as a % of state S.D.)	Collar Suburban Standard Deviation (as a % of state S.D.)
Attitudinal				
GODROLE	2.02	93	107	97
SEXLFREE	1.75	101	99	98
GAYTOL	1.53	100	96	97
FAMLYVAL	2.28	99	109	94
ABORTION	3.82	103	97	98
DEATH	3.68	97	104	99
PROLONG	3.50	98	105	94
Quality of Life				
URBAN AMENITIES	1.94	100	97	96
COMMUNITY LIFE	1.82	95	115	93
INFRASTRUCTURE	1.53	105	101	94
Spending Priorities				
Elementary education	.48	100	92	100
Higher education	.50	100	94	100
Economic development	.49	98	96	102
Aid to farmers	.48	102	98	100
Aid to poor	.49	102	88	100
Public safety	.47	104	87	100
State highways	.50	98	98	100

residents—both inside and outside the Chicago metropolitan area—as might be expected given Illinois' political history since the Civil War. When asked, people in different parts of the state were not likely to admit to similarities between themselves and others, nor did they think others cared much about their welfare. Also, most people did not think the legislative representatives from different regions of the state were concerned with the welfare of the entire state. The differences here were most marked between downstaters and Chicagoans. A good number of downstaters also viewed Chicago as a financial burden. On the other hand, no one was likely to view any other part of the state as a financial burden, and, with the exception of the social stereotypes of suburbanites, the negative stereotypes we examined did not receive much support. Also, hardly anyone wanted Chicago to be separated from the state; most thought such a move would hurt "their" part of the state.

Table 10–18. Diversity within More Refined Regions of Illinois

| | | | Variables | | |
| | | | (as a percent of statewide standard deviation) | | |
Region	GODROLE	SEXLFREE	GAYTOL	URBAN AMENITIES	AID TO POOR
Downstate					
Medium-sized cities (25,000+)	101	97	102	104	102
St. Louis Metropolitan area	88	98	93	93	98
Little Egypt	72	109	103	95	100
Rural and small towns	92	99	101	98	102
Chicago					
South Side	97	98	96	104	69
West Side	103	98	88	95	78
North Side	114	102	99	85	92
White ethnic	99	94	94	99	100
Suburban Collar					
North Shore	110	111	93	95	100
Northwest	94	91	97	87	100
Near west	104	110	101	97	102
DuPage	97	88	97	93	102
South	97	98	90	107	96
Outlying suburbs	92	103	103	98	102

Despite the somewhat mixed picture we got by asking people what they think of others, an entirely different picture emerged when we compared their responses to a common set of questions. Some differences across regions did emerge. But the overall pattern was one of startling similarities across the state, all the more startling in light of the diverse origins and different patterns of economic development that have characterized the state. Most of the differences that did exist were trivial. Using our initial categorizations, regional differences usually accounted for no more than 2–3 percent of the variance in the dependent variables examined, much of which was reduced once demographic controls were introduced. While restricting the analysis to longtime residents did not change this picture, using a more refined set of substate categories routinely increased the explanatory power of region. Even then, in no instance did region account for more than 6 percent of the total variance in any variable, usually much less. What the use of these more refined regional breakdowns revealed more than anything was that, to the extent regional differences exist in Illinois, they do not correspond to the simplistic Chicago-downstate dichotomy so prominent in Illinois' political discourse or even to the more recent Chicago-suburban-downstate trichotomy.

Each of these regions is far more diverse than is acknowledged in casual political discourse. It makes no more sense to talk about the suburbs as a homogeneous grouping than the city of Chicago. The same can be said of downstate Illinois, which, is, in reality, a complex amalgam of medium-sized metropolitan areas, rural areas, and small towns, with smatterings of mining areas, medical and legal centers, university communities, and military installations. The effects of what Wirt (chapter 2 herein) refers to as the diffusion of social pluralism throughout Illinois in the post–Civil War era were quite evident in the examination of the distribution of responses for each of the major regional groups. The spread of responses was, for most variables, as wide in each regional grouping as it was for the state as a whole.

The last point is important because it underscores the real meaning of the extensive regression analyses undertaken here. The general lack of a strong regional effect does not mean "all Illinoisans think alike." On the contrary. There is a wide range of views within the state on virtually any matter of much significance. Not only do regionally distinctive means not exist, but each region mirrors, to a large degree, the diversity that characterizes the state as a whole. Thus, the segmented distribution of responses hypothetically depicted in Figure 10–9 is simply not borne out by data.

This point is important because it enhances our understanding of the regional animosities noted earlier. In light of the results reported here, it would be difficult to support the view that regionally based subcultures exist in Illinois which lead local residents to markedly different political orientations, thereby fueling political conflicts and animosities over the ends of governmental actions. This conclusion does not, of course, mean that the animosities that do exist are solely driven by distributional conflicts. They are more likely based on a combination of misperceptions about those in other parts of the state (what they are like, what they want from government, etc.) as well as genuine conflict over the distributional consequences of governmental policies. While these problems are not easy to address, they are not insurmountable. Indeed, the simple realization that people in various regions of the state are more similar than previously thought may make regional animosities easier to address. This is especially true if the results of this analysis are viewed in conjunction with the Fossett and Giertz (chapter 9 herein) findings that marked disparities in the distribution of government resources are not as prevalent as many would assert.

NOTES

1. In this scheme, we weighted each sample to make it reflect the region's proportion of the state's overall contribution. Our northern and southern regions each composed about 10 percent of the state's population and were accorded a weight of 1.00. The counties in the central region constitute approximately 17.2 percent of the state's population and were given a weight of 1.64. The suburban collar counties were given a weight of 2.31 as they have about 36 percent of the people in the state. Chicago residents make up 26.3 percent of the state population and were given a weight of 1.74.

2. We should note that a small number of people within each of the five major subgroupings that corresponded to our five subsamples identified themselves as being from a more specific subset of that region. For example, 29 percent of those included in the northern Illinois category said they were from northeastern Illinois; 20 percent of those listed under southern Illinois said they were from southeastern, southwestern, or south-central Illinois; and 23 percent of those categorized under central Illinois actually said they lived in east-central, north-central, or west-central Illinois. In the Chicago grouping, 13.7 percent actually identified a neighborhood of Chicago and 13.4 percent of those under the generic suburban label actually identified themselves as being from a subset of suburbs (northwest suburbs, western suburbs, etc.).

3. The fact that around 90 percent of the people interviewed, who could describe where they lived, gave us a label that generally corresponded to one of our five subsamples means only that we guessed pretty well at the

Table 10-19. Correspondence between Sample Source
and Self-Identification

Self-Described Identifier	Northern Subsample % (N)	Southern Subsample % (N)	Central Subsample % (N)	Chicago Subsample % (N)	Suburban Collar Subsample % (N)
Northern Illinois	67.0 (300)	1.6 (7)	1.9 (9)	38.3 (261)	49.1 (343)
Southern Illinois	1.3 (6)	78.5 (352)	3.8 (18)	1.0 (7)	1.4 (10)
Central Illinois	19.0 (85)	8.9 (40)	80.5 (379)	1.2 (8)	2.7 (19)
Chicago	2.0 (9)	0 (0)	0.8 (4)	43.1 (294)	11.2 (78)
Suburban collar	0.2 (1)	.07 (3)	.02 (1)	1.3 (9)	20.6 (144)
Other	5.6 (25)	4.9 (22)	7.6 (36)	9.1 (62)	7.7 (54)
None	2.0 (9)	4.2 (19)	1.5 (7)	5.4 (37)	5.9 (41)
Total	(435)	(443)	(454)	(678)	(689)

labels people put on the various subgroupings of the state. It does not mean that we identified accurately the boundaries of those subgroupings or that they categorized themselves in the same way that we did. Table 10-19 reports the correspondence between their identification of where they live and the sample from which they came. As is evident, the southern and central subsamples have the highest level of correspondence between their identification of where they live and the sample from which they came. Over 75 percent in both subsamples identified themselves as being from southern and central Illinois—79 and 81 percent, respectively. Indeed, if we add the neighboring locale to each of these (the central region to the southern subsample and the northern and southern region to the central subsample), with the idea that people in border counties may legitimately categorize themselves in one region or the other, the level of general correspondence rises to 87 percent for the southern subsample and over 86 percent for the central subsample. Indeed, we get as high a percent for the northern subsample if we include those who viewed themselves as part of central Illinois (86 percent).

The most interesting contrast in Table 10-19 is between the Chicago and ring county subsamples and the others (northern, central, southern). Well less than half of the Chicagoans described their locale as Chicago, while over a third described themselves as being from northern Illinois. The situation is even more extreme for the suburban subsample. Only about one in five listed themselves as being from the suburbs. Almost half of the suburbanites listed themselves as being from northern Illinois; over 10 percent gave Chicago. These data seem to suggest that there is more ambiguity in the northern part of the state—Chicago and its suburbs in particular— about where they fit into the state as a whole. Certainly the view is not supported here that all Chicagoans view the state as "Chicago" and the rest of the state. Less than a majority even view themselves as being from Chicago. The situation is even more ambiguous in the suburbs as most are more likely to view themselves as just part of northern Illinois.

4. For a good explanation of analysis of covariance using multiple regression, see Cohen and Cohen (1975:chapter 9).

5. To examine the impact of regions, we constructed a set of "dummy variables" (coded 1, 0) for each of the samples (north, south, central, Chicago, suburban collar) as well as a downstate dummy variable that included the north, south, and central samples. Using the downstate variable, we can see whether there are significant differences between the three non-Chicago metropolitan areas or whether they can be merged together for comparative purposes.

6. Dummy variables (coded 0, 1) were used to control for the effects of being male, being black, being unaffiliated with a religion, being Protestant, being Catholic, being married, being divorced or separated, being childless, being a two-income family, and renting one's residence. Years of education were used to measure educational achievement, and the NORC (National Opinion Research Center) occupational prestige scale (used in conjunction with a dummy variable to capture cases where the respondent did not have an occupation) was used to measure job status.

7. The instrument used is given in Table 10–20. Respondents were read the following directions prior to the series of statements listed in Table 10–20: "Different people have different values and opinions about things. I am going to read some statements, and for each I would like you to tell me how much you agree with the statement by rating it on a scale from 0 to 10, where 10 means you agree completely and 0 means you disagree completely."

8. Table 10–21 reports the results of the factor analyses, based on an n of 4,100 weighted cases. The variable names correspond to the variables listed in Table 10–20. The results for the FAMLYVAL analysis were termed marginal because only two of the three variables tapping attitudes toward the relative importance of the family were sufficiently correlated to include in the factor analysis. This led to an eigenvalue of only .9 (1.0 is usually regarded as the minimal acceptable value). As it stands, the resulting composite variable is identical with a simple sum of the standardized versions of variables F-2 and F-3 (see Table 10–20).

9. The results of the analysis of covariance for these variables are not

Table 10–20. Statements Relating to Personal Values and Attitudes

Statements about God and Religion:

G-1 The happiest people are those who believe in God.

G-2 The world would be a better place if more people prayed.

G-3 People with a strong belief in God are usually the best kinds of people.

Statements on Gender, Sexual, and Family Issues:

F-1 People should set aside one day a week to spend with their family.

F-2 A woman should sacrifice career advancements for the happiness of her family.

F-3 A man should sacrifice career advancements for the happiness of his family.

G-1 Women make more irrational decisions than men.

G-2 When a company has to lay off employees, the first people to go should be women whose husbands have jobs.

G-3 Policewomen do just as good a job as policemen.

A-1 Women should be allowed to choose an abortion if they desire.

S-1 Birth control information should be available to teenagers.

S-2 Sex between consenting teenagers is okay.

S-3 It is alright for two unmarried adults who love each other to have sex.

Statements on Race:

R-1 I would not like it if someone of a different race moved in next door.

R-2 A poor white and a poor black are just as likely to commit a crime.

R-3 White people work harder at their jobs than others.

Statements on Homosexuals:

H-1 Homosexuals should not be allowed to teach in the public schools under any circumstances.

H-2 Employers should not be allowed to discriminate against admitted homosexuals.

H-3 It would not make a difference if my neighbor was homosexual.

Miscellaneous Statements:

M-1 Judges should be able to sentence people to death.

M-2 Doctors should do everything they can to prolong the life of a terminally ill patient.

reported because they were very marginal and idiosyncratic. For the most part, the regional variables had no significant effect on these variables. Sporadic effects were found, but in no instance did one regional variable affect more than one question in each of the two issue areas. This suggests either that region has no impact or that the individual variables are not stable or meaningful enough to capture regional effects.

10. Each respondent was read the following directions: "Next I'd like to ask about the things that make a town a good place to live. I'm going to read a list of things, and I'd like you to rate each on a scale from 0 to 10,

Table 10–21. Results of Social Attitude Factor Analyses

GODROLE

Variable	Factor Loading
G-1	.84
G-2	.78
G-3	.73
	Eigenvalue = 1.84

SEXLFREE

Variable	Factor Loading
S-1	.51
S-2	.55
S-3	.79
A-1	.55
	Eigenvalue = 1.50

GAYTOL

Variable	Factor Loading
H-1	.68
H-2	−.60
H-3	.67
	Eigenvalue = 1.27

FAMLYVAL

Variable	Factor Loading
F-1	.67
F-2	.67
	Eigenvalue = .90

where 10 means it is very important, and 0 means it has no importance to you at all.''

11. Table 10–22 reports the results of the factor analyses, based on 4,373 weighted cases.

12. Respondents were read the following directions: "Now, some people we have talked to say that the state government should do some things but not others; and some say that some things are more important than others when it comes to where the state should spend its money. I am going to read you a short list of things on which the state might spend tax money. For each, tell me whether you would favor one of four things: Would you favor: no change in either spending or taxes for the thing, increased taxes and more spending by the state on the thing, decreased taxes and less spending on the thing, or decreased taxes and no spending at all by the state on that item?"

13. Despite the vagaries of this categorization process, an examination

Table 10–22. Results of Quality of Life Factor Analyses

URBAN AMENITIES

Variable	Factor Loading
Shopping districts	.49
Vibrant night life	.76
Professional sports	.53
Fast pace to living	.58
Many different restaurants	.47
	Eigenvalue = 1.65

COMMUNITY LIFE

Variable	Factor Loading
Availability of open spaces	.44
Family-oriented activities	.62
Good neighbors	.83
Privacy	.56
	Eigenvalue = 1.58

INFRASTRUCTURE

Variable	Factor Loading
Adequate street lighting	.67
Well-maintained streets	.78
Good hospitals	.49
	Eigenvalue = 1.28

of Getis's (1986) measure of economic health by our categorization of suburbs shows some marked differences. In his analysis Getis (1986:54–62) employs a variety of indicators ranging from median incomes, vacant housing, and percent unemployed to per capita municipal debt and expenditures, Moody's general bond rating, and retail trade per capita to produce an economic health rating for each suburb. The rating ranged from a high of 1.68 (Glencoe) to a low of −4.16 (Phoenix). The average for our suburban groupings were as follows: North Shore, .99; northwest, .54; DuPage, .50; near west, .05; south, −.62; outlying suburbs, −.28.

14. For a normal distributed set of data, two standard deviations on either side of the mean will include 95 percent of all cases in the distribution (Blalock, 1960:81). Thus, the smaller the standard deviation, the tighter the clustering of responses around the mean and vice versa.

REFERENCES

Blalock, Hubert M. 1960. *Social Statistics.* New York: McGraw-Hill.

Cohen, Jacob, and Patricia Cohen. 1975. *Applied Multiple Regressional / Correlation Analysis for the Behavioral Sciences.* New York: John Wiley and Sons.

Getis, Arthur. 1986. "The Economic Health of Municipalities within a Metropolitan Region: The Case of Chicago." *Economic Geography* 62:52–73.

PART V

Conclusions

Understanding and Reassessing Geo-Political Cleavages in State Politics

11

Peter F. Nardulli

We began this set of essays with a brief review of the history of intrasystem, geographically based political conflict. This overview demonstrated that geo-political animosities, in one form or another, have plagued political systems for millennia. Their ubiquity, as well as their tendency to persist well beyond the circumstances that generated them, suggests that they are an independent source of political conflict. The salience of these animosities can be compounded by ethnic and religious differences, political and economic exploitation, and the existence of distinctive, regionally based subeconomies, among other things (Nardulli, chapter 1 herein). But the emergence of regionally based fears, misunderstandings, and hostilities in even the simplest of societies suggests that geo-political cleavages are an integral part of most political communities. Thus, the complications that regional animosities introduce into the political process are likely to persist for the foreseeable future and merit our attention and study. This is true at both the national and subnational level.

More intensive research on these matters must await future efforts. Here we can only attempt to synthesize and integrate some of the thoughts and findings embodied in the essays prepared for this volume. This will help us understand the broader meaning and implications of these works and see where future efforts need to be directed. Some of these reflections and syntheses will relate primarily to the Illinois situation; others will pertain to state politics more generally. These integrative efforts concentrate on three main areas.

One broad focus that runs through many of the essays concerns the forces that foster, deepen, and shape geo-political cleavages. If geographically based political conflict approaches a constant within civil communities, the regional mosaic with which a political system must deal over time does not. Different factors contribute to different fault lines in different societies, and the shape of the geo-political puzzle changes with the ebb and flow of history. Old ruptures are healed and new ones erupt as the torrents of social and economic change make themselves felt. Thus, this essay begins by outlining the evolution of regional cleavages in Illinois' political history and attempting to isolate the factors that contributed to those cleavages.

A careful review of various regional conflicts in Illinois' past also reveals that not all such conflicts are the same. While all are regional in character, they are rooted in very different soil and nurtured by very different ingredients. At least four different dimensions to regional conflict can be discerned. It is important to distinguish among them because each requires a different strategy or set of strategies to resolve; each also says something different about the nature of the political community. Therefore, in the second section of this essay, these different dimensions to regional conflict are outlined, and observations from the other essays are used to say something about the current state of regional animosities in Illinois.

The third section of this essay builds on the earlier two sections, as well as the other essays, but is much more speculative. It lays out some thoughts on how to address the political problems caused by geo-political cleavages at the state level. These thoughts deal with reassessing regional differences in state politics, developing principles for addressing recurring regional conflicts, and strengthening the statewide political community.

The Structure and Evolution of Regionalism in Illinois

If we look at the factors that were influential in the formation and evolution of regional cleavages in Illinois, we can see a blend of geographic, political, military, economic, social, and technological factors. They are so intertwined, however, that it is often difficult to disentangle their various effects. One could point to geographic factors—such as the long latitudinal span of the state, its broad expanses of fertile soil, and the confluence of waterways at its southern and western edges—as the most influential factors in determining its regional structure. These factors certainly had a dramatic impact on the cultural makeup and political allegiances of the state's early settlers, particularly since water routes facilitated the migration by southerners into its southern and southwestern regions (Wirt, chapter 2 herein; Atack, chapter 3 herein).

But too much emphasis on these geographic considerations would ignore the political maneuverings involved in Nathaniel Pope's efforts to override the original outlines of the Northwest Ordinance and obtain an additional forty-one miles of Lake Michigan frontage for the state, including the present site of Chicago, its suburbs, and all of what we refer to as northern Illinois (Sutton, chapter 4 herein). Without this northern tier of counties, the evolution of the state's economic and political bases would be drastically different, as would its regional divides.

The real impact of Pope's achievement, however, was not fully realized until New York's completion of the Erie Canal, a technological and political feat of no small import in 1825. This facilitated the flow of Yankee settlers (and, later, European immigrants) into the northern part of Illinois, laying the groundwork for the early cultural mosaic of the state—a mosaic that fueled nineteenth-century political battles over slavery, education, the structure of government, and prohibition, among other things (Wirt, chapter 2 herein; Sutton, chapter 4 herein). The success of the Erie Canal also provided a model, as well as an impetus, for the Illinois and Michigan Canal, which linked the Great Lakes with the Mississippi River and the Gulf of Mexico via the Des Plaines and Illinois rivers.

The economic and demographic advantages that this waterway system gave to Chicago and the northern part of the state assured that the balance of political and economic power within Illinois would eventually shift from south to north. The emergence of Chicago as a main cog in the nation's emerging east-west railway network simply expedited the inexorable shift of power to the north (Atack, chapter 3 herein). Also significant in this transition were political-military factors. The curtailment of traffic along the Mississippi River by the Union army during the Civil War hampered the ability of the southern river towns to compete with burgeoning Chicago, the economy of which was greatly stimulated by the war (Sutton, chapter 4 herein).

The national forces that benefitted the northern sections of Illinois intensified in the period following the Civil War. But their impact on the state's regional mosaic was not limited to shifting the balance of power within the existing geo-political structure. Rather, they planted the seeds for a new regional alignment, one that obscured earlier cultural differences between the north and south and pitted the city of Chicago against the rest of the state. Rapid industrialization brought both people and wealth into Chicago, as well as the typical problems associated with high-density urban life in the modern era. The people attracted to the city, however, were quite different from earlier "strangers" within the state's "gate" (Wirt, chapter 2 herein). The cultural divide was no longer between Anglo-Protestants from different congregations who migrated from different parts of the eastern United States; the new strangers were Catholics from different parts of the world who spoke in foreign tongues and observed strange customs.

Regional tensions between Chicago and downstate were strained by a number of other factors. The needs of an industrializing economic sector were quite different from those of an agricultural sector, and these different interests and demands were manifested in the legislative process. Labor unions and anti-war activism also contributed to regional stereotypes, uncertainties, and misgivings, as did the early emergence of a powerful political machine in Chicago. All of these factors, and others, culminated in the decades-long battle over reapportionment (Frank, Nardulli, and Green, chapter 8 herein).

The Chicago-downstate distinction characterized Illinois politics for much of the twentieth century, even though a large portion of downstaters lived upstate from Chicago and the two regions tended to vote in tandem far more frequently than not, at least in presidential elections before 1960 (Frank, Nardulli, and Green, chapter 8 herein). While the Chicago-downstate distinction was becoming calcified in the minds of Illinois citizens and pundits alike, significant changes were occurring within the state's population, especially in the post–World War II era. A population explosion occurred in the towns and counties that surrounded the city of Chicago (Chiang and Geraci, chapter 5 herein). Second and third generation immigrant families from the inner city were moving to the suburbs in droves. The suburbs were also attracting highly educated, well-to-do families from outside the metropolitan area.

The advances in transportation and highway systems that facilitated the diffusion of urban dwellers into the suburbs also made possible, along with other factors, the industrial migration from the city to the suburbs. Chicago's economy became more service-oriented, but it lost much of its manufacturing base (Alexis and McDonald, chapter 6 herein). This was all the more unfortunate because at the same time Chicago's white ethnics were moving to the suburbs, blacks from the South were migrating to Chicago and other northern cities and were seeking more lucrative economic opportunities.

Profound political changes followed these social and economic changes. The once proud, powerful, and cohesive Democratic party began to unravel after the death of Mayor Daley. The rush to succeed Daley factionalized the machine as party loyalists were overcome by ambition. The eventual triumph of Harold Washington deepened the split during the days of "Council Wars" and "Mayoral Wars" (Preston, chapter 7 herein). Just as Washington was beginning to solidify his position after his reelection, his death once again unsettled the political situation in Chicago. Remnants of the old machine resurrected themselves to install one of their own members — albeit a black alderman — in the mayor's office. But few believe that the succession issue is resolved, and most expect a flurry of political maneuverings that will exceed those in the post-Daley years.

The maneuverings on the Chicago stage are taking place before an ominous backdrop: the burgeoning social, economic, and political power of the suburbs. While there is a good deal of diversity within the collar counties, it is quite clear that, as a whole, they constitute the most prosperous and dynamic part of the state (Chiang and Geraci, chapter 5 herein). Politically speaking, the suburbs already have surpassed every other region of the state in terms of total votes in statewide elections, and they now provide around 40 percent of the Republican vote. Perhaps more important, if present trends continue, they will shortly surpass the Democratic totals produced by Chicago (Frank, Nardulli, Green, chapter 8 herein). Continued infighting in the city will hasten the decline of its influence in statewide political matters — both electoral and legislative — especially if the white ethnic areas coalesce with the suburbs. Nothing the city can do is likely to reverse its declining fortunes; the suburbs are likely to consolidate and enhance their position over the next several decades.

The real questions are: how will the suburbs use their relatively new position in state politics to affect state matters and how will the other sections of the state react to the preeminence of the suburbs? One point should be kept in mind as political and civic leaders ponder these questions. The emergence of the suburbs is simply part of the continuing evolution of geo-political divisions in Illinois, but it comes at a time when the environment facing states such as Illinois is markedly different from that of just a generation ago. Regional leaders cannot presume that their real adversaries are within the state; nor can they ignore the interdependencies that tie their fate to that of other parts of the state. Broad strategies to address these problems will be considered in the final section.

Dimensions of Geo-Political Conflict in State Politics

Examining the Illinois experience over time and in light of a broader perspective on geo-political conflict has helped clarify several independent dimensions to these types of conflict. In the same way that regional cleavages are shaped and driven by a variety of different forces, these animosities can surface in a variety of different contexts and forms. The distinctions among them are important to note because each is driven by fundamentally different considerations, even if their roots are firmly planted in the same regional crevices. It is also important to distinguish between them because they require different approaches to analyze and different strategies to address.

Perhaps the most widely perceived form of geo-political conflict in state politics is conflict based on regional differences in fundamental values and interests that affect the content of specific public policies. Such conflicts are likely to occur when distinct subeconomies with different needs and interests exist within a state or when distinct subcultural groupings settle in different regions. They are likely to manifest themselves in debates over the desirability of adopting or modifying policies with strong emotive overtones or ones that have differential economic consequences. Examples would include the early debates over slavery, education, the regulation of commerce, labor unions, and prohibition, as well as more contemporary issues, such as those concerning the regulation of banks, the specification of environmental standards, and the consolidation of school districts.

A second type of geo-political conflict concerns disputes over the rules of the game within a political system. They speak to the structure of the process by which authoritative decisions are made and will contribute to regional conflict even in fairly homogeneous states— states that have no history of marked geographic differences in political values or economic interests. The stakes involved in such conflicts are often control of the machinery of government or the structure of power within that government. Disputes over the structure of regime rules will be even greater where geographic differences exist. Regional overtones in decisions affecting the structure of the political process have been evident throughout American political history and at every level of government. The debate over reapportionment is probably the most salient example of this type of geo-political conflict at the state level, but the decision by the Constitutional Convention of 1787 to establish two house of Congress also had marked geographic overtones. At the local level, disputes over at-large as opposed to district elections is an example of a conflict that can have regional implications.

Geo-political conflict over the rules of the game is not limited to representational schemes. Differences over the role of government, the role of individuals in government, and the linkages between the public and the government can affect views on such things as the selection of judges (partisan elections, merit-based), the form of local government, and the desirability of recalls and citizen referenda. To the extent that views on such matters are affected by the size of one's community (rural, small town, or urban metropolis) or by geographically distinct cultural subgroupings, they can take on regional overtones when the issue must be decided by the larger, more inclusive level of government.

A third important dimension to regional conflict is distributional. Independent of regionally based differences over the desirability of adopting a particular program, conflict will arise over the distribution of public goods within that program. The importance of this dimension has increased with the growth of government expenditures and services. The heterogeneity of some large urban states with significant rural sectors and the diversity of state programs that reallocate resources insure that misgivings will arise in various sectors over whether they are getting their fair share. Difficulties in determining what constitutes an equitable distribution of resources (Fossett and Giertz, chapter 9 herein) make this an even more complicated issue with which to deal, especially in states with a long history of regional strife. Using whatever criterion of equity that suits their purpose, political leaders wishing to exploit regional animosities can always point to one program that unduly benefits one section of the state or another. The regional dimension to distributional issues also becomes highlighted in the case of nondivisible goods (e.g., the location of large state facilities or the priorities attached to various building projects).

One final dimension to geo-political conflict at the state level concerns extraction policies; that is, how does government pay for the services that it provides? Again, this is a question that is analytically quite separate from the questions of what policies are to be pursued and how public goods are to be distributed, even if they often are linked in practice. The regional implications of different taxing strategies in economically diverse states are readily apparent. A corporate tax would most adversely affect the more industrialized sections of a state, while the agricultural sectors would resist overreliance on the property tax. Suburban interests, given their large tax base, would be best served by the property tax, especially if the proceeds were used to provide for local services, such as education. Suburban forces would resist income taxes most strongly, especially progressive ones. Big-city interests would be best served by an income tax, especially a progressive one, and an occupation tax.

If we examine the Illinois experience—as reflected in the research reported here—in light of these four dimensions of geo-political conflict (value-based, rule-based, distributional, extractive), we can gain some insights into the foundations of regionalism in contemporary Illinois politics. It is quite clear that the distinctiveness of the peoples that populated the various parts of Illinois in the first century of its statehood interacted with issues generated by national forces to produce geo-political conflict that reflected stark differences over fundamental values. Moreover, many of these issues were ones that presumably had to be resolved in a dichotomous fashion within the state arena. Was slavery to be permitted? Was the state to have a public school system? Should the sale of liquor be prohibited? If we examine the contemporary scene, we see a number of important differences. Relatively speaking, there are very few issues within the state arena that involve the resolution of differences in fundamental values.

Most disputes involving differences in fundamental values in contemporary American society are resolved at the federal level, by either Congress or the federal courts. Most political conflict at the state level involves disputes over how to implement or fund what most agree needs to be done. When differences over what needs to be done arise, they tend not to involve fundamental values, at least not to the extent they did in the nineteenth century. Even when fundamental values are at stake, there is less likelihood in post–World War II society that these disputes will evolve into regional issues. The relative homogenization of society during this period has not eliminated differences in perspectives, but it has made it less likely that perspectives will be determined by wholly local influences. Nowhere was this clearer than in the analysis of the survey results reported earlier (Nardulli and Krassa, chapter 10 herein). The similarities across the various regions of the state, in terms of what people wanted out of life, what they wanted out of government, and what their fundamental values were, were far more striking than their differences. Equally impressive was the diversity of views within the different regions. In many instances the diversity within subregions paralleled the diversity within the state.

Much the same can be said about regional conflict over the basic rules of the game in state politics and government. In Illinois history, there have been both minor disputes (the issue of county versus township government) and major controversies (reapportionment of the state legislature) that have divided various regions of the state. Even today issues such as the method of judicial selection can generate some regional differences. However, several factors have lessened the divisiveness of these disputes. One is the evolution and diffusion of the basic tenets of the American version of democratic constitutionalism.

Most of the basic issues have been worked out over America's two-hundred-year experiment with democratic rule, and most have been socialized to accept the resolution of those issues. While there is no unanimity over all points, neither is there much geographic structure to the differences in views. Perhaps even more important, many of the controversies which do remain and could lead to regional divisions have been removed from the state arena. The increased activism of the federal courts and the evolution of legal thought concerning the meaning and reach of the Fourteenth Amendment have led to the resolution of these fundamental questions in a way that has mooted regional conflict. The reapportionment controversy is the best example of this but not the only one. States no longer quarrel over whether they will redistrict but over how to redistrict. The conflicts are largely over party lines rather than geographic ones.

A very different picture emerges if we consider the last two dimensions of geo-political conflict, the distributive and extractive components. Conflicts over who gets what and who pays for it are the lifeblood of contemporary state politics and will continue to be for the foreseeable future. These issues recur on a regular basis and cannot, in their entirety, be usurped or shifted to the federal level. Nor can such discretionary, patently political matters be resolved by judicial tribunals or by constitutional revisions. Moreover, such issues evoke strong emotions. Few people think they get a fair shake from government and, as earlier analyses demonstrated (Fossett and Giertz, chapter 9 herein), there are many ways to define equity. Modern state governments are complex and multifaceted redistributive systems; exploitative politicians can always point to isolated programs that unduly benefit one region of the state or another. The fact that empirical analyses suggest that pervasive inequities do not exist (Fossett and Giertz, chapter 9 herein) is of little import to those who seek to fan the flames of regional animosities.

Those who would exploit long-standing regional suspicions have a responsive audience. Some of the most striking results of the statewide survey (Nardulli and Krassa, chapter 10 herein) were the findings that showed respondents believed that people and legislators from different parts of the state, especially Chicago, cared little about the welfare of "their" part of the state. This, of course, suggests that the current underpinnings of geo-political conflict have little to do with culturally based differences in fundamental values, but rather with suspicions about who is getting what and who is paying for it. These suspicions are fed by the perception that those in other parts of the state are somehow different and care little about the well-being of others (Nardulli and Krassa, chapter 10 herein).

The prominence of distributive and extractive issues underlying contemporary regional animosities is, in some ways, reassuring. They are more amenable to negotiation and compromise than issues steeped in deeply held values. Obvious inequities in state programs can be resolved by reshuffling funds and tax structures through the will and determination of political leaders. Even siting controversies can be resolved with the inclusion of additional projects favoring other parts of the state. State legislators have developed such practices into an art form. The resolution of issues such as slavery and prohibition did not lend themselves to such compromises so readily.

These differences having been noted, however, the challenges posed by these issues should not be underestimated. While distributive and extractive issues are not as value laden as some earlier controversies that have split states such as Illinois along geographic lines, the principles that underlie them (notions of equity, for example) can be very deeply held by different parties to the dispute. Moreover, these issues touch the economic self-interests of both individuals and geographic regions of the state in a very direct way. Finally, one must question whether tried and true methods of political compromise on fiscal questions are viable in the changed environment that most states face.

Dealing with Regional Conflict

Regional divisions within the American states result from the natural interplay between local factors and national (and increasingly global) forces, whether they be technological, economic, military, or otherwise. This interplay is, to a large degree, both inevitable and desirable. Given the strategic location of Chicago, Illinois could have done nothing about its emergence during the latter part of the nineteenth century. Nor would it have been beneficial to the state had it been able to thwart its growth or the growth of its suburbs in the postwar years. Having said this, however, we should be careful to distinguish between regional cleavages and their political manifestations. While regionally based political conflict may be inevitable, it does not have to be insurmountable.

We can use some of the insights gained from this effort to consider steps and strategies that may be useful in dealing with regionally based political conflict. Three seem deserving of at least cursory comment. First, this research suggests that we should reassess our view of regionalism within state politics in general and within Illinois in particular. Second, given what was said earlier, progress needs to be made in developing a consensus on equitable principles and strategies concerning distributive and extractive practices. Finally, it seems evident that the groundwork needs to be laid for developing a stronger sense of political community at the state level.

Reassessing Regionalism

Heterogeneity of any sort and geo-political cleavages in particular complicate the political matrix with which political actors must deal. These cleavages require compromises that are often suboptimal and frequently quite costly; in some instances, they prevent the accomplishment of goals about which some feel quite strongly. Regional rivalries can obscure similarities and commonalities while highlighting and magnifying isolated instances of conflict. This breeds mistrust, which feeds upon itself by seeping from one conflict to another. These cleavages are all the more pernicious because they are self-perpetuating.

This is the view of regionalism with which we began this examination, and it still holds true to a large degree. However, in the course of examining various aspects of this general problem, a number of points became clear that justify a reassessment of it. They can be illustrated best by a cost-benefit analogy.

At a very general level, this research suggests that the political costs of having a regionally diverse state in contemporary American political life are not as great as they were at the turn of the twentieth century; these costs are less in the sense that the problems generated by regional diversity are more limited in scope. It is also clear that there is a set of benefits that accrues to large, regionally diverse states. These benefits are both economic and political and are of increasing significance for state affairs in the latter part of the twentieth century. These observations are deserving of further comment because they can lead to a greater tolerance for, and appreciation of, regional diversity in the American states. Such tolerance could lead to the debunking of some of the lore that has enveloped regional differences in states such as Illinois, as well as simplifying some of the problems they create for the political process.

The proposition that the political costs of having a regionally diverse state are relatively reduced in contemporary state politics rests upon the assertion made earlier that various changes in the structure of post–World War II social and political life have narrowed the potential scope of geo-political conflict at the state level. Not much more needs to be said about the slim foundations upon which regional animosities in contemporary Illinois (and presumably other similar states) are based. While regional trends in presidential voting may in fact be growing more disparate, the survey and expenditures data reviewed earlier suggest that less separates the various regions of the state than one might think. The mooting of many issues—either through national or judicial preemption—that could exacerbate regional tensions within states has also minimized the significance of regional conflict. Most of the issues facing the American states in contemporary society are simply not regional issues; those that are fall within the distributional and extractive domains.

In reassessing the benefits of regional diversity, we must begin with the recognition that, at least during the post–Civil War era, many regional stresses in state politics were due to the emergence of large cities, with their threatening size and industrial ills. This led to a quite distinctive set of political demands upon state governments, many of which were not consistent with the interests of the state's more rural sectors. In retrospect, however, there were many benefits that accrued to large diverse states, benefits that political actors and pundits alike chose to ignore.

From an economic perspective, it is clear that the regional economic diversity that so often exacerbated geo-political tensions also led to a much more stable state economy that buffered the impact of national economic cycles. Healthy sectors of the economy could offset, to a degree, the effects of economic downturns in other sectors. Alexis and McDonald (chapter 6 herein) made clear the type of economic division of labor that often emerges across regions of a state—one that works to the economic benefit of all concerned. In the late nineteenth century, urban centers provided rural areas with a market for their goods and transportation facilities that helped them reach other markets; they also provided them with up-to-date machinery to enhance their productivity. When astonishing gains in agricultural productivity decreased the demand for farm labor, burgeoning urban areas provided employment for displaced farm laborers. As firms outgrew their increasingly outmoded plants in big cities, suburban settings provided them with an opportunity for easy relocation in a familiar setting, one that permitted them to maintain most of their labor force.

The emergence and growth of major urban areas in the post–Civil War era, while causing havoc in state politics, also usually led to the cumulative development of an infrastructure that smaller, more homogeneous states usually could not support. The economic benefits of such things as a well-developed, integrated transportation network, a prestigious university system, and an established scientific community are clear. There are also intangible social benefits that flow from having an impressive infrastructure; states become defined as "major league." They attract professional sports teams, tourism, and national prestige. This can be clearly seen in the efforts of various cities and states to build sports facilities in the hopes of attracting major-league franchises (or keeping the ones they have). The same can be said about convention centers and other such public facilities. The advantages of these developments in an era in which states are competing vigorously for economic development are all the more clear. They take on added significance because a first-class infrastructure is not something that can be constructed overnight.

Many of the underappreciated political benefits of regional diversity are related to size. Even though there are many anti-majoritarian features of our national political system—such as the Senate and the Supreme Court—there are still important benefits that accrue to large states, those that are most likely to develop the types of regional fissures with which we have been concerned. This can best be seen in the attention given to such states by presidential candidates in election years, despite the prominence of smaller states with early primaries. The winner-take-all system embodied in the electoral-college mechanism insures that the largest and most diverse states will continue to get disproportionate attention. The advantages of this can best be seen by the influence wielded by political leaders such as Mayor Daley during the Kennedy and Johnson years. Unified congressional delegations could enhance the advantages of size even further.

We can also see some political benefits of regional diversity unrelated to size. These occur at the state level, but their effects are much more nebulous and speculative than the national effects just mentioned. They relate to the constraints placed upon governmental action by diversity, and they flow from Madisonian notions of democracy. Simply put, Madison held that the diversity of groups in a large, heterogenous polity would act as a check upon transient majorities that would trample upon the rights of insular minorities.

A good case could be made that, for a variety of reasons (geographic isolation of minorities, malapportioned legislatures), these Madisonian checks have not been very effective at the state level. However, the diffusion of ethnic groups from Chicago to other parts of the state, and from other parts of the state to the Chicago metropolitan area, has combined with other national forces to make various regions of the state less distinctive. This was very apparent in the analysis of the survey data. Much heterogeneity was evident throughout the state, and very little regional distinctiveness was evident. Thus, the significance of Madison's ideas seems much clearer in contemporary Illinois.

Toward a Consensus on Distributive and Extractive Practices

The extent to which regional differences in fundamental values and views on basic rules of the game have been either mitigated or mooted has already been noted. It would be difficult for a major regional dispute over such matters to withstand scrutiny. Such is not the case with respect to distributive or extractive issues. Questions over who gets what and who pays for it are likely to generate conflict for as long as political dissent is tolerated. Moreover, it is unlikely that regional differences over distributive or extractive issues are likely to be mooted by national or judicial usurpation.

Despite the enhanced presence of the federal government in the provision of both social services and revenues to state and local governments, the states have always played a major role in these areas. Indeed, with the "Reagan Revolution" of the 1980s, the role of the states has been enhanced. One could conceive of the national judiciary's laying down principles governing the distribution of selected state services, such as education, but it is presently inconceivable that all such issues could be mooted in the way that reapportionment and other more procedural issues were. Distributional and extractive issues go to the heart of the political process and are fundamentally different from questions concerning rules of the game—questions that often determine who can play the game and how level the playing field must be.

The nature of distributive and extractive questions insures that they will never, and perhaps should never, be resolved permanently by resorting to rigid, fixed principles; their importance suggests that ongoing efforts to address them should not be hampered by distortions emanating from geo-political jockeying and logrolling. Progress needs to be made toward neutralizing the role played by regional animosities in such matters so that distributive and extractive decisions can be based on more pertinent criteria, criteria that will maximize social and economic goals rather than narrow political ends.

Progress toward the negation of regional influences on distributive and extractive decisions can take place only in the highest councils of government and, only then, by the deliberations of political leaders committed to the betterment of the political community as a whole. But this process can be facilitated by the realization that the desires and policy preferences of citizens across the state are remarkably uniform, as seen in the survey results. Another impetus is the recognition that modern states are highly integrated economic entities. What is good for one part of the state often benefits other sections, if only indirectly.

Little can or will be said here about the type of concrete actions that need to be taken to make progress on these matters. Several insights based on this research effort can, however, be outlined. It seems obvious, for example, that deliberations toward reaching a consensus on distributive and extractive equity across regions should begin with the recognition that Illinois, like all other major states, is an organic whole. As such it is composed of different parts that serve different functions and have different needs. The functions served by a region will evolve over time, but in a given era these functions are fairly well set and contribute to the overall composition of the state. They define its personality and image and affect its economic health and vitality.

A recognition of this internal makeup will lead to a better understanding of and responsiveness to the needs of different parts of the state. The overall goal of state government should be both to maximize the comparative advantage of each region of the state and to meet the particular needs of its citizens. Such a broad strategy will enable it to fulfill the obligations of a civilized society to its members and to compete as best it can in the national and international marketplaces that have come to characterize the modern economic order.

The package of state services provided and the distributive and extractive strategies pursued should be assessed in light of this overall goal and the state's internal makeup. A regional "fair shake" should be defined as having its peculiar needs met and not in terms of simpleminded notions of per capita equality. Not all inequalities are inequities, and efforts to balance all expenditures may be counterproductive. Government programs are redistributive by definition, and, as Fossett and Giertz (chapter 9 herein) point out, the benefits of government spending are not always restricted to the locale in which the expenditures are disbursed.

In making adjustments to the existing package of state programs— either to provide for appropriate levels of interregional equity or to respond to legitimate new needs—efforts should be made to avoid "additive" political strategies. That is, programs should not be structured to necessarily provide every segment of the state with comparable levels of the same service. Rather, they should be based on need. To insure interregional equity, a mix and match strategy should be pursued. Trading should occur, as Fossett and Giertz (chapter 9 herein) suggest, across programs, not within programs.

Building a Stronger Statewide Political Community

The pursuance of mix-and-match political strategies requires political leadership and courage as well as interregional trust. None of these commodities is likely to be forthcoming in sufficient quantities or on a continuing basis until stronger statewide political communities are established. The notion of a statewide political community is more vague and nebulous than many of the other ideas introduced here, but it is no less important. By a political community, we refer to the network of political ties that bind a geographically distinct people together. Although the American states are not natural political communities in the sense that some ancient European states were, it is not realistic in the American setting to talk about redefining state political boundaries to correspond more closely with natural political constituencies, even if such entities existed. Efforts to enhance the harmony of these political communities and the bodies that govern them must focus on ways to strengthen them, not reconstitute them. What must be strengthened are people's sense of identification with, commitment to, and support of the political entity and structures that bind them together at the state level.

In largely politically heterogeneous states such as Illinois, citizens' sense of identification with and commitment to the national political community are stronger than to the state; indeed, this may be true of citizens in all states. This is, however, a twentieth-century development. Certainly in the pre–Civil War era, attachments to the states were stronger than to the nation. It may no longer be possible to engender the type of identification with and commitment to the states that existed during the early days of the republic, nor may it be desirable or necessary. What is important, however, is that there exist enough awareness of and commitment to the statewide political community that regional animosities do not handicap state efforts to respond to the diverse needs of its constituents.

Regardless of the factors that undermined the development and maintenance of strong political communities in some states over the past century, much of what has been said here suggests that the time could be ripe for efforts to strengthen these communities in states such as Illinois. People from different parts of the state are not as dissimilar—in terms of basic attitudes, views, and wants—as conventional wisdom has suggested. Moreover, many of the issues that have historically divided the state along geo-political lines have been mooted. All this suggests that the potential for strengthening exists.

The structural changes in the national and international economy also serve as reminders to all citizens and their political leaders that competition from outside the state is more threatening to their well-being than competition from within the state. This realization should serve as the impetus for efforts to work together more harmoniously. Skeptics who doubt the impact that the internationalization of the economic order can have upon the ability of past adversaries to co-operate need only be reminded of its effect upon labor-management relations. Just twenty-five years ago, few would have predicted the enhanced ability of these two groups to understand their mutual destiny and act upon their shared concerns.

How a revitalized state political community is to be developed is an entirely different matter—one that is largely beyond the scope of this effort. Nonetheless, a few comments can be made with respect to laying the groundwork for such an effort. First, any such attempt must begin at the perceptual level. Illinois citizens' views of the state must be changed to conform more closely with reality. This does not mean denying, ignoring, or downplaying important differences in wants, needs, or interests across the state. It does mean, however, that commonalities shared by people should be stressed, as well as the benefits of the diversity that so often breeds geo-political conflict.

This perceptual re-creation of Illinois should stress the national political significance that its size and diversity have brought it, as well as the economic strength and stability they have built into the state economy. It should also emphasize the more tangible fruit that has been produced by Illinois' diverse terrain. Chicago is clearly the cultural and media center of the Midwest and a national convention center. The state has produced a transportation network (highways, airports, railways) matched by few states in the nation. Its agricultural, scientific, and medical centers are among the most productive and prestigious in the nation, as is its system of higher education. It also has an enviable system of national parks and sites.

These structural achievements insure that the long-term prosperity of Illinois is not entirely at the mercy of cyclical shifts and long-run trends at the national or international level, that the state can control its own destiny. These achievements should form the core of an effort to redefine how Illinoisans view Illinois. It is an effort that must be spearheaded by statewide political, civic, and business leaders, media throughout the state, and the state's political parties. But to be successful, it must be accompanied by another change in political mores and practices. These same leaders should work to make the political exploitation of regional animosities as opprobrious as the exploitation of racial or ethnic differences. Political exploitation has been an important force in the perpetuation of regional animosities and stereo-types during a period when their foundations have been crumbling; the changed environment facing American states in the late twentieth century makes continued exploitation of these hostilities no longer tolerable.

Notes on Contributors

MARCUS ALEXIS is professor of economics and dean of the College of Business Administration at the University of Illinois at Chicago. He is the author of *An Economic Strategy for the 1980's, Black Consumer Profiles,* and *Empirical Foundations of Marketing,* as well as numerous articles in scholarly journals. Alexis has sat on many boards and commissions, including the ICC and the Federal Reserve Bank. He is the recipient of several fellowships and awards.

JEREMY ATACK is professor of economics at the University of Illinois at Urbana-Champaign, specializing in American economic history. He received his Ph.D. from Indiana University in 1976 and has taught at Illinois since then. In 1987–88 he was visiting professor of economics at Harvard University. His research has focused upon agricultural and industrial development in the nineteenth century and makes extensive use of federal manuscript census data and quantitative methods.

CHENG H. CHIANG received his Ph.D. in sociology from the University of Chicago. Since 1979 he has been the state demographer for Illinois responsible for demographic projections and the publication *Illinois Population Trends,* of which he is the chief contributor. His current research involves the impact of population change on the state's service programs. He has also taught at Sangamon State University. His research interests include the study of migration and small groups.

JAMES W. FOSSETT is assistant professor of political science at the Institute of Government and Public Affairs of the University of Illinois at Urbana-Champaign. A former staff member of the Brookings Institution, he has published research on a variety of federal and state urban policy issues. His current research deals with access to health care among lower income groups.

MICHAEL W. FRANK is a candidate for the Ph.D. degree in political science at the University of Illinois at Urbana-Champaign. The topic of his dissertation is rational bases for the acquisition and use of politically relevant information. His research interests include the application of prospect theory to political paradoxes and critical mass models of political tolerance.

ANN GERACI is program analyst and coordinator of the Illinois State Data Center Cooperative in the Bureau of the Budget, State of Illinois. She holds both bachelor's and master's degrees from the University of Illinois at Urbana-Champaign.

J. FRED GIERTZ is professor of economics and a member of the Institute of Government and Public Affairs at the University of Illinois at Urbana-Champaign, a position he has held since 1980. He received his Ph.D. in economics from Northwestern University. His major research interests are in the areas of public finance and public finance with special emphasis on state and local taxation and expenditure policies. He served as research director for the Illinois Tax Reform Commission in 1982–83.

PAUL M. GREEN is director of the Institute for Public Policy and Administration and chairman of the Public Administration Department at Governors State University. He received his Ph.D. from the University of Chicago in 1975. He is the author of several books and articles on Illinois and Chicago politics. He also spends a good deal of time working with local government throughout the state of Illinois. He is currently writing a book on the 1987 Chicago mayoral election with Melvin G. Holli of the University of Illinois at Chicago.

MICHAEL A. KRASSA received his Ph.D. in political science from Washington University in St. Louis. He is currently assistant professor of political science at the University of Illinois at Urbana-Champaign. His research examines contextual, environmental, and compositional influences on citizen behaviors and attitudes in democracies.

JOHN F. McDONALD is professor of economics at the University of Illinois at Chicago. He is the author of *Economic Analysis of an Urban*

Housing Market and *Employment Location and Industrial Land Use in Metropolitan Chicago,* and has published numerous articles in economics and urban studies journals. McDonald has acted as a consultant to several commissions and bodies, public as well as private.

PETER F. NARDULLI is professor in the Institute of Government and Public Affairs and the Department of Political Science at the University of Illinois at Urbana-Champaign. He has written extensively in the area of law and politics, criminal justice policy, and state and local politics. He is author or co-author of *The Courtroom Elite, Politics, Professionalsim, and Urban Services, The Contours of Justice,* and *The Tenor of Justice.*

MICHAEL B. PRESTON received his Ph.D. in political science from the University of California at Berkeley. He has taught at the University of Illinois at Urbana-Champaign, the University of Chicago, and is currently professor of political science at the University of Southern California. He does research in the areas of urban and black politics and public administration. His books include *The New Black Politics, The Politics of Bureaucratic Reform,* and *Race, Sex, and Policy Problems* (edited with Marian Lief Palley).

ROBERT SUTTON was, until his retirement in 1983, professor of history and director of the Illinois Historical Survey on the Urbana-Champaign campus. Sutton received his Ph.D. from the University of Illinois in 1948 and joined its faculty that same year. He has been active in a number of professional organizations including the Illinois State Historical Society, which he served as president and for a number of years as a member of the board of directors. Sutton was chairman of the Department of History from 1972 to 1974 and associate dean of the Graduate College for eight years. His special field of interest is nineteenth-century American history, with an emphasis on the Midwest and on Illinois state history. His writings have focused largely on the development of midwestern transportation and the special role of the Illinois Central Railroad in the Civil War. Sutton has authored, co-authored, or edited six books and has had a score of articles published in scholarly and popular journals, as well as numerous book reviews mainly on regional and railroad subjects.

FREDERICK M. WIRT is professor of political science at the University of Illinois at Urbana-Champaign. He is a nationally recognized expert in state and local politics, the policy-making process, and the politics of education. Wirt is author or co-author of *Power in the City, Politics of Southern Equality,* and *The Polity of the School,* as well as several other books and numerous articles in scholarly journals.

Author Index